In Praise of Jaime Escalante

Edward James Olmos (the actor who portrayed Escalante in *Stand and Deliver*, 1988—as reported by Lizette Olmos for LULAC in 2010): "Jaime Escalante exposed one of the most dangerous myths of our time—that inner-city students can't be expected to perform at the highest levels—and because of him, that destructive idea has been shattered forever. This is a legacy that changed American education, and [I] will work to ensure that it continues long into the future."

President Ronald Reagan (April 26, 1988, "Remarks on Receiving a Report on American Education"): "Another star who is with us today is Jaime Escalante. Jaime Escalante has taught calculus at Garfield High School, a predominantly Hispanic inner-city school in Los Angeles, since 1974. And when he arrived there, Garfield was terrorized by gangs and close to losing its accreditation. And Jaime set out to prove that their kids could learn math as well as any—with incredible success. In 1982 his students did so well on the advanced placement calculus exam that the Educational Testing Service in Princeton couldn't believe their eyes. They thought the Garfield students must have cheated. Escalante advised his students to take the test again, and they scored as well or better. Today, thanks to Mr. Escalante, Garfield has one of the best calculus programs in America. A movie about Mr. Escalante, *Stand and Deliver*, has just been released, which is particularly gratifying to me. Too often my old industry glorifies the wrong kind of people. Jaime Escalante and those at Garfield High School are the kinds of people movies ought to glorify, and this time the movies did."

President Barack Obama (2010, tribute upon Escalante's passing): "I was saddened to hear about the passing of Jaime Escalante today. While most of us got to know him through the movie that depicted his work teaching inner-city students calculus, the students whose lives he changed remain the true testament to his life's work. Throughout his career Jaime opened the doors of success and higher education for his students one by one, and proved that where a person came from did not have to determine how far they could go. He instilled knowledge in his students, but more importantly he helped them find the passion and the will to fulfill their potential."

Defying Low Expectations

Defying Low Expectations

What Jaime Escalante Taught Us About Learning

William A. Dembski
Alex Thomas

Description

Jaime Escalante didn't just teach calculus in East LA; he blew up the lie that poor, minority students can't handle serious academics—and then watched the system quietly bury the evidence. *Defying Low Expectations* tells the story beyond *Stand and Deliver*, the 1988 film about Escalante starring Edward James Olmos that became a classroom staple. Here we learn about the immigrant teacher from Bolivia, the maverick principal Henry Gradillas who cleared a path for him, and the forces that dismantled their success once it became too threatening to the status quo. Drawing on fresh interviews, lost online material, and hard data about today's failing schools, Dembski and Thomas show how Escalante created an ecosystem where students did the hard thing—and won big. This isn't nostalgia. It's a blueprint for rescuing American education. Escalante's example exposes low expectations as educational malpractice and shows how disciplined teaching, principled leadership, and moral courage can turn "throwaway" American schools into powerhouses of learning.

Library Cataloging Data

Defying Low Expectations: What Jaime Escalante Taught Us About Learning by William A. Dembski and Alex Thomas
Trim size: 6 × 9 inches
Library of Congress Control Number: 2026930110
ISBN: 979-8-89946-022-7 (Paperback), 979-8-89946-021-0 (Hardback), 979-8-89946-023-4 (Kindle)
BISAC: EDU034000 EDUCATION / Educational Policy & Reform / General
BISAC: EDU029100 EDUCATION / Teaching / Methods & Strategies
BISAC: EDU029010 EDUCATION / Teaching / Subjects / Mathematics

Book Cover Design:
The cover depicts Edward James Olmos (left) and Jaime Escalante (right) on a mural in Los Angeles. Photography for Inkwell Press by Ryan Axe. Cover design by Inkwell Press staff.

Inkwell
PRESS

2321 Sir Barton Way
Suite 140-1032
Lexington, KY 40509
https://press.inkwell.net

Only the educated are free.

—Epictetus, *Discourses*

Table of Contents

Preface (2025) by William A. Dembski

The Backstory to This Book

Jaime Escalante's story is widely known, at least in broad strokes: Escalante took a failing math program at East LA's Garfield High, an inner-city school whose students were poor and largely Hispanic, and transformed it into a math powerhouse that, at its height in 1987, accounted for more than a quarter of all Hispanic students in the US who passed the AP Calculus exam. Only a handful of US high schools had more students pass the AP Calculus exam that year. But Escalante's academic success at Garfield High didn't stop with math. Across the school, academics improved—and not just a little, but dramatically. A rising tide lifts all boats.

What led to Escalante's extraordinary success? What happened to his program in subsequent years? Most people know what they know about Escalante from the Hollywood film *Stand and Deliver*, which dramatized his success teaching math at Garfield High. The film was largely accurate, as this book recounts. But it doesn't explain the groundwork and supporting players that led to Escalante's success. Nor does it explain why Escalante's program capsized once the principal who gave him undivided support, Henry Gradillas, left Garfield High to go elsewhere. We fill in those details in this book.

The story behind this book began in 2014. While working with an educational website, I had the opportunity to revisit Escalante's legacy. Escalante passed away in 2010 at the age of 79, but I had long been a fan. Hollywood released the film about Escalante, *Stand and Deliver*, in 1988. Author Jay Mathews published *Escalante: The Best Teacher in America* in 1989. Both works inspired me. I completed my PhD in mathematics at the University of Chicago in 1988, specializing in probability theory. I was therefore a research mathematician rather than a mathematics educator. Yet I cheered Escalante from the sidelines, hoping someday I might contribute to his efforts to advance math education. This book is an attempt to fulfill that hope.

When I revisited Escalante's legacy in 2014, the first person I contacted was Henry Gradillas. Gradillas, now in his 90s but then just turning 80, had a few years earlier written with Jerry Jesness *Standing and Delivering: What the Movie Didn't Tell* (2010). That book focused on Gradillas's role in Garfield High's "golden age," but also described the aftermath, showing how quickly the lessons that should have been learned and forever internalized about Garfield's success could be forgotten.

One thing that became clear from that book and conversations with Henry is how important his role was in Escalante's success. Escalante, as a rockstar teacher, was in the limelight. But Gradillas, as the key administrator, played a crucial supporting role that was largely ignored in *Stand and Deliver*. Escalante was like the Beatles, getting all the glory. Gradillas was like George Martin, their producer, working in the background to make their success possible. It therefore seemed time to retell the story of Jaime Escalante, going back to his beginnings, extending beyond his glory days at Garfield High, filling in missing details about what made his success possible, and then trying to understand what his legacy means and how, in practical terms, it can be applied.

In heading this project to reexamine Escalante's legacy, I next contacted writer Alex Thomas, who at my urging wrote an article titled "Escalante in the 21st Century—Still Standing and Delivering," which summarized the Escalante story as well as the keys to his success. Around the same time, my friend and colleague James Barham interviewed Henry Gradillas and Angelo Villavicencio. Villavicencio had been one of Escalante's protégés at Garfield and taught some of its AP Calculus classes.

We also enlisted Mary Poplin, a professor at Claremont Graduate University, who was just up the road from Garfield. She had carefully studied teachers in LA County who defied expectations by helping disadvantaged students in otherwise low-performing, poverty-ridden schools do phenomenally well academically. And finally, James Barham interviewed Ben Carson, a world-famous pediatric neurosurgeon, for many years on the faculty at Johns Hopkins University, whose inspiring story about how he was able to overcome Detroit's poor school system complemented Escalante's approach to teaching and learning.

We collected all these pieces to make sense of Escalante's legacy. They appeared for a time online. And then they vanished (unless you know where to look on the Web Archive). These pieces appear in this book as an afterword and appendices. Yet, at the heart of this book is a biography of Escalante that Alex and I wrote. Our aim was to put Escalante's immense contribution to American education into perspective, while also detailing the forces arrayed against him that sought to memory-hole what he achieved and stood for.

The Escalante-Gradillas Prize

This biography, without the afterword and appendices as in the present book, appeared briefly in print in 2016 under the title *It Takes Ganas: Jaime Escalante's Secret to Inspired Learning*. This book was meant to provide a catalyst for reforming American K–12 education. In line with our efforts to highlight the good work done at Garfield High, the educational website that spurred this biography also instituted the "Escalante-Gradillas Prize for Best in Education," a prize worth $20,000 annually. We were serious about cementing the legacy of Escalante and Gradillas.

Stressing the importance of both teachers and administrators to successful student learning, the Escalante-Gradillas Prize was awarded in alternate years to an outstanding teacher or an outstanding administrator, with $10,000 going to the individual (teacher or administrator) and the remaining $10,000 going to the individual's school district.

High school principal Lisa Kaplan received the prize in 2015 and high-school calculus teacher Anthony Yom received the prize in 2016. Then, in 2017, the prize was expanded to include a first, second, and third place winner, with the outright winner and winning school district sharing $20,000, the second and third place winners receiving respectively $5,000 and $3,000— though not for themselves but on behalf of their schools. In 2017 the prize again went to an administrator: superintendent José Espinoza getting first place, principal Sharif El-Mekki getting second place, and principal Woodland Johnson getting third place.

In fact, an inaugural Escalante-Gradillas Prize was first given in 2014 to three recipients. Thus, $10,000 went to Escalante's widow, Fabiola, who was living in Bolivia, to honor Jaime Escalante's memory. Additionally, $10,000 went each to Henry Gradillas and to Angelo Villavicencio for their work with Escalante. It seemed fitting that Escalante, Gradillas, and Villavicencio, so essential to the very reason for this prize, should be honored as its first recipients.

Despite this great start, the prize and the momentum to revive Escalante's legacy stopped abruptly. The sponsoring website was sold in 2017. The new owners immediately discontinued the prize and ultimately removed all traces of Escalante and Gradillas. Their decision to withdraw support from the Escalante project that I had headed was not ideologically motivated but simply a business decision. Underlying this decision was a cost-benefit analysis, weighing the benefit of keeping this material on the website against the cost of sending the search engines confusing semantic signals and thus undercutting the site's SEO (search engine optimization). In short, all this valuable material was removed to keep Google happy.

Rekindling This Project

Because I retained rights to materials associated with this Escalante project, it was now up to me to keep it alive and find another publisher. But finding a suitable publisher was easier said than done, especially because the book had now been "burned" by already having been published and then withdrawn. Also, my plate was full with other projects. Then Covid hit. And after that, my plate was full with still other projects.

Only in 2025, through the remarkable book production technology developed at Inkwell.net, did I finally feel in a position to publish an updated edition of the Escalante biography that Alex Thomas and I had published almost a decade earlier. Getting books written is one thing. Getting them across the finish line so that they are properly copyedited, typeset, printed, published, distributed, and marketed is another. Usually there are lots of speed bumps in the book production process. Inkwell eliminated them.

Revised, and now with an afterword and four interviews to complement it, our Escalante biography was now ready for a new life. Surprisingly—or not—this work has aged remarkably well. In fact, it remains spot-on in assessing what ails and needs fixing in American education.

Coincidentally, in the spring of 2025, education reform advocate Steven F. Wilson published a book titled *The Lost Decade: Returning to the Fight for Better Schools in America*. In it he details the way some K–12 schools in the US that for a time had taken seriously Escalante's no-excuses, high-aiming, discipline-based approach to education subsequently buckled under political and ideological pressure. Thus, in the name of advancing "social justice" and "antiracism" and of rooting out "white supremacy," they were willing to embrace lower expectations, thereby losing their hard-won gains and reverting to the former unimpressive status quo.

The dynamics at play recounted by Wilson are identical to those at play with Escalante. The terminology has changed a bit in the intervening years, but the rationalizations for downplaying achievement and embracing mediocrity are the same. Escalante and Gradillas insisted on high expectations for their students. For instance, they wanted their Hispanic students as quickly as possible out of ESL (English as a Second Language) so that they could continue their education without hands tied behind their backs. With ESL behind them, they could fit into the surrounding culture and be positioned for career success, which would be less available to them without a command of English.

Above all, Escalante and Gradillas wanted their students to be intellectually challenged. Indeed, I don't know how many times in conversation with Henry that I heard him disparage "Mickey Mouse courses"—busywork that merely wastes time and accomplishes nothing. Henry would have liked to see such courses entirely eliminated from American K–12 education. Instead, Escalante and Gradillas wanted students challenged and to rise to the occasion. They rejected lowered expectations as crippling students and preventing them from reaching their full potential.

So now, in 2025, this project to revisit and revive Escalante's legacy, which has been dormant for almost a decade, is again ready to see the light of day. This time it is poised to make a lasting impact—at least that's the fervent hope. A past that is forgotten is a past that might just as well never have happened. Escalante's life needs to be remembered. His work needs to be celebrated. And his success needs to be repeated so widely that it becomes the norm.

A word about the old and new title. The old title, as mentioned above, was *It Takes Ganas: Jaime Escalante's Secret to Inspired Learning. Ganas* is a Spanish word that Escalante used to denote the deep, burning desire needed to achieve outstanding success. The old title, however, doesn't quite capture the essence of Escalante's success. Escalante himself had plenty of *ganas*. But I suspect some of his students persisted and succeeded in calculus not so much because of their own *ganas* but by feeding off of Escalante's *ganas*—which seemed limitless and enough to cover and goad everyone within his sphere of influence.

Also, the term *inspired learning* in the old subtitle doesn't quite capture the type of learning Escalante was trying to elicit. Inspired learning suggests a kind of ecstasy or flow in which all one experiences are green lights. For sure, some of the learning that occurred under Escalante's watch was inspired learning in this sense. But learning is not always fun or exhilarating. Escalante worked his students hard. More often than not they were likely to feel uninspired—something more akin to the old Gary Larson cartoon where a student behind a desk complains to the teacher, "May I be excused? My brain is full."

Consequently, this book has been rechristened *Defying Low Expectations: What Jaime Escalante Taught Us About Learning.*

The subtitle makes explicit the connection with Escalante in his role as master teacher. The title itself underscores Escalante's insistence on rejecting low expectations. In this, it is stronger than a title that merely applauds high expectations. A negation properly phrased can affirm something more strongly than a straight-up affirmation.

For instance, the First Amendment of the US Constitution states that Congress shall make no law to abridge freedom of speech. That's stronger than an amendment that affirms free speech but then tacitly allows Congress to make laws redefining what is meant by free speech. Negation here says, Don't touch this. It allows no wiggle room. Affirmation here, by contrast, potentially allows for rationalizations that undermine the whole point of the First Amendment.

The title *Defying Low Expectations* is in that same vein. People reflexively celebrate high expectations. Only when high expectations collide with prejudices or become inconvenient do we find them no longer celebrated. Defying low expectations, by contrast, denotes a remorseless unwillingness to settle for anything but high expectations. Unfortunately, when push comes to shove, low expectations have a way of sneaking into the educational hen house and consuming the hens.

Low Expectations as Ideology

Anyone who has studied the history of IQ testing and eugenics will recognize the weaponization of low expectations against people deemed inferior and therefore unworthy of receiving a good education. In the early twentieth century that included my own ancestry of eastern European immigrants—hence all the jokes about "dumb Polacks" that I had to endure growing up in Chicago. And of course, with far greater virulence, it included Blacks and Hispanics.

Consider, for instance, Lewis Terman. A psychologist who adapted Alfred Binet's intelligence test into the Stanford-Binet scale, Terman popularized the concept of the intelligence quotient, or IQ, and promoted its widespread use in American education. In *The Measurement of Intelligence* (1916, pp. 91–92), Terman remarked that for "laboring men and servant girls," his test of intelligence "told the truth." What truth was that? As he explained:

> These boys [and girls] are uneducable beyond the merest rudiments of training. No amount of school instruction will ever make them intelligent voters or capable citizens in the true sense of the word. Judged psychologically they cannot be considered normal.
>
> [They] represent the level of intelligence which is very, very common among Spanish-Indian and Mexican families of the Southwest... Their dullness seems to be racial... [T]he whole question of racial differences in mental traits will have to be taken up anew and by experimental methods. The writer predicts that when this is done there will be discovered enormously significant racial differences in general intelligence, differences which cannot be wiped out by any scheme of mental culture.
>
> Children of this group should be segregated in special classes and be given instruction which is concrete and practical. They cannot master abstractions, but they can often be made efficient workers, able to look out for themselves. There is no possibility at present of convincing society that they should not be allowed to reproduce, although from a eugenic point of view they constitute a grave problem because of their unusually prolific breeding.

Granted, it didn't take Jaime Escalante to show that Terman was wrong—the crass eugenics of Terman has long been discredited (though with CRISPR and designer babies, we now face a newer eugenics 2.0 that is more slippery and perhaps even more pernicious). Nonetheless, by taking the very ethnicity that Terman singled out (i.e., Hispanics) and showing that its members could "master abstractions" such as calculus, Escalante provided as stark a refutation and counterexample to Terman as could be desired. In light of Escalante, Terman showed himself to be not a scientist but a bigot who uncritically accepted the stereotypes of his age.

Eugenicists and proponents of early intelligence testing, like Terman, used the term "moron" as a supposedly scientific designation for individuals with low IQ scores. Accordingly, morons could be justly excluded from advanced education and, once public sensibilities were suitably reshaped, even be restricted in their reproduction.

Those like Terman divided the world into the elite upper classes and the moronic lower classes. The dynamic was one of superior versus inferior. Thus, the moronic masses were excluded from a superior education because elites regarded them as incapable of profiting from it. Indeed, why subject the morons to the frustration of trying to learn something they are inherently incapable of learning? Arrogance, pride, and condescension motivated the elite in this attitude.

In our day, this sort of racism is no longer tolerated. Yet a so-called "antiracism" is today tolerated and even embraced. This antiracism is in fact a racism of low expectations. It is rationalized in terms of compassion, equity, and (social, not real) justice. It presupposes an essentialism in which different races or groups are claimed to exhibit deep-seated and ineradicable differences. Rather than thinking of humanity as a whole for which racial or group differences are only skin deep, this antiracism not only glorifies such differences but also sees them as fundamentally dividing humanity.

Take, for instance, Luis Leyva, a professor of mathematics education at Vanderbilt University. In early 2023, he delivered a lecture at a large AMS (American Mathematical Society) meeting in Boston titled "Undergraduate Mathematics Education as a White, Cisheteropatriarchal Space and Opportunities for Structural Disruption to Advance Queer of Color Justice." (https://meetings.ams.org/math/jmm2023/ meetingapp.cgi/Paper/16248) In that lecture, he claimed to show "how Black, Latin, and Asian QT [Queer-Trans] students' narratives of experience reflect forms of intersectionality, or instances of oppression and resistance at intersecting systems of white supremacy."

Leyva is emblematic of Critical Mathematics Pedagogy. This approach to mathematics education traces to the critical theory and Brazilian philosopher Paulo Freire. Freire, best known for his book *Pedagogy of the Oppressed* (1968), understood teaching as an act of liberation rather than as a transmission of knowledge. Critical mathematics pedagogy links mathematics to social, political, cultural, and economic contexts of oppression. It claims to unmask how math both reflects and reinforces power structures, critiques the ways it is used to sustain inequity, and emphasizes connecting such a critique to concrete action for justice and reform.

Suffice it to say that if the conventional teaching of calculus, as practiced by Jaime Escalante, oppresses marginalized groups —as Critical Mathematics Pedagogy would say it does then it needs to be suppressed. In that case, Escalante, instead of being a hero, becomes a tool of white supremacism. For him or anybody to teach calculus to Hispanic or African-American students would then be to impose a white form of learning on them. Because different races are thought to have different aptitudes and predispositions, it would be racist to impose a form of learning devised by one race on another.

Unlike the old racists like Terman, whose racism was hierarchical, with some races deemed superior to others, the new anti-racism is egalitarian. Different races are just different, but the differences are so fundamental that they must be respected, and to disrespect them is to be a hater and oppressor. Accordingly, someone like Escalante, who saw everybody as fair game to be taught calculus becomes a victimizer of those whose race has rendered them unsuited for learning calculus or for being subjected to its teaching.

The practical outworking of both the old racism and the new antiracism, however, is the same. People, on account of their race, need to be excluded from certain courses of education. The old racists justified the exclusion by deeming the excluded inferior. The new antiracists justify the exclusion by deeming the excluded different. But at the end of the day, the sound and valuable education that people might otherwise have received doesn't happen.

One subtlety with the new antiracism is that the exclusion from a top-quality education doesn't have to be explicitly enforced. In the old racism, the so-called morons would be forcibly excluded from a top-quality education because they were officially identified as stupid and thus as incapable of profiting from such an education—no need to waste time and money on them.

In the new antiracism, all it takes is to lower standards and expectations sufficiently so that students fail to learn the prerequisites for more difficult subjects and thus naturally exclude themselves from a top-quality education. One approach actively blocks the path to achievement and mastery. The other redirects it away from the path to achievement and mastery. The end result is the same.

Escalante had no patience for either the old racism or the new antiracism (which, in an Orwellian twist, is of course itself a form of racism—a racism of low expectations that disproportionately harms certain races, ethnicities, and socioeconomic classes). Whatever their guise or rationalization, low expectations were anathema to Escalante. He was implacable in defying low expectations. He insisted on proving them wrong.

As this biography shows, if anyone had reason to wallow in feeling oppressed, it was Escalante. A Bolivian immigrant who had successfully taught mathematics in his home country, he had a difficult time getting educators here in the US to take him seriously as a math teacher, much less to give him the opportunity to teach mathematics—though ultimately he prevailed.

As Henry Gradillas makes clear in his interview (Appendix 2), neither he nor Escalante had any interest in casting themselves as victims or trying to profit from victim status. Both could easily have done so. Yet to do so would have hindered them from doing the valuable work they were called to do with their students. You can embrace your and others' victimhood or you can help yourself and others to transcend victimhood, but you cannot do both. Either one or the other will be your master. Escalante and Gradillas understood this better than anyone.

Low Expectations as Dereliction of Duty

In the previous section, I described two ideological currents used to justify low expectations for students and their education. Yet even without ideology driving low expectations, K–12 public education in America is infested with low expectations and in desperate need to raise them. As I write this in the fall of 2025, the latest National Assessment of Educational Progress (NAEP) reading scores for 12th graders have just come in, and they're the worst they've been since 1992. In reading, only 35 percent of 12th graders scored at or above NAEP's *Proficient* level, while 32 percent scored below NAEP's *Basic* level—an all-time high for below-Basic. In math, only 22 percent of 12th graders reached *Proficient*, and 45 percent scored below *Basic* —likewise an all-time high for below-Basic. Just to be clear, "all-time high" here means bad.

Economist and friend Gale Pooley (coauthor of *Superabundance*—read it!) is a master at estimating the costs of goods and services in dollar amounts. He notes that Americans spend about $1 trillion annually to educate 55 million K–12 students, averaging $18,000 per pupil per year, which over 13 years amounts to $234,000 per student. With a high school graduation rate near 90 percent, he argues the effective cost per graduate rises to $260,000, though before considering proficiency. As just noted, the 2025 NAEP results show only 35 percent of 12th graders proficient in reading and 22 percent in math, averaging to 28.5 percent, or about one in 3.5 graduates. Adjusted for proficiency, Pooley calculates the cost of producing a proficient graduate at $912,281. Moreover, with lingering Covid-related learning losses, he sees the actual number exceeding $1 million. That's 13 years of a Harvard education paying full sticker price.

With most K–12 students in the US attending public schools, these numbers suggest anything but a success story for American public-school education. How could we be spending so much for primary and secondary education (more than any other nation per pupil) and be getting so little in return? Many have written cogently on this topic, and I don't want to rehash what has been written elsewhere on it except to offer a few observations.

Certain dominant themes play into America's overspending and underperforming educational system. The legacy of Thomas Dewey and progressives in valuing self-expression over getting down to business and learning what needs to be learned is one theme. Another theme is experimentation with and perseveration in new-fangled approaches to learning, subsequently shown to have failed, over proven old-school methods. Hence the disaster of the whole language approach to reading despite the proven track record of phonics. Hence the proliferation of methods for "understanding" arithmetic that neither require memorizing the times tables nor ensure the ability to do arithmetic without a calculator.

The fact is, in the absence of an explicitly self-defeating ideology (such as IQ testing, meant to reserve a good education and high expectations only for the elite), most K–12 schools in the US say they want their students to excel—and certainly to meet the NAEP's proficiency standards. At the very least, they pay lip service to high expectations. None of them will proudly advertise that their students are falling behind. So why do they, protestations to the contrary aside, in practice embrace low expectations?

In answering this question, we need to be careful not to paint with too broad a brush. Many public school systems exist in the US whose students do very well and place into top colleges and universities. These schools are often in more affluent communities where parents and community leaders are committed to maintaining high standards for their schools. The people running these schools defy low expectations as a matter of course and hold accountable those who would inflict low expectations on their children.

The NAEP scores recounted above as well as international scores of student achievement (such as PISA—Programme for International Student Assessment), which show the US lagging educationally, are averages that don't capture the variability in educational quality across America. In statistical terms, they give the mean but not the variance. The variance in American education is huge, and if we focused on performance from our best public schools (even leaving aside charter schools), I suspect we would be fully competitive with the rest of the world.

The question remains, with public school education urged on all sides to give students a quality education, and minimally to meet proficiency standards, why do so many school systems continue to embrace low expectations? One hears many rationalizations: Bureaucratic inertia. The stranglehold of teachers' unions, which reward seniority and job security (tenure), over teaching excellence. Breakdown of the family. Poverty. Lack of parental involvement. Etc.

In the end, however, for public schools to embrace low expectations represents a dereliction of duty. We know that circumstances do not render public schools helpless in raising expectations and achieving excellence. Even schools in areas with the worst social problems can do right by their students and empower them to learn in impressive ways, far exceeding proficiency standards. And I'm not talking here about the need to clone a teaching superstar such as Jaime Escalante. There are proven ways for delivering a sound education even in the face of hardship and deprivation.

Consider, for instance, Harvard economist Roland Fryer, writing in the *Wall Street Journal* (September 8, 2025):

> In Houston, a research project I led called Apollo 20 showed it was possible to erase the racial achievement gap in less than two years, by applying simple reform principles to the worst-performing schools. Today, the tools we used sit on the shelf—not because they failed,

but because leaders failed to act. We are watching temporary setbacks calcify into permanent inequality, even though we know how to reverse them.

I've been obsessed with fixing American schools for most of my career. In 2009 I told my team of research assistants and project managers that we would do it by 2025... Fifteen years later, many of the ideas that once filled our conversations are gone—not because they failed, but because the system walked away from them.

In 2012, my graduate student Will Dobbie and I collected unprecedented data from nearly 50 New York City charter schools to see which practices truly boosted student learning. Class size and teacher credentials—political obsessions for decades—mattered little. What mattered most were five concrete, replicable practices: more instruction time, high expectations, frequent teacher feedback, data-driven instruction, and high-dosage tutoring. Together, these five tenets explained roughly half the difference between effective and ineffective schools.

In Houston, Roland Fryer's Apollo 20 project, launched in the 2010–11 school year, proved that the racial achievement gap could be erased in less than two years by applying the five simple reforms he mentions, yielding extraordinary gains, such as four extra months of math learning annually in elementary schools and nearly eight months in secondary schools. Yet despite these unprecedented results, funding was withdrawn once the schools were no longer the district's worst, upon which the program collapsed. Within a decade, the Texas Education Agency took control of Houston's schools. Consequently, Houston demonstrated the promise of large-scale, replicable reform, only to squander it through bureaucratic corruption, shortsighted politics, and failure of will, leaving students once again adrift in a system that knows what works but refuses to implement it.

In parallel with Fryer's conclusions, Claremont education professor Mary Poplin published an article titled "Highly Effective Teachers in Low-Performing Urban Schools" (*Kappan Magazine*, February 2011). Summarizing a study led by her, Poplin described tracking 31 highly effective teachers working in nine low-performing schools in Los Angeles County. Despite serving students in economically depressed neighborhoods, these teachers consistently produced achievement gains far beyond their peers. What set them apart were six key practices:

1. strictness that students recognized as purposeful and rooted in care,
2. instructional intensity with little wasted time and constant engagement,
3. movement around the classroom to monitor, assist, and build relationships,
4. traditional, explicit instruction focused on state standards and clear expectations,
5. exhorting virtues such as responsibility, persistence, respect, and linking success to future goals, and
6. strong, respectful relationships that conveyed high expectations without excuse-making.

Interestingly, these practices described by Poplin don't just repeat but rather complement the practices described by Fryer. Together with the practices he lists, they likely account for most of the difference between effective and ineffective teaching.

Poplin's study found that these teachers' effectiveness had little to do with credentials or trendy instructional fads and everything to do with discipline, clarity, and optimism about students' potential. They rejected excuses based on background, focused relentlessly on core academic and character formation, and consistently reminded students of their futures beyond the classroom. Rejecting helplessness, they gave students hope.

The upshot was that students were engaged, respected their teachers, and made measurable academic gains. Poplin's research suggests that expensive reforms or fashionable pedagogies are less effective than the kind of disciplined, respectful, and explicit teaching practiced by these high performing teachers.

Bottom line: Schools that give in to low expectations have no excuse. The path forward to an effective education is clear and proven. Escalante and Gradillas took that path in the 1980s. Others have taken it as well, with clear success. It can be done. It may mean running against strong headwinds. But for teachers and administrators to reject the path to academic success for their students is a dereliction of duty.

Postscript: A postscript needs to be added here. Dereliction of duty to provide the best for our children's education is never an innocent oversight or excusable failure. It should properly be regarded as criminal negligence and malfeasance against our children and their future. The ultimate cost to our nation in loss of productivity, criminality, incarceration, addiction, mental illness, and premature death because of the failure of our public schools to properly educate our children is enormous.

But don't take my word for it. The US Department of Education has said as much. In 1983, it published the National Commission on Excellence in Education's report titled *A Nation at Risk: The Imperative for Educational Reform*. That report is best remembered today for the following remark: "If an unfriendly power had attempted to impose on America the mediocre educational performance that exists today, we might well have viewed it as an act of war." This warning applies as much today to US education as it did forty years ago.

Calculus and the Challenge Zone

A word is in order about why Escalante focused his energies on calculus. Escalante was a math teacher, so it followed that his impact as a teacher would be in teaching mathematics. Calculus, particularly in its AP form, is the highest level of mathematics taught in most high schools. To master calculus and prove that one has mastered it therefore demonstrates a high level of achievement at the high school level. Given his desire to see his students excel and given his expertise in mathematics, it therefore followed that Escalante would focus his energies on AP calculus.

In an alternate universe, could Garfield High have achieved national recognition by having an Escalante double whose students excelled in AP physics, or AP chemistry, or AP American History, or AP English? Perhaps. I don't mean to overemphasize STEM. But I doubt that high achievement on any other single AP exam would have generated comparable excitement to that generated by outstanding performance on the AP calculus exam.

Perhaps here I'm simply betraying my own bias as a mathematician. But all STEM subjects find their foundation in the "M" that appears in the acronym "STEM," namely, in mathematics. Mathematics is the language of STE, leaving off the M—science, technology, and engineering. Also, there's a sense in which the humanities and social sciences are more widely accessible and less intimidating than mathematics as such. One doesn't hear of history phobias or English phobias, but one does hear of math phobias. Success at math thus suggests the more impressive level of performance.

So, while an Escalante of English literature is conceivable, the Escalante in the actual world, in providing proof of concept that poor Hispanic kids could rise to the highest academic challenges, was providentially a teacher of calculus. Implicit in Escalante getting his students to pass the AP calculus was an *a fortiori* argument, an argument from the stronger to the weaker: if Escalante's students could master calculus, they could master anything. Mastery of mathematics was a huge confidence booster for Escalante's students.

Any story about Escalante will necessarily give pride of place to mathematics—he was, after all, a math teacher. It would be a tragedy, however, if this book merely motivated math teachers to achieve extraordinary levels of mastery with their students to the exclusion of teachers working in other disciplines. Escalante has an important lesson to teach all teachers. To see this, we need to step back a bit and consider the type of teaching that Escalante was doing to get his students to excel in mathematics generally and calculus in particular.

Defying low expectations and insisting on high expectations, Escalante strove for his students to master calculus. Or, if there wasn't enough time because of their lack of background to get them up to speed for calculus, his goal was to make as much progress as possible in helping them master the lower levels of mathematics that were prerequisite to calculus. But what did the day-to-day training of his students look like?

Performance psychologists, such as K. Anders Ericsson (see his 2016 book *Peak*), distinguish three zones of learning: a comfort zone, a challenge zone, and a panic zone. The best learning happens in the challenge zone, where students are challenged to stretch themselves, feeling neither underchallenged in a comfort zone or overchallenged in a panic zone. The comfort zone is too easy. It merely repeats things that were a challenge in the past but are no longer a challenge. The panic zone is too hard.

It makes things so difficult that no incremental successes are possible. In the challenge zone, things can get uncomfortable but not so uncomfortable that no progress can happen.

Escalante, as much as possible, kept his students in the challenge zone. And indeed, all effective teachers keep, as much as possible, their students in the challenge zone. This is the zone where what Ericsson calls "deliberate practice" happens. It is not easy practice. It is often tedious practice, doing drills and routines that are no fun. But it is the type of practice that in the end pays huge dividends. Learning in the challenge zone is resistance training. Indeed, all effective learning is resistance training! This is as much true in athletic development as mental development.

We all know from other contexts about the need for deliberate practice, which only happens in a challenge zone. Consider, for instance, the game of golf. After learning its rules and taking a few lessons, the average golfer tends to improve mainly by playing with others, gaining familiarity with the flow of the game and picking up small tips along the way. However, this improvement eventually plateaus because the golfer is only repeating existing habits rather than refining them. Without deliberate practice—such as systematically working on putting, driving accuracy, or swing mechanics—the player reinforces the same mistakes and fails to push specific skills to a higher level. As a result, casual play alone yields diminishing returns whereas meaningful advancement requires targeted, intentional effort, which is to say deliberate practice in a challenge zone.

Note that all high school sports follow this pattern, with player development depending crucially on deliberate practice. Note also that no one who decries academic excellence as emblematic of white supremacy decries athletic excellence on the same grounds. Yet the learning principles for achieving peak performance are the same in both academics and athletics. If there is an advantage that athletics has over academics here, it is that athletic improvement tends to be more readily observable because performance statistics are meticulously recorded and can be seen to vary in real time. If academic improvement could be as carefully measured and tracked over time (which it can with contemporary technologies), we could get the same real-time record of achievement for academics as for athletics.

In any case, Escalante was all about keeping his students in the challenge zone, engaged in deliberate practice. This is how, day to day, he defied low expectations and kept his students' eyes on the prize. This is how all teachers and administrators, regardless of discipline or grade level, can experience the same type of success that Escalante achieved. The problem is to determine the sweet spot—where students are challenged at just the right level to make the greatest progress. This is a moving target because learning is dynamic, with things that seemed difficult one day becoming easier the next day and routine thereafter. Wisdom in teaching is knowing how to move instruction in tandem with that target. Escalante and Gradillas were exemplary in how they exercised that wisdom. This book was written help readers, especially educators, to do the same.

Technological Developments

Significant technological developments have occurred since the high point of Escalante's work at Garfield High in 1987, and even since the earlier version of this book was published in 2016. The internet didn't become a thing until the 1990s. Charter schools also took off around that time, with the internet lowering barriers to entry and acting as an enabling force in their expansion. Moreover, since 2016, digital technologies for online education have proliferated. And then, beginning around

2021–22, artificial intelligence (AI), especially in the form of LLMs (large language models) such as ChatGPT, disrupted all aspects of education.

I want therefore next to turn to technological developments that are impacting education, and what they mean in connection with Escalante's legacy, which is the story of one person inspiring others to learn and shine by standing on their own feet and thus without the props of technology. The short of it is that nothing that's happened since the 1980s or in the last decade in any way invalidates Escalante's legacy. If anything, subsequent technological developments make the lessons of his legacy all the more urgent. Let's turn to a few of these developments, though in no particular order and without any pretense at completeness.

In the years since this book first appeared, distractions that Escalante's generation never faced are now omnipresent and embedded: smartphones, social media, streaming services, pornography, and immersive gaming have grown from novelty to default leisure for adolescents. According to a 2024 Pew Research report (pewresearch.org), 72 percent of US high school teachers see cellphone distraction as a major problem in the classroom. High-school students are accessing their smartphones for non-academic activity during class time. The old script—"turn the phones off and get to work"—now must be complemented by classroom cultures that integrate digital fluency into serious learning, rather than simply banning devices. Educators inspired by Escalante must design lessons where technology is a tool, not a distraction, and must adopt protocols for rigorous engagement that match his relentless energy and expectation.

Further, instructional design itself has evolved dramatically. Adaptive-learning platforms and AI-driven tools are no longer the novelty they were a decade ago; they are part of many high-school math classrooms. Yet while these tools offer personalization, they cannot substitute for the kind of high-expectation classroom climate, teacher-student rapport, and uncompromising curriculum mastery that Escalante emphasized. Work in 2023 by Danielle Thomas and collaborators (arxiv.org/abs/2312.11274) suggests that schools which pair high-quality adaptive software with vigilant teacher oversight ("hybrid human-AI tutoring") outperform those relying solely on technology. Thus the lesson remains: tools can amplify learning effectiveness, but it all begins with the teacher—an Escalante who serves as cultivator, guide, and facilitator of learning.

Artificial intelligence (AI) is the biggest development since Escalante's day as well as since this book was first published in 2016. AI is widely viewed as a threat to education, allowing students to cheat in ways unimaginable in the past, helping to write their papers, do their problem sets, and in general bypass the hard work of learning. All such problems for education, however, arise because teachers are not monitoring their students closely and making sure that they can do their academic work standing on their own feet. It's a false dilemma to think that students will either cheat using AI or must be prevented from using it to learn successfully. The third option is to use AI as a way of honing students' skills and knowledge, helping them learn more effectively than before.

By analogy, consider computer chess. In 1996, IBM's Deep Blue defeated Garry Kasparov, who at the time was regarded as the strongest player ever to have played the game. Since then, computer chess has become far stronger than any of the world's grandmasters. Yet human chess players today are the strongest they've ever been because they are able to leverage computer chess in their training. It would be one thing if players in their play constantly asked a chess program what their next move should be in a game. That would be using computer chess as a crutch. But except for machine versus machine chess tournaments, chess tournaments pit humans against humans and prohibit machines from interfering in the game. Consequently, human players can now use chess programs to make themselves better at playing other humans.

There's no reason the same cannot be done using AI in education, especially by judiciously taking advantage of LLMs such as ChatGPT. To facilitate the learning of academic subjects by students, AI cannot be used indiscriminately. In particular, it won't do to sit students in front of an LLM and simply tell them have at it and learn something. In education, AI always needs to be in clear service of a well-defined curriculum. Moreover, AI must be used only in ways where its reliability is proven or can be corrected. This may involve teachers and curriculum builders prompting an LLM for study materials, but then vetting and editing the LLM's output carefully so that questions and answers are not misleading.

LLMs are known to make stuff up ("hallucinate") and they can betray bias in their training data. Educators using AI need to control for such problems. Above all, teachers must always be ready to block AI in educational activities that require students to think on their own feet. As in chess, there always comes a time in education to put the machine aside. Students tend to take the path of least resistance. AI can save what otherwise is a lot of wasted effort trying to track down certain information. At the same time, students need to be able to act without the prop of AI. A sound education will know where to draw the line.

Interestingly, leveraging AI in this way doesn't require a full-fledged teacher, though it always helps to have one available. With the AI vetted to deliver accurate instruction through an LMS (learning management system—a technology that did not arise until the late 1990s), it mainly needs a *monitor*. A monitor needs to know a lot less than a full-fledged teacher. A monitor just needs to confirm that the student isn't cheating and is answering questions correctly. The teacher, by contrast, needs to know the subject, set the lesson plan, make up tests, determine the answer key, and above all guarantee that the instruction offered is accurate.

Ben Carson, in the interview given in Appendix 4 of this book, describes how his mother got him to read two books a week when he was young. She herself had only a third grade education, and so was limited in what she could teach him. But she could ensure that her son spent time reading the books and then quiz him on their content, getting him to summarize and answer questions about it. Carson's mother here acted as a monitor, not as a teacher. Yet she had a profound impact on Carson's education, and he credits her insistence that he read books as the key to his success in life, especially in becoming a renowned pediatric neurosurgeon on the faculty of Johns Hopkins.

Carson's mother took an old-school approach to his education. She did not, in the progressive tradition of Thomas Dewey, ask Carson to peer deeply into his heart to determine whether he really wanted to read books, and from there decide whether to become a reader. His mother did not give him that option. Initially, reading was for him a chore. But eventually he came to love it. And it made all the difference for him. The pain was worth the gain. That's always the way it is with a sound education.

Artificial intelligence is promising to fundamentally transform education, leading to vast increases in efficiency of learning. Consider Alpha School. Founded in 2014 and refashioned under tech entrepreneur Joe Liemandt, Alpha School represents a radical experiment in K–12 education—an AI-driven, mastery-based model that compresses core academics into just two hours a day. Backed by $1 billion of Liemandt's own funding, Alpha's TimeBack system uses adaptive AI tutoring, personalized pacing, and focused time management to accelerate learning.

Alpha School students are said to advance an average of 2.6× faster than peers on nationally normed MAP (Measures of Academic Progress) tests and frequently score in the 99th percentile. The remaining hours focus on life skills such as entrepreneurship, leadership, and communication. Teachers, called "guides," earn salaries starting around $100,000 and function as mentors rather than lecturers. Tuition runs from $40,000 to $75,000 annually—the high end being charged in places like San Francisco, where the cost of living is high.

Alpha is at once a luxury brand and a highly disruptive educational model. It vastly reduces the time spent on learning academic subjects. It completely restructures traditional schooling. And it justifies such disruptive changes by claiming stupendous increases in academic results. Obviously, its cost puts it out of reach of most students and their families. But even though early adopters are paying premium prices, this educational model may in time become affordable and widely available.

Actually, a model similar to Alpha's that is affordable is already available. It's not as deluxe as Alpha, focusing instead strictly on academics, and thus, at least for now, lacking Alpha's life-skills amenities. Victoria Garmy, founder of StudiaNova.org, created this model. She draws inspiration from her upbringing in a one-room schoolhouse, her background as a mechanical and aeronautical engineer, and her passion for eliminating inefficiency in education. Applying an engineer's precision to education, she has designed a "microschool" model that maximizes learning intensity while minimizing waste. Her approach reimagines the one-room schoolhouse for the digital age—lean, high-tech, and yet personal—allowing students to achieve mastery in a fraction of the time consumed by conventional schools.

In Garmy's model, students attend school for just three hours a day in concentrated learning sessions. During that time, they work independently at computer stations, moving through carefully sequenced online courses while a teacher-supervisor circulates to answer questions, provides one-on-one help, and monitors progress. Garmy's school runs like a modern office. Like employees, students begin work by logging into their workstations. They then move through rich, interactive courses complete with videos, eliminating the need for live lectures or Zoom calls.

This "white-collar" classroom ensures that every minute serves a learning goal. The short day is enough, Garmy argues, because it eliminates non-instructional time: no cafeteria meals, no hallway transitions, no lengthy assemblies, and no distractions from unfocused instruction. The result is sustained intellectual engagement—three hours of genuine learning intensity, surpassing the diluted six- to eight-hour grind of traditional schools.

Her business model is as streamlined as her pedagogy. A single storefront equipped with twenty desks and repurposed Linux computers can accommodate forty students—twenty in the morning, twenty in the afternoon. With each paying $3,600 for nine months ($400 per month), annual revenue comes to $144,000. Studia Nova's tuition cost is a small fraction of Alpha's, making it widely affordable.

A single educator can, according to Garmy, operate such a self-sustaining one-room schoolhouse without grants or bureaucracy, making the model easily replicable nationwide. Garmy finds that total revenue of $144,000 is enough to cover rent, utilities, insurance, and an educator's salary. The startup cost for laptops and desks is minimal. This is a lean operation. No cafeteria or food costs. No sports. No frills.

Outcomes have been striking: Students quickly reach grade level within a year, even those arriving multiple years behind. After that, the sky's the limit. For students way behind in their reading level, reading while listening to the text being read combined with a writing exercise in which they give chapter summaries has proven remarkably successful at bringing readers up to speed. Three other features stand out:

1. the model's adaptability, enabling personalized pacing and mastery learning;
2. its simplicity—Garmy has built a model any committed educator or parent can reproduce, restoring both efficiency and excellence to American K–12 education;
3. its incentivization of good behavior and engaged learning because students themselves much prefer a short three-hour work day versus the typical six to eight hours at a traditional school—they don't want to jeopardize having to go back to the old model.

The compressed study time at Alpha and at Studia Nova contrasts with the long hours that Harvard economist Roland Fryer, in the *Wall Street Journal* article cited earlier, found was important for learning in traditional public schools. KIPP (Knowledge Is Power Program), a network of charter public schools, also emphasizes long hours, adding two hours to the typical public-school workday.

Which of these approaches is better for a sound education —short hours or long hours? Long hours have the advantage of allowing more time for students to socialize, play sports, do extracurriculars, etc. Students who attend microschools (or homeschools) may be able to participate in these activities at a local public school while foregoing its academics, but arranging that will require some additional effort by students and parents.

The question now arises, How many of the long hours spent at traditional schools are spent doing intense concentrated mental work (work in the challenge zone) that delivers significant learning outcomes? In posing this question, we need to keep in mind that people can sustain intense, deliberate focus for only so many hours per day before cognitive fatigue sets in, leading to sharply diminishing returns in productivity and output. This limit arises from the need for recovery (periods of rest or diversion) to maintain high-level attention and performance, as excessive effort beyond this threshold triggers errors, reduced creativity, and burnout. It seems, then, that Alpha and Studia Nova have found a way to make the learning experience much more efficient than conventional schooling.

Victoria Garmy's Studia Nova is attempting to spur an educational movement across the US and beyond that builds and empowers microschools at a vast scale. For now, however, her efforts remain fledgling. Yet there is a thriving educational option whose schools are even smaller than microschools. Those are the homeschools. Homeschooling in the US, at the time of this writing, educates about 4 million K–12 students, or about 7 percent of the primary and secondary school population. Started in the late 1970s by persons dissatisfied with traditional schooling, the homeschooling movement grew from 10,000–15,000 students in the early 1980s to millions by the 2000s, achieving legalization in all states by 1993.

Homeschooled students often outperform public-school students on standardized tests, excelling in self-directed learning. Homeschooling leverages technology extensively, using LMSs (learning management systems) from their inception in the late 1990s, online curricula like Khan Academy, and AI tools like

ChatGPT to personalize learning, enabling efficient, mastery-based education akin to models like Studia Nova's three-hour daily sessions. On average, homeschoolers spend about four hours per day on focused academic work, varying by age and curriculum, with younger students often at the lower end closer to two hours and high schoolers closer to six hours. Like Alpha and Studia Nova, homeschooling avoids the inefficiencies of traditional schools' longer hours, fostering high achievement while avoiding, through parental oversight, the pitfalls of AI misuse.

With the wise use to technology, students can learn much more efficiently than past generations of students, greatly accelerating their education. In particular, the wise use of technology avoids so much wasted time and busywork that burdened academic life in the past. Need a journal article? Find it instantly online as a pdf. Compare that to me finishing a book in 1998 and needing to spend half a day visiting a university library that had a journal article I needed, driving there, finding it in the stacks, photocopying it, driving back home, and then transcribing by hand any quotes from it. All this activity was necessary back then for me to finish the book. But it was not edifying—I did not become an intellectually more able scholar because of my library visit.

Or consider a baseball analogy. I used to coach baseball at the middle and high school levels. In a game, nine players from a team are listed in the lineup, and it's necessary for each player to take a turn at bat before a player can bat again. Understood as a learning opportunity, each at bat is therefore only one ninth of the total at bats, and so a player is only learning one ninth of the time that players on his team are at bat. For learning to improve one's game, this use to time is therefore highly inefficient. That's why games are not a great way to hone a player's batting skills, and separate practices are needed. Unfortunately, much of traditional K–12 education is inefficient in this way, focusing on the activity of one or a small group of students in a classroom while the rest of the class sits idly watching.

Besides improving the effectiveness and efficiency of learning traditional academic subjects, AI-driven technology promises to open entirely new frontiers in K–12 mastery, extending learning well beyond the traditional curriculum and enabling students to acquire high-level, once-rare skills. Consider the following possibilities:

1. **Accent and Pronunciation Refinement in Language Learning**
   Speech-recognition AI can analyze intonation, rhythm, and articulation down to the phoneme, offering individualized correction and visualized feedback, especially for non-native speakers who want to eliminate an accent. Students can practice repeatedly with voice models until their accent aligns with native fluency—an outcome rarely attempted, much less achieved, in traditional classrooms.

2. **Creative Writing with Rhetorical Precision**
   AI editors can train students to identify and employ rhetorical devices—analogy, parallelism, irony—and revise for tone, cadence, and argument strength. Instead of vague feedback, students get detailed stylistic analysis mapped to classical rhetorical devices. Classical schools would likely be early adopters.

3. **Polyphonic Music Composition and Performance**
   AI-guided keyboard and ear-training software can help students not just *play* Bach's music but *think* contrapuntally. Thus they will learn voice-leading, harmony,

and music theory generally not in the abstract but in real time as they compose or perform. Feedback systems can identify harmonic tension, suggest corrections, and let students iterate toward mastery of multi-voice textures.

4. **Advanced Sight-Reading and Aural Skills for Musicians**

   AI ear trainers can generate exercises dynamically, listening to a student's singing or playing and giving instant corrective guidance. Learners can progress through increasingly complex rhythms, keys, and harmonic progressions—achieving conservatory-level fluency before college.

5. **Scientific Experiment Simulation and Inquiry-Based Discovery**

   Students can design and run virtual experiments in physics, chemistry, or biology with AI labs that model real-world variables and data. The system can prompt hypotheses, predict outcomes, and help interpret anomalies—cultivating genuine scientific reasoning. Anyone anywhere with an internet connection and a computer can thus become a budding scientist.

6. **Mastery of Mathematical Intuition and Visualization**

   AI-driven virtual-reality environments can help students visualize abstract mathematical concepts dynamically, letting students manipulate parameters and *see* underlying relationships. Over time, learners internalize mathematical structures through direct experiential interaction rather than rote formula use.

7. **Fine Motor and Artistic Skill Development via Gesture Feedback**

   Vision-based AI can analyze brushstrokes, pen pressure,

or sculpting motions, giving immediate feedback on proportion, perspective, and technique. Students can thus master skills like calligraphy, drafting, or figure drawing once possible only under expert tutelage.

8. **Debate and Argumentation Coaching**

   Sufficiently advanced natural-language processing will be able to listen to and comprehend dialogue, assessing claims, evidence, and logical coherence in real time as students engage in debate. The AI coach can suggest stronger evidence, point out fallacies, and help students strengthen persuasion.

9. **Emotional Intelligence and Empathy Training through Simulated Dialogue**

   Conversational AI avatars can role-play complex emotional and social scenarios, letting students practice empathy, negotiation, and conflict resolution. Feedback can highlight emotional cues and alternative responses, cultivating social maturity rarely addressed in standard curricula.

10. **Advanced Memory and Visualization Techniques**

    AI tutors can train students to organize and recall large bodies of knowledge by turning abstract information into vivid, memorable stories or spatial patterns. Using adaptive prompts and personalized review schedules, learners can develop exceptional recall and deep understanding across subjects—from history dates to scientific classifications.

This last skill, if achievable through AI and becoming widespread among students, would be of both practical and historical significance. Before books and literacy became commonplace, cultures were largely oral, and a strong memory was a virtue. One concern about Gutenberg's press was that human memory would weaken on account of it. That concern is, given the internet, greatly amplified, with so much of human knowledge now being instantly accessible, requiring very little of our capacity for recall. Use it or lose it—and people in developed nations have lost a lot of their memory capacity. AI can reverse this trend, empowering the memory of student learners, and thereby helping them to be better learners generally. Indeed, who wouldn't find a powerful memory useful in their studies?

The goal of using technology in education—as sketched here and consistent with Escalante's legacy—is humanistic, not transhumanistic. The goal is edification, not enhancement. It is to grow by learning things that make us fuller, more vibrant versions of ourselves. It is not to remove inherent defects in ourselves and ultimately replace ourselves through technologies aimed at dissolving our humanity.

My prediction is that the humanistic vision will prevail, leading to far more actual human flourishing than the transhumanist vision, which is all about using technology to fix and upgrade humanity. The humanistic vision is natural, like promoting health through good diet, exercise, and proper rest. The other is artificial, like relying on pharmaceuticals to achieve wellness.

I close this section with two postscripts. The first is some advice to parents: Edify your kids, don't enhance them. We are organic beings, not gadgets to be improved with newer and better modules (like the newest computer chips). We are alive and need to strive for becoming fully alive. So far, we haven't tapped into the full potential of our humanity.

So why look to transhumanism, whose aim is to so transform humanity as to render it unrecognizable? Transhumanism tempts us with FOLO (fear of losing out): enhance your children or else they will get left behind, unable to attend Ivy

League schools, second-class citizens in the wider culture. Yet edifying your children is not only proven to make them thrive but also known to do no harm. Neither can be claimed for transhumanism.

The second postscript is this: There is much talk these days among journalists, talking heads, and podcasters about artificial intelligence (AI) turning into artificial general intelligence (AGI), where AGI matches and then exceeds our cognitive faculties, in the end so putting us to shame that AGI will take over the world, supplanting us and ultimately ridding the world of humanity.

This fear is unfounded. "Model collapse" of LLMs (there's now even a Wikipedia entry on the topic) suggests that these systems face inherent limitations that will ever keep them from reaching AGI. But a deeper theoretical reason for the inherent unachievability of AGI derives from conservation of information in search, which demonstrates mathematically that computational systems can never output the novel information needed to attain AGI. For the demonstration, see my monograph *The Law of Conservation of Information* (available for free at BIO-Complexity.org).

Choosing the Harder Path

In closing this 2025 preface, I need to stress a final crucial point: *defying low expectations admits no exceptions.* In conversations about education reform, one hears talk about no excuses and zero tolerance. Typically the point of such talk is that some boundaries are so inviolable that for students to cross them requires drastic intervention and discipline. Such boundaries do exist, like students threatening or disrespecting their teachers.

But defying low expectations is not about imposing draconian measures on students, teachers, or administrators. Students, especially, need grace because they are young, green, and mistake-prone. Rather, the point about defying low expectations is that anyone in education always needs, as much as possible, to resist lowering expectations, whether in regard to the learning of students, the teaching of teachers, or the administering of administrators. It matters not whether you justify lowered expectations in the lofty moral terms of compassion, self-esteem, or equity. Once you begin to tolerate lowered expectations, the education you offer is on the path to mediocrity, under-achievement, oblivion.

Of course, some caveats apply. We don't want to set impossibly high expectations, as typified by the overbearing parent who berates a child for getting "only" an A rather than an A+. Nor should we set expectations for classroom discipline so severely that minor infractions born of immaturity rather than defiance bring down the wrath of heaven. High expectations need to be set to encourage success, not to underscore failure.

That said, we need to be clear that to follow the example of Escalante is to choose the harder path. Defying low expectations is the harder path. It offers great promise of return. But it comes at a personal cost, and often with nasty opposition from those eager to take the easier path and insist that others join them: "Wide is the gate and broad is the road that leads to destruction, and many enter through it. But small is the gate and narrow the road that leads to life, and only a few find it." (Matthew 7:13–14, NIV) Escalante gave us a blueprint for academic success. You'll find that blueprint in this book. But can you be honest with yourself about how serious you will be in following this blueprint?

At a total cost of about $1 trillion annually, American K–12 education is big business. There's a lot of money in it. It's therefore unsurprising that education attracts many grifters who want some of that money, yet without delivering educational value. The easy road is easier. Teachers need to exert more effort to get students to learn than to sit back and watch them fail. Teachers' unions are appropriately named: they look out for the interests of teachers first and foremost—not the students. They consider it a job well done when mediocre teachers with seniority are able to keep their jobs at the expense of excellent but more junior teachers. In education, the forces of corruption are thus always in play to lower expectations.

William James, in his *Briefer Course* on psychology, notes that we find it easier in the abstract to recognize good things than in the concrete messiness of life. To illustrate this point, he describes a Russian lady at the theater. She weeps over the fictitious people experiencing tragedy on stage. Yet she is oblivious to her coachman who freezes to death on his seat outside. According to James, this sort of thing happens everywhere, though rarely with such force and clarity.

The point? Nobody I know who has watched *Stand and Deliver* regards Escalante as a villain or cheers on those in the film who try to thwart him. Yet the real-life Escalante was hard-nosed, wouldn't take no for an answer, and experienced serious opposition. It's easy to pat ourselves on the back and assure ourselves that when push comes to shove, we would have had Escalante's back. But if people universally had Escalante's back, his legacy would not need to be retold, as in this book.

The path forward is clear. We have the power to take it. Taking it brings immense reward. But it's not easy. And many prefer the easier path.

William A. Dembski, Ph.D.
Aubrey, Texas
December 2025

Foreword (2016) by Henry Gradillas

Henry Gradillas, a veteran, author, and educator, was Jaime Escalante's principal at Garfield High School from 1981 to 1987. The school, located in inner-city Los Angeles, struggled with gang violence and poor academic performance. Gradillas and Escalante worked effectively to improve the school academically, healing its toxic environment and ushering in Garfield High's "Golden Age."

At some point in life, most of us want to hit full throttle and give our best effort, regardless of what stands before us or what challenges others set against us. As an airborne-qualified US Ranger, I felt that I had given all I could—my best—in the training I gave to young army recruits. All of the rigorous tasks that my trainees had to successfully accomplish were geared to one main goal: survival on the battlefield.

I faced my challenge and found that my determination and strong desire to produce the best-trained soldiers brought enormous positive results. At one time, my trainees received a commendation for being the most aggressive soldiers and for receiving the highest rifle marksmanship scores ever attained at the recruiting camp.

After completing six years of active military service, I decided to end my military duties and return to civilian life. My desire to work with youth prompted me to return to college and obtain a teaching credential. My first teaching assignment was in East Los Angeles at Belvedere Junior High. This was the same school that I had attended, and one of the schools that sent students to Garfield High School.

After leaving that job, I managed a thousand-acre produce ranch. Yet my deep hunger and yearning to feel that pride again—that wonderful rush of being responsible for my young soldiers' extraordinary achievements—would return to me time and again. The years since those heady days in the military had taken a toll—I felt time was running short. So, I returned to teaching in South Central Los Angeles. Ever since, I have dedicated my life to training young minds to achieve success in their chosen fields.

In my first assignment back teaching, I was sent to Garfield High in East Los Angeles to teach biology. There I met a highly gifted and unusual teacher—an immigrant from Bolivia. I would end up partnering with him in an extraordinary educational project that would go on to become celebrated around the world.

Who was this teacher who hurried students into classrooms, at times holding his students in a line outside his room, asking each student a question before allowing them to enter? His name was Jaime Escalante, and he taught mathematics. We soon became good friends, working together to keep the halls free of lingering students and at times intervening to prevent altercations between potential troublemakers.

Escalante had arrived at Garfield shortly before me to begin his first teaching assignment in America. He experienced a big disappointment his first day on the job. The computer science classes he was scheduled to teach had been cancelled. What happened in the days that followed was the start for him of many challenges and disappointments.

Escalante cracked down on any behavior he considered to be a barrier to learning. He strongly believed that students need to be challenged and inspired in an environment that promotes learning. He convinced the then-principal to allow him to teach mathematics since the computer program was on hold. This is how one very small class of advanced placement calculus was started. Escalante had a powerful message for his students: *it can be done, no matter where or who you are.*

To return to my part in the story: After obtaining an administrative credential, I was promoted to Dean of Boys. This new assignment allowed me to give Escalante greater support. I was subsequently reassigned to several administrative positions within the Los Angeles Unified School District.

Then, in the summer of 1981—with no hint of what lay ahead—I enthusiastically accepted the position of principal of Garfield High School. What an amazing, once-in-a-lifetime opportunity to work with young minds again in a school community with which I was well familiar! I knew most of the staff, and many of the students knew me from my work in their junior high schools. Escalante was more than thrilled. He came to my office and loudly proclaimed, "We can do it, sir. Now we can do it!"

Unfortunately, my exciting new assignment began with one gigantic, troublesome, and quite extraordinary challenge. The Educational Testing Service had accused the Garfield AP Calculus students of cheating by improperly sharing answers with other students. They claimed there was evidence of similar wrong answers. The testing service disqualified 14 of the 18 scores and urged that students whose scores were disqualified retake the test if they wished to get college credit for AP Calculus. All of this was happening as I accepted the position as principal of Garfield High.

Escalante was extremely upset over this accusation against the AP Calculus students. So was the entire school and community. As their teacher, Escalante opposed the students' being required to retake the examination. He felt that if they took the test a second time, it would be an admission of guilt. Working closely with Escalante and discussing various options with him, I was able to help him think through how best to move forward. He reluctantly agreed to have the students retake the exam. Twelve students successfully completed the examination a second time, some with even higher scores.

Soon after this turmoil subsided, Escalante and I had a long and serious discussion. He explained how he needed to be able to count on me, as principal, to help him with his advanced placement program. He described his burning desire—what he called *ganas*, in Spanish—to teach calculus to dozens of kids. He said that with my backing and support, he would put Garfield on the map.

I committed to doing all I could to help this amazingly dedicated teacher succeed in attaining his goal. I knew that as principal I would not have direct hands-on contact with the students. However, I could certainly do all that was in my power to support Escalante. With my backing, he enthusiastically transformed his classroom into a wacky wonderland that intensified student interest and increased a strong desire among Garfield students to master advanced mathematics.

Over the next several years, the number of AP Calculus students at Garfield continued to increase. But students were not just taking Escalante's AP Calculus course in droves; they were also with impressive numbers passing the AP Calculus exam. The high-water mark came in 1987 as the AP Calculus program saw over 80 students pass the exam, more than at neighboring Beverly Hills High. One statistical survey documented that 27 percent of the Mexican-American students in the entire country who passed the AP Calculus college exam that year were from Garfield High!

Unfortunately, after I left Garfield in 1987 and a new administration took over, this spirit of innovation and commitment was lost. As the authors of this book clearly and accurately describe, the spirited, strategic, and successful advanced placement course Escalante had created with my support quickly declined. It ultimately returned to the mediocre program it was before Escalante came on board.

After so great a success, the new Garfield administration withdrew the support that Escalante had previously enjoyed. The destruction of Escalante's AP Calculus program is well documented, though not so well known. Most people think of Escalante as he was depicted in the film *Stand and Deliver*. That film, however, ends at the pinnacle of Escalante's time at Garfield. It misses the quick decline that came soon after.

Escalante's successes stemmed in large part from the rapport he built with his students and the attention he gave to them. In return, his students showed great respect and admiration for him and for his teaching methods. Today, decision-making and control have increasingly been transferred out of the classroom—out of the teacher's hands and into those of administrators occupying the higher rungs of the national educational bureaucracy. Attempts to improve our educational system have led to questionable programs such as "No Child Left Behind" and "Common Core." Testing has become a runaway train nationwide.

In 2011, Claremont Graduate University education professor Mary Poplin led a team that studied 31 highly effective teachers in the most economically depressed neighborhoods in Los Angeles County. As becomes clear from her Afterword to this book, Escalante epitomized the qualities of these teachers.

According to Professor Poplin, education is common sense: "We should observe what works and what does not; then we should build on the one, discarding the other." She also notes that it takes desire for excellence—*ganas*, again—on the part of educators to buck the system, or go around it, in order to create an environment where students can excel.

I strongly and enthusiastically endorse this inspiring book. The authors convey well the impressive heights attained by Escalante and the program he built.

Escalante's most valuable gift to his students was not a knowledge of calculus. It was the proof that they were capable of so much more than the world expected of them.

—Henry Gradillas, Ed.D

1. Renegade

Jaime Escalante was an amazingly effective teacher. Yet his effectiveness came at a cost: wherever he went, he created waves. For many of the educators who worked with Escalante, that wasn't a problem. Escalante's students achieved such remarkable success that fellow teachers and administrators were often willing to cut him slack. The new principal at Garfield High, however, thought otherwise. She ran a tight ship, and she wasn't about to let anything rock her boat.

Maria Elena Tostado had risen through the ranks of the Los Angeles Unified School District. Like many of her fellow career educators, she had taken the safe and steady path to success. The surest way to regular promotions was to follow procedures, obey instructions, and make sure employees who reported to her did the same. She wasn't about to jeopardize her professional standing to placate a prima-donna math teacher who was a royal headache at district headquarters.

In the main office—known by many in the school system as "Downtown"—Escalante was notorious for his endless demands and insistence on bending the rules. And when rules got bent, complications arose: angry parents, unhappy administrators, unsettled unions, unfriendly politicians. The California state educational code was 2,300 pages long. Tostado's responsibility was to deliver its promises and policies, not circumvent them, to 3,500 mostly poor and Hispanic students that crowded into the

Garfield campus in East LA, built more than sixty years earlier and badly frayed by decades of overuse and underfunding.

Her predecessor, Henry Gradillas, had handled Escalante like a rockstar, giving him what he wanted and shielding him from the wrath of students, parents, and school administrators who chafed under his high expectations and low tolerance for mediocrity. Gradillas's sympathetic view of Escalante and his unorthodox teaching techniques would be swept away by Tostado's new vision. Maybe Gradillas was willing to spend his own personal and professional capital to insulate this renegade from the consequences of his behavior; but she was not.

Within five years of Tostado's arrival at Garfield, every teacher and teaching method associated with the controversial and divisive Jaime Escalante would be gone without a trace. And so would one of the most spirited, innovative, successful, and famous Advanced Placement programs in the history of American education, replaced by a system that failed in every way except that it followed the rules. Tostado ensured the elevation of procedure over results, the return to mediocrity from hard-won excellence, the triumph of indolence and apathy over talent and industry. Indeed, few have been as successful as she at snatching defeat from the jaws of victory.[1]

1.1. Advanced Placement Calculus

Escalante taught his first Advanced Placement calculus class in 1978, four years after he came to Garfield, cobbling a curriculum together from old test questions and handouts he scrounged himself because there was no budget for textbooks. Five students survived his intense regimen of drills, before- and after-school tutoring, and lunchtime review sessions to take the Educational Testing Service national AP exam at the end of the year. Two of them passed.

Gradually attendance increased. In 1982, eighteen students took the AP calculus test and for the first time everyone passed. That was also the year fourteen of the pupils were accused by ETS of cheating. Shocked and angered by the accusation, Escalante, Gradillas, and a growing national chorus accused the testing company of discrimination, despite the fact that students' identities were unknown to the graders who read their answer sheets. Twelve of the fourteen agreed to retake the test (the others had already moved on with their educations) and all twelve passed.

This spectacular vindication transformed Escalante and Garfield High into celebrities. All the Advanced Placement courses on campus surged in popularity, with AP calculus enrollment growing every year. In 1987, 127 Garfield students took the AP calculus exam and 85 of them passed. That meant 27 percent of all Mexican-American students in America who passed AP calculus that year were students in Jaime Escalante's program.

1.2. Hollywood Comes to Garfield

Also in 1987, production began on a Hollywood version of the 1982 controversy over whether Escalante's students had cheated. *Stand and Deliver*, starring Edward James Olmos and Lou Diamond Phillips, was filmed that summer at Garfield and at nearby Roosevelt High. It dramatized the story of poor Latino kids whose parents were gardeners and hotel maids, who pinned their hopes for the future on passing an elite national test, and who proved the doubters wrong by passing a retest with the encouragement of their incredible and gifted teacher.

What the movie didn't show, and what Mrs. Tostado and other like-minded educators fretted so about, was the price of this success to everybody outside the AP calculus bubble. By the time *Stand and Deliver* celebrated its Oscar nomination for best actor, the seeds for the destruction of Escalante's calculus program were already sown.

After Henry Gradillas was promoted from dean of discipline to principal in 1981, he had used his position to help Escalante build his program. He helped scrape up money for advanced math textbooks even though most Garfield students struggled with far simpler problems. In the aftermath of the 1982 publicity, so many students signed up for AP calculus that Escalante requested a new, larger classroom. Gradillas gave him a big music rehearsal hall and assigned the other calculus teacher, Ben Jimenez, to a second music room. A member of the school board appropriated $25,000 for air-conditioning to make Escalante's room more appealing to summer school students. Escalante also eventually arranged facilities and funding for high school summer classes at East Los Angeles Community College a few blocks from Garfield.

Escalante took a dim view of activities that detracted from math. Indeed, he thought of students who engaged in such activities as "murderers" insofar as they "killed" time that could have been spent more productively on math. Time was, for Escalante, the most precious commodity and he filled every available minute of his young students' lives with mathematical training. He opened the old band hall, MH-1, at seven a.m. every school day and kept it open late. Students came by for tutoring during lunch. They came on Saturdays and kept working through the summer.

Escalante was always playing catch-up, having to cover a vast amount of remedial ground. Students entered Garfield in the tenth grade, most of them with the barest grasp of arithmetic and basic algebra. To prepare them for AP calculus in only three years was a massive challenge that took all their focus and concentration. Escalante discouraged them from cheerleading, band, football, and anything else that distracted them from his assignments. He also discouraged after-school jobs, even though many students needed to help support their families, work in the family business, or take care of younger siblings.

To keep them interested, Escalante transformed his classroom into a wacky wonderland. He decorated the walls with posters of his beloved Los Angeles Lakers, rewarded correct answers with candy, and threw pillows at students who gave wrong answers. Some days he made them answer a question before they could come in the door. Sometimes he brought doughnuts or hamburgers to class. He might demonstrate a math idea by cutting apples into pieces with a meat cleaver, or using an E.T. doll as a puppet. Steps to problem-solving were transformed into basketball or hockey moves. He patrolled the aisles, dishing out encouragement and criticism in equal measure, commenting on a haircut here, a fashion statement there. He mimicked a cheerleader one minute and a gang member the next. When the class needed a change of pace, he blasted "We Will Rock You" and pounded his desk along with the class. Or he might play music from a favorite opera, or folk tunes from his native Bolivia.

In Jaime Escalante's view, this was what it took to cram five or six years' worth of math into three. It was a matter of having the *ganas*, a Spanish word he often used to describe the desire to learn. Anything was worth the sacrifice to give these students a chance to compete for a college track that would take them out of the barrio and into a successful, high-paying career. Escalante's students were accepted into top colleges around the country. At one point fourteen of his former students were at Harvard, Yale or MIT at the same time. MIT professor and audio system inventor Amar Bose gave an open invitation to any Escalante student who wanted to enroll there, and helped pay their expenses.

Escalante's principal, Henry Gradillas, steadfastly supported this enthusiastic teacher who devoted so much time and energy to students and poured himself into their lives. That level of dedication deserved all the help the principal could give him. Gradillas, formerly a captain in the elite Army Airborne Rangers, respected the school district's rules and regulations but found many creative ways around them. He charged in with confidence where rules were ambiguous or absent. And there were times when he conveniently looked the other way, convinced that the results Escalante achieved were worth veering a bit from those 2,300 pages of regulations.

But it was also true that Escalante made other teachers feel shortchanged. Why didn't any of them get a bigger classroom? Air-conditioning? Off-budget textbooks? After he became math department chairman in 1981, why didn't he do his required faculty service, the administrative work he was supposed to do along with his fellow teachers? What right did he have to make a student give up band practice? The football team? An after-school job?

The counseling office sometimes told students who wanted to drop Escalante's classes that they couldn't, which was not exactly true. Parents complained about the long hours and endless quizzes and homework. "Downtown" complained about the money. The teachers union disapproved of the long hours and large classes, believing they were against the work rules and set a bad precedent. Yet, upstream to administrators and downstream to teachers and parents, Gradillas tirelessly ran interference for his friend and colleague who worked harder than anybody and got spectacular results. When even the janitor complained about Escalante's long hours, Gradillas gave the teacher his own key.

Nineteen eighty-seven was a pivotal year. It was the year that, by hogging resources and irritating a wide range of people,

Jaime Escalante developed and led a calculus program that produced more than one-fourth of all the Mexican-American students in America who passed the AP calculus test—leaving Beverly Hills High in the dust and besting all but three high schools in the nation in the number of exams given. It was the year the Hollywood film *Stand and Deliver* went into production, which soon would make Jaime Escalante a media celebrity far beyond the world of education. It was also the year that Henry Gradillas decided to take a sabbatical to finish his doctoral dissertation, "Characteristics of Capable Teachers," explaining, "I wanted to show the kids you're never too old to learn."[2] And it was the year that his successor, Maria Elena Tostado, began to dismantle the program Escalante had built and Gradillas had protected in order to replace it with her own.

In an interview in the fall of 1987, Tostado hailed Escalante as "one in a million. Everyone is trying to get into his classes. He and his students seem to feed off each other with their energy and enthusiasm." She added that the surge in interest in AP classes was continuing. "He's had a huge impact on the whole school." And yet at the same time, the first steps for undermining Escalante's calculus program were already under way.

The following spring, *Stand and Deliver* was released and Edward James Olmos received an Oscar nomination for his portrayal of Escalante. Suddenly, everyone wanted to interview this remarkable teacher and see him in action. Vice President George Bush stopped by his classroom, and President Ronald Reagan applauded Escalante's drive and success. Escalante began going on speaking trips, sometimes accompanied by Tostado. Participation in AP calculus was down a bit compared with the year before, and results down even more: 119 students sat for the exam and fifty-five passed. Escalante blamed the drop on the distraction of so many visitors and the false impression of moviegoers that passing the AP test was easy. Years of actual classroom preparation had been squeezed into one academic year in the film. But the interest in advanced calculus had sparked enrollment in other subjects as well so that 443 students campus-wide took at least one Advanced Placement exam, ranking Garfield thirty-third out of 8,247 public and private high schools nationwide, and more than any other inner-city school.

"It was Mr. Escalante, who has followed his own grinding trail of self-improvement, who was the catalyst for the sparkling gains the school has made," Tostado said in 1988. "Jaime is a master teacher above all."

Within a year, Escalante was the subject of a biography, *Escalante: The Best Teacher in America*, by Jay Mathews, the host of a Peabody Award-winning PBS series titled *Futures*, and had been invited to the White House to consult on education (he declined, but met President Reagan in California later on). A feature article in *The New York Times*[3] described an animated Mr. Escalante standing in front of his class with a baseball and glove explaining trajectory in terms of a pitch. On the wall was a poster reading, "Calculus need not be made easy: It is easy already."

John Bennett, director of the AP program at Garfield, sounded one note of caution in the *Times* article: "I think a lot of people feel Escalante has built a little empire. That has been divisive to some extent, but the overall effect has been really positive."

"The good [teachers] are not jealous of him," Tostado responded. "The ones I find making the noise are the ones who are not measuring up."

1.3. Escalante's Support Structure Destroyed

But as these glowing comments went out in the national press and Jaime Escalante's star continued to rise, the support structure that made his success possible was being destroyed and the new leadership was beginning to reveal its true colors.

In the fall of 1988, Henry Gradillas finished his doctoral dissertation and returned to Los Angeles. Not only was he renowned as the principal who had supported and encouraged Jaime Escalante, he was also praised for his skill in reducing gang violence, managing discipline, and raising academic standards. With his new Ph.D., he might have expected an assignment that put his abilities to work system-wide. Instead, he was put in charge of asbestos removal.

A spokesman for the district explained that it was a temporary assignment until they "found something good for him." However, Escalante believed office politics were involved and one unnamed administration source admitted that Gradillas was "too confrontational." Jaime's friend was being sidelined because he stirred things up "Downtown." "He eliminated a high percentage of the teachers who were teaching from the desk, not doing their jobs," Escalante remarked. Tostado pointed out that Gradillas had sharply reduced the number of shop classes and "some people downtown are philosophically at odds with that."

In fact, Gradillas had curtailed shop classes because, as he explained in a later interview, "boys were sitting around in woodshop making shoeshine kits. It was a waste of time. The auto shop had an old car with a carburetor. What's the point of learning to fix [an obsolete] carburetor when cars don't have them anymore?" He wanted the classes to be useful or be eliminated and the space used for more productive learning.[4]

"When someone like Henry makes a drastic change in curriculum or in policy," Tostado continued, "he ends up fighting not only his faculty, to convince them of the need of it, but ends up fighting with the powers that be that determine such decisions." It was a kind of fight Tostado preferred to avoid.

One administrator who asked not to be named told the *Washington Post* that Gradillas had "offended his superiors by being 'fiercely, unbelievably dedicated to children … A number has been done on him.'" Another colleague added, "A maverick in this district … is in trouble." Garfield's career counselor, Joe Lopez, told reporter and author, Jay Mathews, that Gradillas' treatment was payback from "Downtown" for the disruptions his high standards and dedication to students caused. "Henry proved them wrong in everything they did."[5]

By 1990, Escalante could no longer depend on the Garfield administration for the help he needed to maintain his celebrated but unorthodox program. Tired of facing irate parents and unhappy students, counselors now allowed students to drop Escalante's class when they felt overwhelmed. Under Gradillas, the administrators had encouraged, even cajoled, students to tough it out and had worked to convince parents that the sacrifice was worth it. When a counselor let a student drop calculus for more practice time with the swim team, Escalante believed the school had lost sight of what he was trying to achieve.

Escalante was now under more pressure to conform to district policies. In the past, any student who wanted to take one of his classes could do so with his permission, even if they didn't have the required prerequisites. Now those exceptions became problematic. He raised administrative hackles when he wanted to use an aide for calculus that was hired for remedial instruction. There had been complaints about the money designated for his use that he received from corporations to fund his summer school at East LA Community College, saying it should instead go to the college math department for them to distribute. (When they threatened to commandeer the money, the sponsor in turn threatened to withdraw it, saying it was for Escalante's program specifically.)

Also in 1990, Escalante was replaced as chairman of the math department by his protégé Ben Jimenez. It's likely that Tostado and others were weary of their celebrity teacher having the title and the extra $500 per year and yet not fulfilling his assigned administrative duties. Escalante believed it was a ploy by the teacher's union to undercut his ability to assign students to their classes and funnel promising prospects into his advanced sections. The union had turned teachers against him and promoted his young colleague. The first vote was a tie; Jimenez won on the second ballot. Escalante resigned his union membership after his defeat.

That year he decided to move to another school.

Stung by the "ingratitude" of parents and teachers he believed didn't appreciate academic achievement, Escalante announced in February 1990 that he would resign from Garfield to teach elsewhere or take a job in computer design. A story in the Los Angeles Times[6] reported that his main reason for leaving was receiving letters from parents who wanted their children to drop advanced math classes to spend more time with sports and other interests. He claimed these parents "don't see education as the way to succeed in this country." He also said he had received threatening phone calls both at the school and at home. What's more, Escalante complained of a "lack of district support" and what he believed was jealousy on the part of other teachers.

It was true that some teachers resented the attention Escalante received because of the film Stand and Deliver. They thought he was arrogant and demanding. It was also true that

Jaime lacked subtlety when judging fellow teachers who failed to meet his high standards. In one often-repeated exchange, Escalante bluntly criticized a teacher for her students' poor performance. When the teacher exclaimed that she'd been teaching students for fifteen years, Escalante replied, "Well, you've been teaching them the wrong thing." Others resented the idea that for them to be considered good teachers the public now expected them to be as flamboyant and spend as much time in class as he did. Some colleagues also resented that President George Bush had visited Escalante at Garfield High, and that the teacher had openly supported Bush for president.

Though many students loved him and worked hard to earn his approval, some were glad to hear he was leaving. One Garfield graduate who had been in Escalante's classes for three years commented, "I think once he leaves, the school will go back to normal and start doing good things. The movie really made things bad for us at school."

Days after his announcement, Escalante changed his mind. Following a meeting with the assistant superintendent of Los Angeles schools and Tostado, he said that he would stay at least until the end of the school year. "I was going to quit in two weeks," he told reporters. "I was going to be a bad boy, but I looked at all the kids and decided I couldn't do that." In addition, he wanted to continue developing a summer program he had started at nearby East Los Angeles Community College (ELAC). When administration policy kept him from teaching the courses he wanted in summer school at Garfield, Jaime had arranged to teach his summer classes on the ELAC campus. Under sponsorship of the National Science Foundation and funded by ARCO (now a subsidiary of British Petroleum), the program had grown to 1,000 students a year from schools all across the district studying math, science, English, and teacher training in the Escalante method. Other corporate sponsors included Xerox, IBM, GTE, and the Carnegie Foundation, all donating specifically to Escalante's summer program.

1.4. Escalante Leaves Garfield

But in the spring of 1991, Escalante again announced his departure. This time he made good on his threat. He blamed "faculty politics and petty jealousies" for his decision to leave Garfield after seventeen years for a teaching position in Sacramento. Henry Gradillas would never have let a teacher who got such results leave his school; he would have done whatever it took to keep him. But while calling him "excellent" and "an undisputed leader of his profession … a master," Tostado also told the *LA Times*, "Here, he is just one of the faculty. No one makes a big to-do about Jaime. I don't think that's strange. It's just the way it is."[7]

Lucy Romero, a faculty member at Garfield for more than thirty years, remembers Tostado as a "very, very insecure person" who "wanted to make her mark" as a principal.[8] Three years into Tostado's tenure, the faculty petitioned the district unsuccessfully to have her removed. She left after nine years on the job.

Angelo Villavicencio, who started teaching at Garfield the year Gradillas left and taught calculus alongside Escalante, believed Tostado was jealous of Escalante's success and notoriety and wanted him gone. "She did not want any Escalante legacy at Garfield," Villavicencio recalled later, "and brought in her own team of teachers she believed were better. She tried her best to get rid of any Escalante legacy, and she succeeded."[9]

Ben Jimenez, Escalante's protégé and successor as department chair, left at the same time, and Villavicencio took Escalante's place. A year later, Villavicencio followed his mentor out the door. "I saw the writing on the wall and said, 'I'm not going to last,' he says of those days. He was identified with the Escalante regime, and, he says, the new principal's attitude was, "My team is better than Escalante's team." Tostado declined his request to add a third class of calculus in order to reduce class size, and in fact threatened to make matters worse by taking away the large music classroom he had inherited. She shied away from supporting Escalante's strict standards in the face of continuing complaints from parents and district officials. Don Mroscak, a counselor at Garfield from 1967 to 1994, remembers that "expectations fell off" during that time. "There was no more push."[10] Concludes Villavicencio, "There were some narrow-minded people there. They were jealous of his success ... It took four or five years for the whole thing to go down the drain."

In a 2002 article, Jerry Jesness, who later collaborated with Gradillas on a book, wrote of Escalante's legacy at Garfield, "By 1996, the dynasty was not even a minor fiefdom."[11] Reporting Escalante's death from cancer in 2010, *The New York Times* observed, "Without him, Garfield's calculus program withered."[12] Results prove the point. In 1996, five years after Escalante left Garfield, eleven students passed the AP calculus exam, down from the historic high of eighty-five in 1987. When Villavicencio offered to return to the school to relaunch the calculus program, the administration told him they were doing fine and didn't need any help.[13] In 2009, fifty-five Garfield students sat for the AP calculus exam; thirteen passed.

As a team, Jaime Escalante and Henry Gradillas produced an educational system that outperformed anything before or since. But it was of necessity a renegade operation that strained, evaded, or ignored the rules and put their professional careers at risk. When Gradillas left, Escalante lost the protection of a sympathetic principal and was hounded from his job. Their results had been historic, but their methods were an administrative headache. Weighed in the balance by "Downtown," administrative harmony trumped student performance.

In any other field or venture that puts a premium on results, Escalante's success would have had the world beating down his door to copy it. Anything impeding such astonishing results would be swept aside in the quest for excellence—people replaced, polices changed, priorities and resources reordered. But history and experience show us that the world of education is a different world.

Does great teaching have to be a renegade operation? Do the best results have to come from outside the educational mainstream? Unconventional teachers, along with parents desperate for unconventional results, may spill out around the edges but more often leave the system entirely to find a better way. The legacy of Jaime Escalante proves we can achieve incredible results in education by doing an end run around the system. It also proves that the system resists end runs and is only too happy to embrace mediocrity.

Why is that? And what will it take for the American educational mainstream to encourage and support a teacher like the Bolivian immigrant who wore funny hats, played loud music, annoyed his colleagues and superiors, and proved to the children of immigrant gardeners and hotel maids that they could get into Harvard, MIT, or any other top university that they might want to attend?

Throughout his career, Escalante hammered home that we all can do far more than we think we can. And that includes educators as well as students.[14] But it takes setting your sights high, which means defying low expectations.

2. I Will Succeed

Jamie Escalante did not look like anybody's idea of a celebrity. One of his favorite nicknames for students, Corcho, would have been a good fit for Jaime himself. He was built like a corcho —a cork. Solid and chunky with big hands, a burly neck, and short legs. One observer said he looked like the school mascot: a bulldog. His dark features were framed by oversized glasses that emphasized the roundness of his face. A scraggly comb-over was often hidden under his trademark newsboy cap. His daily wardrobe tended towards chinos, plaid shirts, and shape-less pullover sweaters. His thick accent persisted decades after leaving his native Bolivia for the barrios of East Los Angeles.

Certainly the first forty years of Jaime Escalante's life gave no clue he would ever be the subject of feature articles in *The New York Times* or an Oscar-nominated Hollywood film. Or that his legacy as a teacher would drive discussion and debate about education in America down to the present day.

When people met Escalante, their first hint of something extraordinary was his eyes. They darted and sparkled like a child's on Christmas morning. He was always observing, absorbing, analyzing, deducing. He would figure out what each student needed—discipline, encouragement, extra time, more explaining, a victory doughnut—and make sure it was there for them. A sense of constant activity radiated and pulsed around him, animating his explanations and propelling his stocky frame up and down rows of desks with unexpected agility. These bursts of motion complemented a brilliant mind teeming with enthusiasm for his young pupils, for the mysterious processes and secrets he was demystifying for them, and for the bright future he envisioned for his poor Latino students even if nobody else did.

From his own experience growing up in the suburbs of La Paz and teaching at a Jesuit school there, he knew all about children's ability to overcome challenges and obstacles in their lives; the value of consistent high standards and expectations; the importance of taking time to teach and learn well; and the power of convincing his pupils that with enough drive and desire—*ganas* in Spanish—they could do the impossible.

2.1. Escalante's Early Life

Jaime was born the last day of 1930 in La Paz, Bolivia, because the village of Achacachi where his parents lived didn't have a hospital. His mother, Sara, spent several weeks before the birth with relatives in the city so her child could be born there rather than in the three-room apartment they rented on an unpaved street with open sewers. She had traveled down from the hills where the working class and poor people lived into the valley below where the good hospitals, roads, and fine houses were. He was the family's second child and first son. Another son and two more daughters would follow.

Sara and her husband, Zenobio, were teachers, assigned by the government to their schools. According to the Bolivian system, administrators decided where teachers would work. The family tradition of teaching reached back another generation to Sara's father, José Gutiérrez. Though Señor Gutiérrez was retired from the classroom by the time Jaime came along, the old man enjoyed teaching him word games. Jaime loved learning from the start.

The boy looked forward to visits with his grandfather. They were likely a welcome distraction from the tension at home. Zenobio drank, sometimes too much, and sometimes beat Jaime's mother in front of him after stumbling home from a bar. Escalante's biographer, Jay Mathews, writes that "the father's wrath also occasionally fell on his small son." One night when Zenobio didn't come home at all, Sara decided to leave him and take the children to La Paz—except for Jaime. Loading the rest of the family into the flatbed truck that served as the local bus, she handed the boy a piece of bread and told him to explain things to his father when he finally returned. Eventually Jaime joined the rest of the family in La Paz, making the six-hour trip by himself and carrying his few belongings wrapped in a towel.

His first day at school the children made fun of his clothes, styled after the Aymara Indian tradition of his old neighborhood. Yet soon he impressed them with his skill at arithmetic and sports, especially handball. He was a master on the court, or *frontón*, and made his own handballs by heating strips of old tires then molding them around a small rock.

Jaime developed an insatiable curiosity about almost everything. When pursuing an answer or experimenting with ideas, he focused so completely on the task that he blocked out any distractions and ignored what might happen if things didn't go according to plan. He started building experiments and enlisted his sisters, Olimipa and Bertha, to try them out. The girls endured a long series of mishaps. Younger sister Bertha was driving a car her brother had cobbled together when it catapulted her head-first into an open manhole, covering her in sewage. Another time he reached out pretending to shake her hand and shocked her with a small hidden generator. Their older sister, Olimipa, once had her foot burned to the bone after Jaime dropped a caustic liquid on it. Chasing a handball that had bounced off a roof into the gutter, Jaime became curious about what else might have fallen down the same spot. When he climbed a ladder to investigate, he fell and broke his arm. He also gashed his forehead, leaving a scar he carried for the rest of his life.

Poor though she was, Jaime's mother was proud of her social position as a teacher. She recognized that her elder son was bright and capable, and vowed to give him what help she could to improve his future prospects. Except for math and science, he cared a lot more about handball than schoolwork. But when he was fourteen, she enrolled him in San Calixto, one of the top high schools in La Paz. Its campus was up the hill from the presidential palace in an old mansion that was the home of former Bolivian president Andrés Santa Cruz, whose gift had endowed the school.

Entering the grounds of San Calixto, Jaime left behind the dirt and bustle of the city for a series of quiet, cool courtyards with fountains and beautiful lawns. He found his place among the other 750 boys as a star handball player who loved math, science, and mischievous—sometimes outrageous —practical jokes.

He and his new friends played handball at recess every day. It was on the *frontón* at San Calixto that he first used the word *ganas*, meaning "drive," "desire," or "passion," to talk about what it took to win the game. Desire was everything, and success was the reward. To extend their playing time, Jaime convinced a friend to wedge a twig beside the clapper of the bell announcing the end of recess. The time it took the teacher to figure out what was wrong gave him a few extra precious minutes on the court.

His report card showed that he excelled in subjects that interested him, offset with a warning that he talked too much and told too many jokes. To keep the unfavorable news from his mother, Jaime mixed his report card up in a stack with his siblings' and tried to trick her into thinking she'd seen his card when she had seen one of the others twice. When she finally saw his report, she paused for effect before insisting that next time she would not sign it if he brought home such low grades again—a dramatic technique Jaime would work into his teaching style years later.

Saturdays Jaime usually spent on homework, sometimes studying with classmates. When they came to a math or science concept he understood, Jaime stood beside a small blackboard and explained it to the others. He devoured information on subjects that interested him. He loved puzzles, and craved new concepts in math and science. He read ahead until he reached the end of the textbook, then borrowed more advanced books from Olimipa. Visiting a friend's house one day he asked to borrow a physics book he saw on the shelf. When his friend said no, Jaime sneaked it out under his shirt.

Jaime cultivated friendships with teachers, always looking for new challenges. Even at so young an age, he started absorbing teaching methods he admired and would mimic later on. One teacher who responded to Jaime's enthusiasm was Father Descottes, a gaunt Frenchman who taught physics. Jaime convinced him to let him borrow books and spend extra time in the lab in exchange for keeping the lab clean.

Jaime especially liked his physics teacher, Mr. Portus, who combined a fast-paced classroom style with biting, sometimes humiliating humor. Jaime loved both characteristics and would adapt them to his own style in a milder form. If a student took too long to answer a question, Portus would snap, "You sound like you had s---- for breakfast!" The teacher would ask students to repeat a joke he had told the day before. Jaime would not only retell the joke but also embellish it, typically making a bawdy punchline even bawdier. Jaime enhanced his growing reputation as a comic with tricks like tossing firecrackers under the school director's robe during graduation.

Jaime's ravenous curiosity extended outside the walls of San Calixto and into every part of life. He enjoyed talking with the shoeshine boys who worked the square around the presidential palace a few blocks from school. His mother disapproved—these were low-class boys and not the type her aspiring young scholar should associate with. Jaime didn't care. He talked with them anyway. After his mother rented a room in their home to a carpenter, Jaime learned enough from him to build his own room off the kitchen and light it with pilfered electricity.

His parents had lived apart ever since his mother escaped to La Paz. Once in a while, Zenobio Escalante would show up, usually drunk. The children tried to avoid him. He belittled Jaime's love of learning and exemplary reading skills. The last time he came he collapsed on the couch and died the next day. At the funeral, Jaime learned for the first time that his father had another family with three children that none of his brothers and sisters had ever met. His death was such a relief that Jaime wept for joy.

Jaime dreamed of going to engineering school after graduating from San Calixto. But his widowed mother had no money to give him, and other relatives couldn't (or wouldn't) help with his expenses. So he put his future on hold, picked up some odd jobs, and tried to decide what to do next. A short-term solution appeared in the form of revolution taking place in Bolivia, the latest in a succession of battles against a weak and unstable government. At nineteen, Jaime Escalante joined the army, spent most of his brief career as an observer, then returned home to scrounge up work day-to-day and think again about his future.

2.2. Escalante Becomes a Teacher

His childhood friend Roberto Cordero decided to take the entrance exam at Normal Superiór, a teacher's college founded recently by the government, and suggested Jaime take it too. Though Jaime still had hopes of engineering school, he applied at Normal along with Roberto. Both passed the test and were accepted. One of the instructors, Umberto Bilbao, had taught Escalante in elementary school and remembered his antics and intelligence. Jaime's second year at Normal, Bilbao joined the education ministry. When a physics instructor at the American Institute died suddenly he offered Escalante the job.

Jaime Escalante was twenty-one, still a student himself, and had no teaching experience. Even so, Bilbao was convinced that this young scholar had the drive, imagination, and skill to excel in front of the classroom. Escalante did not impress the principal at the American Institute. He hesitated to hire someone so young and with no university degree. Jaime suggested he let him teach for a week, then visit the class and see how he was doing. There was no class textbook; he would have to assemble teaching materials from his own physics books, notes, and whatever references he could collect. He had never been in a school with girls, but some of his twenty-eight pupils would be girls. He spent the first class period writing furiously on the blackboard: diagrams, notes, examples, questions. Though he scarcely turned to look at his students, they followed his explanations closely. He worked weekends on his preparations, neglecting his own studies at Normal and even cutting back his time on the handball court to come up with more proofs, better explanations.

In order to maintain accountability, upper level exams in Bolivia were given by visiting teachers, usually from other schools. The first test of the year for Escalante's students would be proctored by a teacher from the rival National Bolívar, a public high school nearby. Four weeks ahead of the scheduled exam, Jaime gave a practice test. Almost half the class failed. He decided that the problem was he had tried to teach too much material. He organized after-school study sessions two days a week to drill the basics. Encouraged by his attention and impressed by his tireless energy, almost all the students came to the help sessions. Their success on test day was a testament to their hard work and commitment, and to their young teacher's skill.

Along with more hours of instruction, Escalante pressed for better facilities for his students. When a new modern high school was built in a wealthy neighborhood, Jaime joined a group of teachers and others who occupied part of the new building, demanding their students share in the new space. Officials of the Education Ministry agreed, and gave students from Normal Superiór some of the new classrooms and use of the pristine new basketball court.

In April 1952 another revolution rocked the country. Though it lasted only three days, the economy was upended as the new regime turned land over to the Indians and nationalized the copper mines. Escalante's friend, Umberto Bilbao, remained with the Education Ministry and offered Jaime a new job at National Bolívar. Jaime noted that he was only starting his third year at Normal and had no license to teach. But with his position, Bilbao could get him a job anyway. "It's hard to find people who don't have to teach because often they make the best teachers," Bilbao observed.

Jaime got off to a rocky start. The principal at Bolívar criticized his teaching technique. He wrote too much on the board and kept his back to the students. He didn't emphasize homework enough.

Jamie was fascinated with a teacher named Tito Meleán. His approach was part-teaching, part-theater, and all intimidation. He carried a bone in his hand as he walked between the rows of desks. Rumor was that it was a human bone. When students were too slow to answer or seemed not to pay attention, he whacked them with the bone and barked, "I'm talking to you, stupid!"

Jamie asked Tito for advice. "Anything you produce, anything that works, stop and analyze it," the older teacher answered. "If it works, use it. Save it. Study it. And you have to know how to tell dirty jokes to the seniors. Anything to get them to class."

Athletic, witty, and always smiling, Jamie had become a ladies' man. He liked girls who liked to party. But around this time he met a fellow student at Normal named Fabiola Tapia. His friend Roberto's wife, Blanca, encouraged him to pursue her. She was quiet and studious, not the loud, fun-loving type he was typically attracted to. And she was a Protestant—rare in a country that was overwhelmingly Catholic. Her father had a degree from Biola University in California and worked as a teacher while writing tracts on New Testament prophecy. The family had lost its potato farm in the 1952 revolution when it was given by the government to their tenants. In contrast to Jaime, she and her parents observed a strict no-alcohol policy.

Escalante had been skipping his own classes at Normal to prepare his teaching lessons but began returning to campus at the 11 am break to bring Fabiola *salteñas*, a baked turnover filled with meat, spices, and vegetables. She asked him to help her and a friend with their math lessons. He borrowed a classroom and amazed them with how well he could explain the subject. He eagerly shared his world with her—his favorite *salteña* snack bar, his conversations with shoe shine boys on the square, his love of handball.

Escalante got a call to give a final exam at San Calixto. While he was there, a young math teacher asked if he'd like to join the faculty. They needed a physics teacher. Jaime explained that he still hadn't finished his studies and didn't have his teaching credentials. (He finally finished his last credit —a math class he "never bothered to attend"—a year after the rest of his class graduated.) The director of the school said it didn't matter since this was a private school. And so at age twenty-three, Jaime Escalante began teaching at his alma mater. Rather than give up his other work, he juggled a series of jobs at the same time, working day and night to prepare the lessons. He taught mornings at San Calixto, afternoons at National Bolívar, a late class at Commercial High School, then tutored or taught at a military academy into the late hours. His energy seemed endless and his passion for teaching insatiable.

Always on the lookout for a way to test and improve his students, he enrolled the best of them in a competition sponsored by the Major San Andreas Engineering School. All seven came home empty-handed. Disillusioned at first, Jamie took the result as a challenge to change the curriculum. To him it underscored how important it was to learn by doing. He would drill a concept until the whole class knew it backwards and forwards. Each morning he wrote a problem on the board. The first student to finish it had to explain it to the rest of the class while they corrected each other's papers. Based on the wrong answers, he kept adapting his explanations until most of the class got their answers right. When students seemed about to crack under the stress, he took them outside for a game of handball or a cigarette. He became intensely focused on winning the Major San Andreas competition. The second year his students did win, and won every year afterward as long as he taught there.

Jaime realized that he couldn't remember students' names and started giving them nicknames instead. The heaviest kid in class was always Gordo (Fatso), the talkative one was Chiuanco (a bird with a shrill call), and the short stocky one was Corcho (cork). He encouraged rumors that he had been a street fighter. As a former trickster and troublemaker himself, he knew how to deal with restless and unruly students.

Jaime and Fabiola were married November 25, 1954, at the Baptist church in Cochabamba. Her parents consented to the marriage after Jaime promised to be baptized as a Protestant (which he never got around to). Fabiola maintained her strict social code including no alcohol in the house. The jovial Jaime met with friends and colleagues on his own, leaving her at home. She thought moving to America might separate him from what she considered a questionable social life. Her brothers were going to college in California as her father had done.

Escalante developed a reputation for being strict and ruthless in grading. Giving exams to physics students from another class on one occasion, he said what he should really do was flunk the teacher. He even flunked his own brother and cousin. In 1960, a small group of students demonstrated outside Escalante's house. Another student went to Jaime's mother and begged for help to reverse a failing grade so he could graduate. Jaime grudgingly gave in only after his mother insisted.

By the next year, Escalante was settled with his family in a comfortable three-room duplex with a kitchen he built himself. They bought a blue DeSoto and hired a driver who used it as a taxi when he wasn't working for the family. Escalante's students were star pupils and he had more job offers than he could accept. But the government was as unstable as ever and the economy was a constant roller coaster. Many of the brightest graduates moved away for better opportunities.

Escalante spent a year in Puerto Rico in a special program for teachers under President Kennedy's Alliance for Progress. The teachers went from there on an American tour that included Niagara Falls, Washington (where he shook hands with President Kennedy), an education conference in Pittsburgh, and a Tennessee high school with a physics laboratory more complete and elaborate than anything Jaime could imagine.

2.3. Escalante Begins Again in America

Fabiola continued to push for the family to emigrate. The trip to America made Jaime more willing to consider it. Eager for the slightest hint of agreement, Fabiola pressed her case even harder. He considered his low salary and lack of opportunity. His friend Roberto was thinking of giving up teaching for a job in the customs office. Some National Bolívar teachers complained about Jaime teaching simultaneously at San Calixto, doubling up on salary and seniority. Others complained about how hard his tests were. And there were still rumblings about an incident years earlier that continued to dog him.

He had chaperoned a busload of San Calixto boys on a field trip to Copacabana. When word got out that they had spiked their Coca-Cola with wine, thirty of them were sentenced to be expelled. When they begged Jaime to intervene for them, he refused. He advised them instead to stick together and say that if the thirty were expelled the whole class would leave. The administration backed down, suspending the guilty for three weeks instead. The students won the standoff, but resentment still simmered within the administration.

Along with these concerns, Jaime considered that, as his wife often reminded him, if he wanted to be a great teacher, he had to get away from the city where his friends were always calling him up to go for a drink and where there were so many distractions. Fabiola jumped into action, handling all the immigration requirements and convincing her younger brother Samuel to be their sponsor. Jamie would go first, while she and their son Jaimito went to live with relatives. The family sold everything, including the prized DeSoto and the land on which they planned to build a new house.

Jaime couldn't bear to say good-bye to his mother. Instead, he wrote her a note, which she kept under her pillow every night for the rest of her life. "Querida Viejita [Dear Little Old Lady]: ... God grant that I may return home some day to live in peace. It is my destiny to elevate the name of my family and I am optimistic that I will succeed ... The lessons of yesterday will be good for tomorrow ..." He met an old friend for one last beer and *salteña* on the square, then took a taxi to the airport.

Sam Tapia, Jaime's brother-in-law, greeted him at the Los Angeles airport on an overcast Christmas Eve, 1963. Sam and his brother David lived in Pasadena, where rents were low and the local Pasadena City College welcomed immigrants. There weren't that many South Americans in Los Angeles at the time; that year the immigration service had allowed fewer than 800 Bolivians to come to the United States.

One of Jaime's first moves in the United States was to spend $2,400 (about $25,000 in 2025 dollars) of the $3,000 he brought with him on a brand-new light green Volkswagen Beetle. Fabiola encouraged him to enroll in community college at Pasadena where Sam had gone. Jaime wanted to wait. He didn't know any English and preferred to get a job first so he could learn English and save some money. Across the street from the entrance to Pasadena City College (PCC), was Van de Kamp's Restaurant. Jaime walked in and, in halting English, introduced himself to the manager, Karl Polsky, and asked for work. Polsky answered that the floor needed cleaning and to show what he could do. Escalante tackled the assignment with his usual energy and enthusiasm, mopping the floor spotless and stacking the chairs on tables. Polsky took a look around and said, "See you tomorrow, Jaime."

Sam, who shared Fabiola's sensitivity to social class, was appalled that a graduate of the Normal Superiór with a reputation as a fabulous teacher would take a job cleaning floors. Jaime saw it as a first step to his new life in America. Sam drove Jaime to PCC to take the entrance exam for night school. Jaime chose the math exam because it required the least English.

The instructor gruffly explained that Jaime had two hours to take the test and could not get up or ask questions after the test started. Twenty-five minutes later, Jaime left his seat and gingerly approached the teacher's office door. "Damn it, it never fails!" the instructor bellowed. "I told you, no questions. It's a two-hour test." "But ... I finished," Jaime said quietly, handing up the answer sheet. The teacher checked his answers on the spot. He'd earned a perfect score.

By the time Fabiola and Jaimito arrived in May 1964, Jaime had been promoted to cook and couldn't get away from Van de Kamp's to meet them at the airport. Sam rented his guesthouse to the family: a bedroom, kitchen, and sitting room. Their eight-year-old son entered the fourth grade (his brother, Fernando, would be born in 1969). Fabiola was distressed that Jaime was working at such a menial job. Even though his salary was more than the $100 a week he'd earned as a teacher in Bolivia, cooking in a restaurant was too working-class. She didn't like the smog or the alien culture of Pasadena either. But this whole move had been her idea, so she realized she should make the best of it.

When he felt he was ready, Escalante wrote to the California department of education to apply for a teaching position. He was renowned in La Paz as a superior teacher and had shaken hands with the President at the White House! The response he got was a terrible disappointment. He was crushed to learn that his Bolivian credentials were worthless in California. He would need four years of American college and a year of graduate school for a teaching certificate. Cooking during the day and going to night school it would take forever.

He considered going back to Bolivia where he could have his pick of prime teaching positions. Fabiola encouraged him to change careers instead, stay in California and go into electronics. In the end, they decided to remain in America for their son's sake. This was the land of opportunity where, presumably, anyone could succeed. In 1967, Fabiola got a job on the assembly line at Burroughs Corporation. Jaime applied too and was offered a job the next day. With overtime he'd been earning $200 a week at the restaurant, but took a pay cut to go to Burroughs. Fabiola thought it was where he belonged. He started out filling orders, but was soon troubleshooting components as they came off the assembly line. At the same time, he continued his education at night at Cal State.

Burroughs had gotten its start in the 1880s making adding machines. The company moved to California in 1956 to get into the computer business. In those days computers were room-sized cabinets filled with vacuum tubes and miles of wiring. The company's first customers were banks. Later they marketed their machines to airlines looking for a more efficient way to manage their overburdened reservation networks. The 1960s brought a surge of interest from the government for its space program. The floppy disk and microprocessor, both introduced in 1971, marked a new era in electronics technology.[1] The business was a perfect match for Jaime Escalante—fast-moving and full of new challenges. In 1972, Burroughs offered Jaime a supervisory job at a new plant in Guadalajara. He took a look, but didn't want to interrupt his son's American education. Also he was about to complete his degree at Cal State.

2.4. Escalante Begins a Teaching Career in America

One of his professors there encouraged him to go into industry. When Jaime said he wanted to teach, the professor told him about a National Science Foundation scholarship. He could go to school full-time and be teaching in a year. It would mean a pay cut from the $16,000 (about $103,000 in 2025 dollars) he made at Burroughs to the scholarship award of $13,000 (about $84,000) per year. There were three parts to the scholarship competition: a written test, an oral test, and a classroom teaching exercise where "students" staged interruptions.

Jaime completed the two test portions, then went into his classroom where two students were staging a fight. "I'm glad to see you fighting," he told them. "Fighting is great exercise." He added that he'd fight them both after class. As he started his lesson, another student yelled that he wanted to talk about sex. "Let's do this first," Escalante answered, "then we'll talk about sex." He spent his time showing the class a shortcut to memorizing multiplication tables. Although they were supposed to be acting disruptive, the students forgot about their roles as they were drawn into the lesson.

When he finished he turned to the student who had interrupted him earlier. "You said you wanted to talk about sex, right? Why not? Why don't you start? Tell us all you know on the subject." A week later, Escalante had the scholarship.

In 1973, Hispanics passed African-Americans as the largest minority in Los Angeles. More than a fourth of all students in the city were Latino, but only five percent of teachers were. The next year Jaime interviewed with the Los Angeles Unified

School District. When the interviewer asked him where he wanted to teach, he didn't understand the question at first and thought his English was failing him. In Bolivia, teachers were assigned to schools; he hadn't imagined he would have a choice. The interviewer showed him a map with black, Chicano, and Anglo neighborhoods color-coded.

Jaime said he wanted to teach Chicanos because he knew their language, was an immigrant himself, and one of those areas was closest to his home in Monrovia. He quickly got a job offer with his choice of Belvedere Junior High, Roosevelt High, or Garfield High. All three of these schools were in Hispanic East LA, and he would start in the fall of 1974.

Escalante visited Garfield first and met with the principal, Alex Avilez. "I see you have a lot of experience with computers," the principal noted. "Well, I think we're going to make you a computer teacher. We have a new program here." Uncertain of his English, Escalante asked him to repeat the offer. Avilez said it again. Escalante could scarcely believe his ears. It was a dream job. "Wonderful! O thank you, sir," he exclaimed. "That is exactly what I want."

He called to share the good news with Fabiola, then cancelled his appointments at the other two schools. He was already imagining how he would prepare for the class using his experience at Burroughs and books and equipment from home. IBM had recently introduced the sealed disk drive, revolutionizing computer memory technology. The first "portable" computer (it would weigh 55 pounds) was less than a year away. Computers were poised to revolutionize education and Jaime was right in the thick of it all, ready to lead a generation of students into the computer age. He couldn't wait to get started.[2]

3. Kemo

The Los Angeles school system that Jaime Escalante joined in September 1974 was part of a community fractured by distrust and political turmoil. It was the product of a nation confused about its educational objectives. Lucky for us that Escalante didn't know what he was getting into, or else he may never have taken the job.

An undercurrent of racial tension ran through the culture of the city. Identity politics affected every policy decision, every allocation of resources. In the 1920s, Los Angeles had been one of the first big cities in America to adapt specific residential covenants excluding African-Americans from owning houses in 95 percent of the city's neighborhoods. Yet the city was also the site of a historic legal ruling in *Mendez v. Westminster and the California Board of Education.* This 1946 Supreme Court decision held that maintaining separate educational facilities for public school students with Mexican heritage was unconstitutional. The *Mendez* case laid the groundwork for the more famous *Brown v. Board of Education* case eight years later in Kansas that made racial discrimination illegal nationwide.

Garfield High School was built in 1925 when its East Los Angeles neighborhood was home to white, lower middle class families. Beginning in the 1950s, a demographic sea change surged over East Los Angeles so that by the 1970s the neighborhood was overwhelmingly Latino and much more densely populated. (Garfield today is 99 percent Latino.) Cultural and language barriers were serious hurdles to the Spanish-speaking community. Poverty, drugs, and gangs introduced still more problems.[1]

Historically, American public schooling was a local institution, led by a school board and funded with property taxes. But by the 1970s, a trend toward top-down control was gaining momentum. Most other countries had always controlled their school systems at the national level. This was the model Jaime Escalante had grown up with in Bolivia and where he became a master of his craft. The United States, with its federal model, preferred putting the local authorities in charge to set up local funding. As early as 1785, the Continental Congress reserved the income from a portion of each township in the country for "the maintenance of public schools."[2]

The federal government stayed largely out of the education business until the Department of Health, Education, and Welfare was established in 1953. Opponents of federal oversight argued unsuccessfully that a Cabinet department overseeing education was unconstitutional, since there was no provision in the Constitution dealing with education.

One of the earliest steps in shaping national curriculum standards was the National Defense Education Act. This legislation was a direct response to the Soviet Union's launch of *Sputnik*, the world's first artificial satellite, in 1957. Soviet and American scientists had been in a heated contest to see who could lift a payload into earth orbit first. Afraid of the consequences of losing the space race, the US encouraged schools to teach more math, science, and foreign languages. By influencing the high school curriculum, the government hoped to raise technological standards against international competition. This, it seems, was one of the first objectives of a national educational policy.

In 1965, a series of events marked a new level of government involvement in American public education, and a new sense of urgency in dealing with poor urban neighborhoods like Garfield's. The Elementary and Secondary Education Act, part of President Lyndon Johnson's historic "War on Poverty," provided federal funds to schools to help low-income students; and Project Head Start established preschool programs for the poor. These federal programs funneled many millions of dollars into school districts along with rules and controls required to qualify for the money. These and other programs of the era set up a relationship between funding and control that has defined federal involvement in education ever since.

Also in 1965, a study released by the Labor Department sent shock waves through the world of education. *The Negro Family: The Case for National Action* was written by Daniel Patrick Moynihan, a future US Senator, then an assistant department secretary.[3] His conclusion was that a child's home environment was a more important indicator of success in school and in life than the educational environment. Specifically, Moynihan focused on the number of black children born out of wedlock versus the number of white children. In the 1960s, about 20 percent of black children were born to single mothers as opposed to less than 3 percent of white children. The poverty and social instability of families headed by single mothers, Moynihan reported, was a principal cause of poor school performance.

Moynihan was harshly condemned as racist and elitist for his reporting. The resulting political fallout muted the impact of his study and kept policymakers and scholars away from the topic for years. This is all the more ironic because Moynihan himself was raised by a single mother and once worked as a shoeshine boy. The next year another major report, *Equality of Educational Opportunity*, supported the idea that student background and socioeconomic standing had a larger impact on academic success than school funding.

Latinos poured into Los Angeles in the 1960s and 70s, eventually outnumbering the blacks who had come west by the thousands to work in the factories and shipyards during World War II. Racial tension was constant and pervasive in area high schools, where principals had to deal daily with gang activities, fights, and other disruptions. Only a few miles west of the Garfield campus on East 6th Street in the Eastmont neighborhood was the livid scar of the 1965 Watts Riots, where a major neighborhood thoroughfare had been torched to the ground and never rebuilt. What started as a routine traffic stop escalated into four days of arson and looting, fed by contempt for a militarized police department accused of deep-seated corruption. Thirty-two people were killed and four thousand arrested.

The election of Los Angeles' first African-American mayor, Tom Bradley, in 1973 had not yet brought harmony to the city by the time Jaime Escalante stepped into a classroom at Garfield. And the national government was distracted with a crisis of its own. On August 9, 1974, a month before Escalante taught his first day, the President of the United States resigned from office for the only time in history. The cultural, social, and political upheaval of the times produced an educational environment that was unsettled, unsure of itself, and on the defensive. In East LA the students struggled, the budget was strained, and the facilities were frayed. The new teacher from La Paz would have his hands full.

3.1. Escalante Arrives at Garfield High School

Jaime Escalante pulled his green Volkswagen into the parking lot at Garfield High School and walked happily across the parking lot to his meeting with other math teachers. At last, after ten long years of reestablishing his credentials, Jaime was about to fulfill his dream of teaching in America. And not just any teaching job—a job guiding students through the exciting new world of computers. Based on what he saw in his years at Burroughs, he was convinced that computers were a pathway to success in the future and, more important, a ticket out of the LA barrio to a well-paying career.

On his way inside he noticed graffiti on the walls and trash blown up against the chain link fence. The place could use a little sprucing up.

The meeting began with handing out class schedules to each teacher. Glancing over his sheet Escalante saw "High School Math" for his first period. Next was another "High School Math," then three more. His whole day was teaching five sections of this mysterious course. He politely asked what the course was. "It's basic math," the administrator explained. "Most of our new teachers start with it."

Escalante was confused. "But Mr. Avilez told me I would be teaching a new computer course." "Didn't they tell you?" the man answered. "We weren't able to get that course." The principal had hoped computers would be part of the curriculum that year for the first time, but it didn't happen. Probably the funding he had hoped for never materialized.

Escalante walked to his next meeting in another building on the campus. A dozen or so teachers there listened to Michael Litvak, a math teacher who was also in charge of Garfield's Title I program for mathematics. This far-reaching section of the 1965 Elementary and Secondary Education Act awarded federal money to schools to help educate students from low-income families. To qualify, a school had to show that at least 40 percent of its students lived below the federal poverty line, and had to follow strict rules about how the money was used. One of the ways schools justified their need was to pull eligible students out of regular classes and concentrate them in remedial classes.

Mr. Litvak showed them games and exercises designed to make math more interesting to students who weren't learning by traditional methods. Students would cut pictures out of a book then measure the cutouts. Jaime thought to himself that in Bolivia this would be elementary school stuff. First he had faced the disappointment of not teaching a computer class, and now he thought about the time he would waste watching teenagers cut pictures out of workbooks. Maybe his wife had been right that he should never have quit his job at Burroughs.

Classes started the next morning. As a new teacher at the bottom of the pecking order, Escalante didn't have a classroom of his own but moved from room to room each period. To start, he needed directions to the office where he would pick up his classroom assignments. A well-dressed, soft-spoken young man gave him directions. As he spoke Escalante noticed the pistol under his coat: he was a plainclothes security officer.

In the office he waited an hour for directions to his first class. By then the period was over, so he hustled down the hall to his second period in room 801. He walked in to see desks pushed into a semicircle and the students talking in a loud and rowdy way. The boys tended toward tapered jeans, white T-shirts, and long hair held back by bandannas. Girls wore tight, revealing clothes calculated to distract. As he wrote his name on the blackboard he heard one student yell, "Hey, what class is this?" "Sex!" came the answer from the front row. It was an eerie replay of his teaching test in La Paz. The laughter peaked and then changed to a low rumble as he explained the class rules and started a math lesson. His audience had no interest whatever in what he was saying and no plans to listen. To Jaime, who loved learning and whose students in Bolivia had been so eager and appreciative, his first day at Garfield was deeply disappointing.

Escalante decided that Fabiola was right. He would go back to Burroughs at the end of the school year. But when he told the principal his plans, Mr. Avilez begged him to wait until the spring to decide. As an incentive, he told Jaime he would give him a classroom of his own. He could move into room 801 for good. The classroom was in sad shape, not cheerful or welcoming, not a place that encouraged learning. With the help of a few trusted students, Escalante transformed the space over a weekend. They painted the walls, scrubbed the desks clean of doodles and graffiti, and put up posters of the Los Angeles Lakers. The principal was so surprised and impressed that he sent other teachers over to look at Escalante's handiwork.

Once he had a clean, inviting classroom, Escalante turned his attention to how he could keep his students' interest. They didn't see math as having any relevance in their lives. It was boring. It was pointless. It was for somebody else. One subject the kids did seem interested in was sports. So he started using sports metaphors in class. He also challenged pupils to handball games after school: if they won they got an A; if he won they had to do their homework. Though he was putting on weight, his experience and skill paid off. He always won.

As he had in Bolivia, he gave students nicknames when he couldn't remember their real ones. To engage them he made comments about their clothes, their makeup, or whatever he could think of that would get their attention and provoke a reaction. They in turn gave him a nickname. *The Lone Ranger* was a popular Saturday morning cowboy show. The title character's faithful companion, Tonto, often referred to the Lone Ranger as "Kemo Sabe." His students christened him Kemo and the name stuck. He was Kemo from then on.

Jaime challenged any behavior he considered a barrier to learning, whether it was actually against the rules or not. There were relatively few rules at school, and the ones they had were poorly enforced. Yes, there were armed guards to protect the campus against gang violence and keep weapons off the property, but the students were often rebellious, irresponsible, and rude in ways that chipped away at administrative authority in a thousand little ways every day. It was as though the school had ordained these were poor students whom a failing educational system had badly prepared for high school. As a consequence, they couldn't be expected to do any better. They had no tradition of respect for education or academic achievement, so the best the school could do was push them through the system and collect those federal dollars.

3.2. Students Need to be Challenged and Inspired

Jaime disagreed. He believed his kids had it in them to learn. But they had to be challenged and inspired, to have an environment that promoted learning, not one full of distractions. A girl who sat in the front row of one of his classes sometimes wore nearly transparent blouses. Finally one day he explained to her that if she kept dressing that way, the highest grade he could give her was a C. "How can you do that?!" she demanded. "It just makes a bad impression," he answered.

When the girl threatened to see the dean, Escalante encouraged her to go ahead. Returning a few minutes later she grandly announced, "The dean says this is within the dress code and

I have a right to wear it." "You do have the right to wear it," Escalante said, "just not in my class."

Jaime was determined to set standards for dress and behavior that encouraged learning. Later in the day, he went to the dean to plead his case. If the office didn't back him up, he insisted, whatever rules he tried to enforce were meaningless. His authority and control over the kids would evaporate. The dean disagreed. This was consistent with what Escalante would face all year: administrators who enforced the bare letter of the law because that was the path of least resistance and the way to making the fewest political waves in the educational bureaucracy. People who kept systems running smoothly and didn't rock the boat were the ones rewarded with better jobs up the ladder.

As the year went on, Escalante kept sending unruly students to the office, and they kept returning with notes saying the dean had spoken with them. No discipline, no consequences. Administrators didn't know what to do with the new math teacher who kept pressing for better standards and was so proud and particular about how his classroom looked.

The lax attitude toward discipline affected the school on a wider scale. Gangs were a longstanding problem in the neighborhood. In order to appeal to gang members so fewer of them would drop out, Mr. Avilez gave each gang a school-sanctioned place to post its logo and invited them to register officially with the school. Eighteen gangs signed up. They divided stairways and halls among themselves, confusing and terrorizing everyone else as they staked out their turf. Even teachers avoided the spots where gang members hung out. The cafeteria was especially hazardous.

At the same time, he argued for higher standards of behavior, Jaime also lobbied the math department chairman for more challenging basic math textbooks. The chairman said no.

Students' test scores were already low. If they couldn't learn the math now, how could they possibly tackle anything more challenging? When Escalante pressed his point, saying that at least some of the kids could grasp it, the chairman told him there was no money for new books.

That summer Jaime thought about his future while working at two electronics plants. The year had been a real disappointment, and he hadn't signed a permanent contract to teach. It would be easy to transition into something else. He finally decided to go back for one more year, then take Fabiola's advice and switch to a career in electronics.

3.3. A New Direction

Jaime was getting his classroom ready for the first day of school when he heard that the principal had been reassigned. Mr. Avilez, whose administration was later described as "tragically unsuccessful," along with every other administrator at Garfield was gone."[4] In the spring of that year, an accreditation team visited the school and threatened to close it. Teacher morale was low, half the students dropped out, and the half that stayed were struggling. Shocked into action, the school district brought in a whole new team.

The new principal, Paul Possemato, took the school in a completely different direction. Out went the gang placards. Where students were routinely five or ten minutes late for the start of class, now they had to be in their seats on time. The school had become a meeting place for non-students to hang out, flirt, and be seen with members of their gangs. Possemato locked the doors and declared that outsiders were no longer welcome. Those who tested the new rule were arrested by police. Gang symbols and graffiti were washed off and painted over. The new principal organized banquets and other events to create a sense of community.

Mr. Possemato noticed Escalante's way of reaching out to kids to make math interesting. Escalante saw past the teenage bluster and attitude to the young person who could learn and wanted to learn but needed encouragement and approval. The principal understood how proud of his classroom Escalante was, how he took such care to decorate it and keep it clean. He also saw that Jaime was on the brink of giving up teaching.

He asked Jaime what he would like to do at Garfield. "Teach math," was the quick reply. "Isn't that what you're doing now?" the principal asked. "No, sir." To him the elementary lessons he was required to teach didn't live up to the name. The principal moved him to a better classroom more central to the campus and promised him he could teach algebra.

Another change Possemato made was to appoint a new dean of discipline. Henry Gradillas was chairman of the biology department when Possemato arrived. Before teaching, Henry had spent six years in the army as an Airborne Ranger instructor, teaching some of the military's toughest soldiers how to jump out of airplanes. Henry had a heart for students, whom he believed needed discipline and high expectations to offset a life of low achievement and little encouragement. He was 210 pounds of military muscle and had no hesitation about wading into a fight to bring it to a speedy conclusion. When students swore at him like they did other teachers, Gradillas roared back that they would never speak to him that way no matter how they talked to other people.

Gradillas had been born in East LA and graduated from Garfield's neighborhood rival, Roosevelt High. He had seen all sorts of administrators and programs that gave Latino students little chance for success. And he had seen the self-fulfilling prophecy of these low expectations, which delivered failure upon failure. A widespread feeling existed that these young people, many from broken homes and with so many other problems, couldn't handle being criticized for their academic shortcomings. It would damage their fragile self-esteem. Gradillas cared far less about their self-esteem than about pushing them to achieve their full potential. In his view, school should not mirror the low expectations and poor results of the neighborhood but challenge them: Garfield should be a way up and out to a better life by consistently meeting high standards.

This view paralleled Escalante's outlook exactly. In the new dean of discipline he soon found a soul mate who was devoted to education and convinced that every student had potential to succeed. Not all were equally gifted, but all should be equally encouraged and all could accomplish far more than a distraught educational system could imagine.

As he learned his first day at Garfield, Jaime had to get his students' attention before he could teach them. How could he explain math to them if they sat down in class and tuned him out? The solution was classroom instruction with a healthy dose of theater mixed in. Early on in his teaching at Garfield, he was trying to explain fractions but wasn't getting very far. When his students sauntered into class the next day, he was wearing a chef's hat and apron he'd saved from his restaurant job. He lined up a row of apples in front of his surprised audience. To warm them up he attacked the first apple with a meat cleaver, chopping it to bits. Then he cut the next apple into quarters and handed one piece to a student in the front row.

"How much of the apple do you have?" he asked. "A fourth," the student replied. "And how much is left?" The student looked at the slice in her hand and then at the rest of the apple. "Three fourths." "Right!" Escalante exclaimed. "For your reward you can eat your apple slice!" Now the rest of the class watched with rapt attention as Escalante chopped another apple into thirds. "How much of the apple is this?"

"One third," a couple of voices rang out. "And how much is left?" "Two thirds!"

He picked up two slices and held them side by side. "And which is bigger, one fourth or one third?" Looking at the three dimensional example in his hands, students saw the concept of fractions suddenly emerge from the fog of theory into something concrete they could touch and understand. Take away a fourth of an apple and you have three fourths left. A third is bigger than a fourth. By now the whole classroom was eager to answer, munching happily on their examples.

Treats were an easy and effective way to energize students and do something out of the ordinary that they could look forward to. On quiz days, he handed out candy as a bribe so students wouldn't skip class that day. As they hunched over their test papers, Escalante walked up and down the rows putting a piece of candy on every desk and saying a word of encouragement to each student.

In 1977, Jaime lost two of his allies at Garfield. Paul Possemato was transferred to another school, and Henry Gradillas became assistant principal of a junior high in the district. The new principal was Jessie Franco. To Escalante she seemed nice enough, but not interested in challenging or pushing the students. Escalante felt there was a world of untapped potential waiting to be unleashed. But they had to have more advanced material and take school more seriously. Even the algebra 2 class used what Jaime thought were simple grade school problems.

Jaime raised administrative hackles for criticizing another teacher's lessons as too elementary. He was only trying to offer suggestions for helping students more, but the teacher took it as a professional slight and Escalante got a warning from a vice principal to get along with his colleagues. Escalante was establishing a habit of frank assessment and criticism that got him into trouble repeatedly over the years. He had no patience with teachers who didn't, in his view, work hard enough. To put Jaime in his place, this particular teacher pointed out that he'd been teaching fifteen years. "The only problem," Escalante responded, "is you're not teaching the right stuff."

3.4. High Standards

Beginning his fifth year at Garfield in the fall of 1978, Kemo had mastered the craft of making his students pay attention in class. Other teachers, desperate to gain control over their own classrooms, visited his class to learn his secret. There they saw students who sat quietly, paid attention, and worked hard. The simple tools he had developed to achieve this result eventually became the foundation of his historic success.

The first rule was consistent high standards for academics and behavior. Without a classroom environment that invited learning, every student was at a disadvantage. Escalante once traded classes with Ben Jiménez, a new teacher at Garfield who couldn't get his unruly charges under control. Escalante began the class by demanding quiet and obedience. He ejected one student who kept talking; then another, then another. After the third one had been sent out, the room got quiet. The next morning he gave a quiz that many students flunked. Now he had their attention. As Escalante biographer Jay Mathews observed, Jiménez realized that the key to Escalante's success in class was "quick, harsh action at the first sign of trouble." He didn't wait for the situation to become unbearable. The longer a teacher waited to deal with disruption, the harder it would be to fix.

Every detail that improved a student's chance of success, no matter how small, was worth Jaime's time and attention. He taught his students respect and responsibility as well as math. He hated wasting time, and there was no excuse for parents and administrators not holding these kids accountable. He believed that they were used to getting away with lazy behavior, and that was no way to learn. It irritated him when students came in late day after day, or skipped class entirely, and got a tardy slip from the office admitting them to class without any consequences. He had some slips printed up and offered to give them out himself if students would tell him honestly where they were. If they didn't want to say, he declared he would charge ten cents per slip.

Escalante chafed more than ever at the low standards and elementary material his students had to work with. But his principal insisted there was no money for new textbooks. Hearing that news, Escalante asked to transfer to another school. That threat yielded results. The principal had praised his "excellent classroom organization and lesson plans." He was a teacher who worked hard and saw his kids' potential realized. She scraped together three thousand dollars and got him the new books.

3.5. Advanced Placement Calculus Launched

With these new materials, Escalante could launch a plan he'd been developing to start an advanced placement (AP) calculus class. AP classes were a rarity at Garfield High. There was AP Spanish and a small program in AP history and physics. Advanced placement tests were given nationwide by the College Board, which also administered the Scholastic Aptitude Test (SAT). By passing an AP test, high school students were awarded college credit for advanced instruction. Escalante had never heard of AP when he came to Garfield. Nobody there talked about it or promoted it or encouraged students to try it. After all, AP was designed for students at elite prep schools like Exeter and Andover, or for students at rich public schools like Beverly Hills High, twenty miles west of Garfield on I10, but not for the poor Latinos of East LA.

In planning his first year of advanced placement teaching, Escalante faced off against his relentless enemy: time. There weren't enough hours in the school day to teach an AP calculus curriculum to students who'd never had a challenging algebra course, or trigonometry, or any other advanced math. And unlike high schools in many American cities, Garfield started in the tenth grade, not the ninth. So Escalante only had three years instead of four to bring them up to speed.

Escalante convinced fourteen students to enroll in his AP class that fall. He told them they would have to come to class early every day, take a daily quiz, and have a test every Friday. Within two weeks half the students had dropped out. Two more quit before the year was over. When he complained to one of the counselors that she was making it too easy for the students to quit, she told him that the material was too hard; these kids could never master it.

Jaime drove his advanced students hard every day, yet also worked to make it encouraging and fun. He handed out candy, talked in sports metaphors, played music in the classroom, and did everything he could think of to build team spirit. On the wall, he put the big sign that would later become famous: "Calculus need not be made easy; it is easy already."

Shortly before it came time to take the advanced placement test, Escalante learned there would be a testing fee of twenty-one dollars each. This was a reduced rate for poor students, but even so his kids couldn't come up with the money on such short notice. Jaime quickly organized a car wash to raise the funds. For years afterward, he and his students would sponsor car washes, bake sales, candy sales, and whatever it took to raise the testing fees.

In the spring of 1979, Escalante's first AP class of five sat for the exam. A score of 5 was the highest possible; 1 was the lowest. A 3 or better was considered passing by most schools and worthy of college credit. Of the five who took the test, two scored 4, two scored 2, and one scored 1.

The two passing grades encouraged Escalante to redouble his efforts. The next year, nine students took the test and seven passed. In 1981, fifteen students took the exam and fourteen passed, including one with the first-ever score of 5 at Garfield.

Along with extra hours and zany demonstrations with apples and meat cleavers, Escalante expanded his repertoire of tricks to toys that helped students remember particular things: a pair of wind-up shoes to remind them to go step-by-step, a monkey climbing a pole for inverse functions, a goofy cutout of the cartoon character Charlie Brown repeating the Escalante instruction, "Factoring! Factoring!"

He also threw in basketball terms. "Give-and-go" to illustrate absolute value; "three second violation" to underscore the three possibilities of an absolute number. He lined his students up outside the classroom and made each one answer a question before they could come in. If they were wrong, or if they hesitated, they had to go to the back of the line. "Ten minutes," the teacher would order. "Maybe you spend the time studying your book." Some had to go through several rounds but all finally made it inside. It was hard but it was fun, challenging, and part of being on a special team.

Escalante's hard driving approach and take-no-prisoners attitude got results in the classroom. It also created headaches for the administration. Escalante always wanted his students to try harder, to do more. That meant he was always lobbying for more materials, more time, and more support from the principal and others. He was quick to criticize other teachers he thought weren't working hard enough or pushing their students.

He had no patience for teachers who read the newspaper in class and let their assistants do their work. He was incensed to overhear another teacher working on a real estate deal and soliciting business from other teachers. When he complained to the principal, she explained that teachers were protected by union seniority rules and there was nothing she could do. Counselors complained about Kemo's strong-arm tactics both to enforce his rules and to keep students from dropping his classes. When pupils came to him to sign a transfer form out of his class, he tried to make them believe they weren't allowed to drop.

Once again Escalante thought about changing jobs. He applied for a position at another school closer to his house in Monrovia, and reconsidered picking up his electronics career at Burroughs. He had no doubt they would welcome him back. Monrovia High surprised him by rejecting his application, saying their students didn't have the problems Garfield's did and that they didn't think his intense approach would be successful there. He resolved to give Garfield another shot. He'd seen real progress the last few years; maybe there was hope for the future.

In 1981, Garfield made Escalante chairman of the math department. They may well have done this to get even with him for his criticism of some teachers and what some considered his high-handed ways. The bureaucratic duties that went with the job would have been a nuisance—if Escalante had done them. However, early on he told the rest of the faculty that he had no interest in boring meetings or reports and would not be participating in them. He would not be responding to administrative bureaucrats from the district office. The advantage of his new position was that he could scour the student body for promising math students and encourage them to take advanced courses that would equip them for AP calculus. Junior high schools didn't prepare their pupils for higher math, and Garfield only required one year of basic math to graduate. Finding likely prospects for calculus among the school's 3,000 students at the time was hard work with few rewards.

3.6. The AP Calculus Exam—1982

Also in 1981, Henry Gradillas returned to Garfield as the new principal. Henry and Jaime rekindled their friendship and reinforced their belief in the value of pushing students to achieve.

That year Escalante had eighteen students in AP calculus. It was the largest advanced math class ever at the school. His satisfaction was somewhat offset by knowing that he could have had twice as many if only other algebra teachers taught more advanced material and hadn't let students transfer out of their classes without a fight.

Escalante could be harsh on his students, even the outstanding ones. Students who didn't turn in homework were berated in front of the class and ordered out. He warned those who missed extra study sessions to go to marching band or cheerleading practice—or even another time-consuming subject such as chemistry—to drop it all and concentrate on math. Some did, and some didn't. Pressing for a still higher level of commitment, he required parents of AP students to sign a contract saying their children would do their homework and come to class. He scheduled extra sessions before school, three hours after school, as well as during lunch. Sometimes he drove his students to tears. When the pressure was too much he gave them a break, just as he had done for his students in Bolivia. He brought them all doughnuts or hamburgers, or adjourned for a game of volleyball.

On the morning of May 19, 1982, eighteen nervous students
filed into room 411, sat down at widely spaced intervals in
the room, and began the advanced placement calculus exam.
Andreda Pruitt, the head counselor at Garfield, proctored the
test. When the test was over, she gave the completed answer
booklets to John Bennett, the AP history teacher, who combined them with the history, English, and Spanish tests and
sent them in a special envelope to the Educational Testing
Service in New Jersey to be graded. There were sixty-nine
exams in the packet, a record for Garfield.

By the middle of July, letters started arriving from the
ETS giving Garfield students their grades. So far every single
student had passed and some had earned 5s. Jaime was already
thinking ahead to how he could improve the program for next
year. It was a Saturday afternoon when he took a call at home
from his student Elsa Bolado. She'd already told him she had
received a 4 on the exam. Now she had gotten a certified letter
from ETS saying that graders "found close agreement of your
answers with those on another answer sheet from the same test
center. Such agreement is unusual and suggests that copying
occurred. The Board doubts that these grades are valid ..." The
letter offered three choices for resolving the question: cancel the
grade, provide proof there was no cheating, or retake the test.

Fourteen of the eighteen Garfield students who took the AP
calculus test got the same letter. Based on the similarity of
their wrong answers, the Educational Testing Service accused
them of cheating.[5]

4. Star Rising

The summer that the Educational Testing Service questioned the AP calculus scores of Garfield students,[1] Escalante was teaching in the Upward Bound program at Occidental College in the Eagle Rock neighborhood. This was a federally funded effort to prepare poor high school students for college-level courses. Escalante had approached Cal State, the University of Southern California, and East Los Angeles College (ELAC) hoping to set up a summer school for his own students since the Garfield campus had no money for the classes he wanted. ELAC invited him instead to teach math to their Upward Bound students, some of whom had attended Garfield High six blocks away.

Jaime turned them down for the time being because he wanted to establish his own program. His students were not likely to excel in higher mathematics, but Jaime loved teaching them, loved seeing the light come on in the eyes of students who never expected to catch on. It was a sign of how much he loved his profession that after a grueling academic year at Garfield, including tutoring an hour before school and three hours afterward, plus hosting Saturday help sessions, he still wanted to teach summer school.

The Monday after Elsa Bolado informed him about the ETS accusation of cheating, Jaime attended a meeting to discuss what to do.[2] At the meeting was Ralph Heiland, a physics teacher who was also the union representative at Garfield, two people from the district office, and as many of the accused students as they could round up. Henry Gradillas was at Brigham Young University in Utah for the summer working on his doctorate, so he was unable to attend.

Heiland passed around a copy of the letter from ETS. Raúl Arreola from the school district's Mexican American Commission saw it as a clear case of racial discrimination. Eastern intellectuals couldn't imagine poor inner city Latinos doing so well in advanced calculus and therefore assumed they had cheated. He knew of a recent case where two Anglo students accused of cheating had the charges dropped after their parents hired attorneys. (ETS said the attorneys never contacted them, but that they dropped the charges for lack of evidence.)

When one person at the meeting asked Escalante what he thought they should do, he said he needed time to gather the facts. Later that day he talked with Jesse López, another calculus student who had received the letter. He asked Jesse if there was any way students could have cheated. He said that there was no way because Mrs. Pruitt, the proctor, had been in the room watching the whole time.

After several days of trying to reach her, Escalante finally got through to Antonia A. Rosenbaum, who had signed the letter to the accused students. She had already fielded a call from Mr. Heiland and told Escalante the same thing she had told him: the students' privacy rights meant she could only talk with the students directly. Jaime explained he was their calculus teacher and wanted to do what he could to clear up any doubt that they had cheated. He tried to explain that he had a certain way of teaching and that it shouldn't be unusual for students who studied with the same teacher to work a problem the same way. Rosenbaum politely held her ground. She could not talk to him but only to the students. They would have to decide soon whether they wanted to retake the test.

Heiland and others strongly opposed a retest, saying it would be an admission of guilt. Furthermore the retest would be under far different conditions from the original test in May. That had been at the end of a school year after months of hard study and drills. Everything was fresh in their minds. Now it was the middle of the summer. They hadn't studied in months. Like athletes or musicians who haven't practiced in months, they were rusty. Moreover, the textbooks were in storage and out of reach. All they had to prepare for a retest was their notebooks and other materials in their possession.

The wife of Henry Gradillas called him in Utah and told him about the mess. Henry returned to Los Angeles as soon as he could, and he and Escalante continued to ask ETS for details about the supposed cheating. Together they pressed the theory that because Jaime gave such vivid examples and drilled with so much repetition, students would answer questions in a similar way. At the request of the testing service, Escalante answered three of the questions himself and sent his answers to ETS.

As recounted in Jay Mathews' biography *Escalante: The Best Teacher in America*, answers to one question in particular were what raised the test graders' suspicions. There were forty-five multiple choice questions and seven story problems (called "free response" by ETS) on the AP calculus exam. Problem six listed the costs per square meter for building the sides and base of a tank, then asked for the cost of the least expensive tank of a certain volume. Escalante's class had had a key lesson in volumes from a substitute teacher while Jaime was sidelined with an attack of gallstones.

What had aroused the graders' suspicions was that several test booklets had the same two unrelated mistakes. Graders would not know that the students were from the same school because booklets were shuffled and assigned at random to various graders, and all the identifying information about the student and the school was covered with a flap sealed by the student at the test site. When one grader noticed two booklets with similar mistakes, he took them to one of seven "table leaders" who supervised a team of graders. The leader reviewed the booklets then took them to the chief reader for AP calculus, who opened the sealed flap and for the first time learned the students had taken the test together in the same room.

Over the years, the ETS had developed a clear protocol for suspicious test booklets. About 1/10 of one percent of all exams were flagged for scrutiny. These were subjected to an independent statistical analysis and, in the case of the AP calculus, to review by mathematicians. A three-member board then discussed the findings. They had to agree unanimously before a test booklet could be thrown out. In about seventy percent of cases, the booklets were cleared and results certified. Of the ones rejected, almost half were because of copying (plagiarism) and most of the rest were because the handwriting on the test did not match the signature of the student.

ETS found twelve of the eighteen Garfield tests had wrong answers to problem six that were the same to a very unlikely degree. Two more exams had other answers that were extremely similar. In some cases the likelihood of agreement was one in 10 million.

Escalante felt pressure not only from his students and the Garfield administration but from Hispanic activists and other civic leaders who were convinced that discrimination was behind the accusation of cheating. They wanted him to criticize the testing organization for racial bias. The local ETS representative, himself a Latino and East LA native, tried to explain to Jaime that the graders who originally flagged the exams had no idea the students were Hispanic.

"That's bulls--t!" Escalante barked. He insisted on seeing their test booklets. The official tried, as others had, to explain that they could only talk with the students and that the booklets were private. When the representative took a phone call, Escalante left the room, fuming. His students had been disgraced. He was hurt and furious, and barely knew where to direct his anger.

While Escalante and his colleagues in LA had been searching for answers, Antonia Rosenbaum at ETS kept telling them they would soon have to take a retest or have their scores disallowed. Finally, on August 24, she sent them word that a retest was scheduled for August 31. Escalante met with the accused students and told them he thought they should retake the test. It was the only way they could prove they knew the material. The group asked Jaime to leave the room. After a lively discussion, the students agreed to retake the test. Then they lined up at the telephone in the math office to tell Rosenbaum they would accept the offer.

4.1. Garfield Students are Vindicated

This was on Friday. The test was on Tuesday, four days away. They had no textbooks, no organized plan, and even some of their notebooks had been sent to New Jersey to try and prove their innocence. Before they had all finished their turn on the phone, someone started shouting the school mascot: "Bulldogs! Bulldogs! Bulldogs!" which then morphed into "Tuesday! Tuesday! Tuesday!" They would retake the AP calculus test and prove their detractors wrong.

At 7 a.m. the next morning, Jaime opened his classroom and the students got to work. After several long hours of intense review, the teacher dispatched a group to bring back lunch from

McDonald's. Following the break they tried to work some more but found they were completely tapped out.

Two students had decided not to retake the exam. One was already in a summer program at Columbia and the other was in the army. The other twelve met Tuesday morning at 8:00. Mr. Gradillas scheduled the test in a science room with individual desks and air conditioning. The principal refused to send one of his own teachers to proctor the retest, so two women from the local ETS office were there as monitors. Mrs. Pruitt, who had proctored the original exam and was still stung by the charge that she had allowed cheating, was there but only as an observer. Escalante decided to stay home. There he waited nervously until Elsa Bolado called him around 12:30. She told him it was a hard test. "Don't worry about it," Escalante reassured her. "It's over now."

Two weeks later the results finally arrived: five 5's, three 4's, and four 3's. Every student had passed the second test.

The first news of the Garfield AP calculus drama appeared in the September 29 issue of the weekly *East Los Angeles Tribune.* The front-page account emphasized an angry reaction from Garfield as well as hints of racism in the ETS action. On November 16, KNXT television in Los Angeles picked up the story reporting, "The incident suggests that the test givers harbor stereotypes about Hispanic performance levels: when the kids do well, people don't believe it." Advocacy groups started rumbling about a lawsuit against ETS. Others wanted to sue Garfield for not standing up for their students' rights. ETS tried to explain that the questionable answers had been so similar for the original test, but were not similar in the retest. By now the whole matter was national news.

The AP calculus students were heroes and ETS was the villain. Escalante could fairly claim credit for a triumph that put Garfield on the map. In late 1982 and into the next year the national media descended on Garfield. Many of them wanted to speak to the stocky, balding teacher with the thick accent who seemed able to do the impossible with his students. What Jaime liked most about the notoriety was that it attracted students at the school to AP calculus. He used his media spotlight to sing the praises of higher math.

4.2. Carta Blanca

Henry Gradillas, himself a results-oriented man of action, appreciated Escalante more than ever after the testing crisis. In the wake of the media attention, he told Jaime that he could have *carta blanca* to do whatever he wanted as long as it helped his students to keep excelling. Escalante asked for more textbooks, a teaching assistant, and a new classroom. He said there was a big music room that was empty several periods a day. It was dirty and full of junk.

Gradillas moved a guitar class and a small choir to another space and granted Escalante his wish. An admirer of Escalante's on the school board appropriated $25,000 to air condition the room as another incentive to prospective students. Gradillas explained that it would be a while before he could get maintenance workers to throw out the broken instruments, old band uniforms, and other trash. Escalante marshaled some help and a pickup truck, and moved everything out himself. It was three days before the band director noticed his uniforms were missing.

When Jaime learned that maintenance crews were too busy to paint his new space, he corralled some of his students to help him paint it. He brought spare stereo equipment from home and scrounged extra furniture and supplies from other classrooms. He created his own little world at Garfield in old Music Hall 1. There he stalked up and down the room, its floor tiered originally for band rehearsals and looking like a college lecture hall. He barked out instructions, encouragement, warnings, tossing off sports metaphors to help students remember math steps, handing out candy. "Face mask!" meant a mistake early in working the problem. "Marching band!" was a reminder to follow the usual steps to an easy answer. "Secret agent!" noted a minus sign outside parenthesis, which reversed all the signs inside.

Kemo was quick to criticize a student for failing to turn in homework and even quicker to send him out of the room for misbehaving or otherwise falling short of the standards he set. "Go to the beach" meant "Go tell your counselor to transfer you out of this class." Students, sometimes in shock and sometimes in tears, would leave class and go as ordered. The counselor would then return with the student and plead for another chance. It was all choreographed in advance and Escalante, reluctantly yet invariably, let the student back in. As hard as it was and as much as he drove them, as much as he taunted and hazed them, they *wanted* to be in his class. He had a team of winners.

There were forty-two students signed up for calculus in the fall of 1983. With a practiced air, Jaime assigned them nicknames, challenged them from the first day to do more and do better, kept in touch with their parents by phone, and worked with them every possible minute before and after school to fill their minds with the mysteries of mathematics. Thirty-three of them took the AP calculus test that spring and thirty passed. Escalante was fairly pleased, though he didn't think the kids had tried as hard as the class of '82.

Money for summer classes at Garfield remained a problem. But his conflict with the ETS had made him a celebrity in Los Angeles. One of his biggest fans was George Madrid, director of the Upward Bound program at East Los Angeles College, an East LA native and a Marine Corps Vietnam veteran.

He had tried before to convince Escalante to teach for him in the summer instead of at Occidental. In 1983 he had the enticements he needed. The Department of Health and Human Services awarded the college a grant every year to encourage minority students to study medicine. They'd never get to medical school if they didn't know math, so some of that money could be diverted to Escalante's program. ARCO, the locally-headquartered petroleum giant, donated another $10,000 to the effort. When the ELAC math department chairman read news of the donation in the press, he demanded it go to his own staff instead of a visiting high school program. But the donor insisted the gift was specifically for Escalante's use. Escalante and his allies held firm and hung onto the money.

Escalante and a trusted younger colleague at Garfield whom Escalante had mentored, Ben Jiménez, developed a summer program to cram two calculus prerequisites, trigonometry and analytical geometry, into a single two-month crash course. They would also offer Saturday classes during the school year to students who had trouble keeping up. They hoped they could attract fifty students to their summer school; the first morning more than a hundred showed up. Jaime was elated. Madrid saw the response as a vindication of his faith in the program. Jaime had also pressured him to find after-school jobs for the summer students as an extra incentive to enroll. Madrid came up with work for eighty of them.

After the Garfield cheating story made national headlines in early 1983, Escalante had been invited by the White House to come to Washington to focus attention on education of the poor. Escalante declined the invitation, and declined again when President Reagan was scheduled to present a new federal study titled *A Nation at Risk* in California. George Madrid and others believed that if Jaime accepted the invitation it would give him influence in keeping federal money for the summer school flowing. Every year it seemed they were on the verge of losing their federal funding. To convince him, they persuaded some of his students to talk to him. If he wanted to improve education, here was his chance to talk about it with the president of the United States! Escalante agreed, and met President Ronald Reagan during a ceremony unveiling the study in the Pioneer High School gym.

Sure enough, when funding for the summer school seemed in jeopardy in 1984, Escalante wrote a letter recalling his and the president's shared goals for "personal and national self-sufficiency and excellence through education and work." The next year the dean of instruction, Kenneth L. Hunt, contacted the White House and got a two-year renewal of funding. When that ran out, other supporters cobbled together donations and grants to keep the summer program going. At one point ARCO increased its contribution to $40,000. At last Hunt and Madrid hit on the idea of calling Escalante's summer school a non-credit remedial adult education course. Under funding guidelines, the community college network could then cover the cost itself. And so a new course was born: Transitional Mathematics, a "remedial" "college" course to prepare high school students for the AP calculus test.

Over the next several years, two related trends defined Jaime Escalante's work at Garfield High. The first was a calculus program that grew from strength to strength on its way to ever greater national acclaim. The second was an expanding aura of resentment, jealousy, and exasperation from students, parents, colleagues, and administrators at the price of this success: a demanding, single minded, all-or-nothing focus on math that shoved everything else aside.

In 1984, Escalante doubled the number of students taking the AP calculus exam from 34 to 68. Ben Jiménez taught a section of calculus that year, the first year Jaime had allowed anyone else to teach the subject. Sixty-three of the 68 scored 3 or better, a 93 percent pass rate compared with a national average of 76 percent. Between his department chairmanship, lobbying the teachers of other math classes, and keeping an eye on promising students, after ten years at Garfield he had an excellent feeder system that brought promising students to his calculus program. He cajoled, bribed, begged, and argued to convince kids to enroll and then to stick with it when they began to feel the pressure of learning so much in a single year.

As was his *M.O.*, when students wanted to give up, he refused to sign their transfer paper out of his class. When they needed time to study, he talked with parents to convince them they should let their children take time off from after school jobs. If his pupils wanted to take time-consuming courses like chemistry or computer science, he tried to talk them out of it or insisted they couldn't do it. He made calculus an identity at Garfield. Members of the calculus class sometimes had their own jackets or T-shirts, held pep rallies, raised their own money for test fees with car washes and candy sales, hung out together before and after school, and sometimes ate together in their calculus classroom.

1986, there were 151 Garfield students enrolled in calculus. At the end of the school year, in May 1987, 129 Garfield students took the AP calculus exam and 66 passed with a grade of three or better. That year Garfield ranked fourth in the nation in the number of students taking the calculus exam. Twenty-seven percent of the Mexican-American students in the country who passed AP calculus were students at Garfield High. It was a soaring, irrefutable seal of approval for Escalante's severe but effective methods. It was the high water mark of his program.

4.3. Rockstar

Jaime's star had been rising in the media world ever since he stood up to the ETS cheating accusations. Now in educational circles he was approaching celebrity status. Teachers, administrators, politicians, policy makers, and reporters all wanted his opinions on how to make education better. He spoke around the country, sat on panels, went to seminars, and gave interviews. He embodied the educational ideal: proof that hard work and determination could lift up even the poorest and most unlikely to snare their piece of the American dream.

A lot of his professional peers, however, were unimpressed. To them he was rude, selfish, and narcissistic; a grandstander who hogged scarce resources, poached students from other classes and activities, and had too high an opinion of himself. He earned extra money as math department chairman but wouldn't attend the meetings or deal with the district office the way he was supposed to do. He made even more money teaching high school students at a community college in the summer, which had been at times a gray area as far as allocation of funds.

He was treated like a rock star. He had an air-conditioned classroom when most other teachers did not. The principal and counselors showed favoritism by letting him cherry-pick his students, refuse to transfer them when they wanted out, and then send them away if they failed to follow his orders exactly. They knew parents complained about his browbeating and insistence that their children drop after-school jobs and other hobbies. When he was away speaking or consulting, the school had to hire substitutes, which meant less money for other educational initiatives. Escalante criticized other teachers' classroom skills, their after-hours jobs, and their willingness to let students drop a class without challenging or arguing with them.

He seemed not to care what others thought of his black-and-white worldview and strong-arm tactics. When teachers complained that his work as department chair wasn't getting done, he responded that it was a waste of time and that he wasn't going to do it. When cheerleaders or band members or basketball players came to him saying they needed time for their activities he said, "Too bad." If they wanted to be in calculus, they had to make sacrifices. For all the trouble he caused, the district found it difficult to reprimand Escalante because he brought in so much good publicity. Donors gave generously to keep his summer school going.

Meanwhile, two other Escalante admirers were about to send his star higher than ever. Ramón Menéndez was a recently graduated film school student in the summer of 1983 when he read about Escalante and the cheating scandal in the *Los Angeles Times*. After he shared the article with his friend and collaborator Tom Musca, the two decided there was a great movie in the story of poor Latinos who overcame the challenges of the barrio and institutional discrimination, and in the larger-than-life teacher who inspired them.[3] Menéndez, a native of Cuba, contacted Escalante and pitched the idea of a biographical film. Jaime resisted at first, but the next year agreed to sell an option on the rights to his story for one dollar.

In the fall of 1984, the producer of the PBS series *American Playhouse* gave Menéndez and Musca $12,000 to develop their idea. The filmmakers spent two months in Escalante's classes, discovering what the *Los Angeles Times* later called his "brilliant improvisational theater" where "Mr. Escalante hits the boys with a red pillow, requires the entire class to shout out answers" and "uses a rubber gorilla held upside down as a clue to a problem." They noted that the first day of class Kemo didn't even mention math; he talked about basketball and the NBA stars whose posters were on his classroom wall.

American Playhouse approved a budget of $500,000 for a made-for-TV film. Menéndez and Musca figured their film would cost nearly three times as much. When ARCO, which had generously supported Escalante's summer programs, offered $350,000 toward the project, the filmmakers decided to produce the project on their own, raising money along the way, and then finding a theatrical distributor once the production was finished.

4.4. Hollywood Comes to Garfield

It was a good time in Hollywood to pitch a film with Hispanic heroes. Edward James Olmos, who had recently won an Emmy for his role in the hit TV series *Miami Vice*, was signed to play Escalante. Lou Diamond Phillips, fresh from his role as Ritchie Valens in the hit movie *La Bamba*, played a character that fused the stories of several actual students together. Andy Garcia, lately featured in *The Untouchables*, was cast as an ETS official.

The movie went into production in 1987, the same year Garfield had its best results ever in AP calculus. Olmos and Escalante soon became fast friends. The actor spent days watching Escalante in the classroom and recorded more than thirty hours of conversations. He thinned his hair and gained forty pounds to look and move more like his subject.

One question the screenwriters wanted to put to rest was whether the class of '82 had actually cheated or not. They had all steadfastly insisted they were innocent. Escalante and Gradillas believed them unflinchingly. Mrs. Pruitt insisted there was no way they could have copied. And yet there was the evidence of the test booklets, the similar wrong answers that beat odds of 10 million to one.

Jay Mathews, who had written numerous stories about Escalante for *The Washington Post* and was at the time working on a biography of him, was asked to investigate.[4] With the students' permission he looked at the answers to the infamous question six in ten of the test booklets. Nine of the ten took the same wrong steps and got the same wrong answer (the tenth booklet had the correct answer). As agreed, Mathews sent all ten students copies of their answers and a copy of a detailed memo to him from the chairman of the ETS board of review explaining their decision.

Two of the students came forward and said they and some other students had copied the answer from a sheet someone passed around. Four others denied they had copied and three did not respond to questions from Mathews.

When reminded of a group letter to Escalante he had recently signed saying there was no copying, one of the two who admitted cheating said he signed it because he felt Mathews had coerced a statement from him; then he changed his story to say he had copied the incorrect answer from another student and shown it to others; then he changed his story again saying he had not cheated and was playing a joke to see if Mathews was working for ETS. The second student who admitted copying later said the issue was old and irrelevant and would not discuss it further.

Mathews concluded, "I decided simply to report what I had seen and heard, and hope it would be taken in context. I was convinced that, whatever occurred during that first 1982 examination in Room 411, it had ceased to have much meaning for what was happening at Garfield. What was important was that twelve students, obviously frightened and upset and handicapped by lack of preparation time and textbooks, had taken the retest and had passed ... They earned valid AP college credit and proved that they had had sufficient grasp of the material all along."

During an interview in the fall of 2014, Angelo Villavicencio, a colleague and admirer of Escalante's who eventually replaced him as the calculus teacher at Garfield High, insisted the class of '82 had never cheated. "I was an AP calculus reader for the ETS for five years," he said. "You see all kinds of crazy things. It may have been the right move to take a closer look at those booklets with similar wrong answers, but there's an easy explanation."

"Escalante gave very vivid, unforgettable examples to explain his concepts. Because his teaching style was so flamboyant, and because he used so much repetition, kids remembered what he said and repeated it back exactly the way he said it. Sometimes he made mistakes at the blackboard. We all make mistakes once in a while. Remember that Escalante had only been teaching AP calculus for a few years when this happened. He was still refining his approach. He always moved hard and fast—drilling, drilling, drilling. If he explained something the wrong way, it would stick with them."

"It was during the time he was sick with gallstones that he went through this stuff on volumes. He was in pain, he was in and out of class. But he kept going and this is what he ended up with and this was incorrect. The students learned it, imprinted it, incorrectly, and they all learned it the same way." But what about the long odds of the wrong answers being the same? What about the two students who admitted they cheated to Jay Mathews? Villavicencio was adamant: "The idea that they cheated is bulls--t. They did not cheat."[5]

In the end, the screenplay assumed the students were innocent and that the second test only underscored their truthfulness. Menéndez and Musca raised the money to finish the film themselves, with Musca producing and Menéndez directing. *American Playhouse* and Olmos Productions shared in the production credits. The picture was shot on location at

Garfield, with some scenes filmed at nearby Roosevelt High. Warner Bros. bought the theatrical distribution rights. The premiere was set for March 11, 1988. In an interview with the *Los Angeles Times*, Tom Musca commented, "I wonder what effect we will have on Jaime's life." By the morning of March 12, he had his answer.

5. Don't Give Up

"'*Deliver*' Receives High Marks," declared *Los Angeles Times* film critic Sheila Benson, introducing her review of *Stand and Deliver*. "Talent like [Escalante's] is a miracle," she added. "Pride is contagious. It has infected Garfield High, where Escalante still holds his standards high and dares kids to follow."[1]

Already well-known in educational circles, Jaime Escalante became a national celebrity overnight. It was an unusual subject for a Hollywood hit. As director Ramón Menéndez explained to *New York Times* film critic Aljean Harmetz, it had been a tough sell to distributors. "Try to describe a film about kids taking a math test."[2]

But it worked. Harmetz wrote that "the heart-pounding excitement comes not from car chases, gang warfare or invented crises in the life of the teacher but from the Advanced Placement calculus exam …" The script took certain liberties with the truth, compressing the timeframe and combining the lives and experiences of many students into a few on-screen characters. Aili Gardena, a veteran of the 1982 test, commented that the movie made students look "so dumb" at the beginning.[3] Those who took the '82 AP test in real life had been preparing for years. They were seasoned Escalante veterans, hand-picked for their potential and drilled endlessly. Another fictitious addition was the hoodlum played by Lou Diamond Phillips. Escalante would never have allowed a student like that in his program. And if anyone had ever thrown a chair in class, Henry

Gradillas would have transferred him to another school the same day.

For all its fictitious details, the core of the film—Escalante's incredible energy, innovative classroom technique, and limitless dedication—captured the main points of his career and shared his triumph with the world. *Stand and Deliver* was also a financial success. Made for under $1.5 million, the film was acquired for distribution by Warner Bros. for $3.5 million and earned $14 million (or $38 million in 2025 dollars) at the box office.[4]

5.1. "Jaime Must Stay!"

Considering Escalante's fame and the film's popularity, few would have guessed that within three years Jaime Escalante would be gone from Garfield, and soon afterward the math department that made them both famous would be undone by new leadership weary of the administrative trouble his program had caused. Still, the professional accolades kept coming: the Jaime Escalante Educational Fund to assist Bolivian and Latino students in 1989; the Jaime Escalante Mathematics Teacher Award also in 1989, presented by the Los Angeles Educational Partnership and sponsored by ARCO; Escalante receiving the American Education Award in 1990 from the American Association of School Administrators. His PBS television series, *Futures*, received a Peabody award in 1990. Yet as we have seen, that was also the year Escalante was replaced as chair of the math department. Finally, in 1991 he resigned from Garfield under pressure after being there seventeen years.

Jaime Escalante may be the only teacher ever to give the commencement address at his school the same year he was forced from his job. It is yet another indication of the ambivalence and divisiveness surrounding his legacy. Most of his students loved him; parents and community leaders held a rally in his support, hoisting signs that read, "Jaime Must Stay!" Members of the PTA and even the teachers union expressed disappointment that he would leave. Los Angeles newspapers bewailed that their school district would let this valuable resource, this celebrity teacher befriended by US presidents, star of his own television show, and educational consultant in demand across the country, slip away.

Escalante considered going back into the computer or electronics fields, but his heart was in teaching. A representative of his generous benefactor ARCO predicted that Escalante "will find another Garfield and do his thing all over again. He will never stop teaching. He will die in the saddle teaching."[5] Escalante accepted a new position at Hiram Johnson High School in Sacramento beginning in the fall of 1991.

5.2. Hiram Johnson High School

While Los Angeles media couldn't believe the district would let their star teacher go, Sacramento could hardly believe its good fortune. The superintendent there praised Escalante lavishly, saying he was "elated" to welcome him, and prepared a showcase classroom to his specifications.[6] It was a large former auto shop classroom, newly air conditioned and furnished with new, oversized desks, both donated by Escalante supporters. There was an observation area with large one-way windows to accommodate the steady stream of visitors that had become the norm at Garfield in the years since the movie made Escalante a national figure.

Unfortunately, Escalante quickly encountered a taste of the same professional friction at the new school that had dogged him at Garfield. Some Hiram Johnson teachers said they learned about Escalante's arrival on their way to work the first day of school. Others were jealous of the press coverage even before then. Certainly there were colleagues who envied his classroom.

As he had done at Garfield, Escalante began by teaching lower-level math courses—arithmetic and basic algebra to freshmen and sophomores. His third year he taught precalculus; and only with that course finally under students' belts did he teach the full-fledged calculus class. Yet during seven years at Hiram Johnson, Escalante never approached the success he'd had at Garfield. Part of the reason was his health. When he moved to Sacramento in the fall of 1991 Jaime was sixty years old, the survivor of a heart attack and gall bladder surgery during his tenure at Garfield. He was sixty-five when he taught his first class of AP calculus at Hiram Johnson. It is an inopportune season of life to begin again from scratch so difficult a challenge.

But the main reason his program never gained the momentum it had before was that the administration and parents in Sacramento failed to back him up when it came to maintaining the standards necessary for results. Teachers and parents allowed students to drop his courses. They took exception to his heavy-handed classroom technique that included badgering and barking at students, giving them sometimes unflattering nicknames, and demanding long homework assignments.

Hard-edged nicknames were part of the Hispanic culture, but now for the first time in his career, Escalante taught mostly non-Hispanics. Only 19 percent of the student body at Hiram Johnson was Hispanic, while 61 percent were either white or Asian. As Don Mroscak, the veteran Garfield counselor, recalls, "The families in Sacramento were less pliable." At Garfield, threatening to call a parent was often all Escalante had to do to make a student toe the line. He had a rapport with the Latino families there that he lost among the Asian, Anglo, Latino, and African-American mix at Hiram Johnson. Now the response from a student to his threat might well be, "Call anybody you like!" Without the family and community support he had counted on before, Escalante lost the leverage he previously had to keep students in class when they wanted to give up.

By 1995, Escalante was able to reestablish his early morning and lunchtime help sessions, and was prepping thirty or so students for the AP calculus exam. But two years later, the calculus program at Hiram Johnson was fading fast. Though he was able to improve the school's math performance, he never repeated his historic results at Garfield. In 1997, only eleven students took the AP test. The next year only seven signed up for advanced calculus and the class was deleted from the curriculum. That year Escalante taught no calculus at all. A third of his algebra students dropped during the school term, leaving twenty young teens rattling around in his giant show-case classroom by the spring of 1998.

Also that year Escalante weathered withering criticism for publicly backing a state referendum to phase out bilingual education in California classrooms. He believed the policy of keeping students in Spanish-speaking classes hampered their academic progress and reduced their job prospects. The threat-ening phone calls he received both at school and at home no doubt influenced his decision to retire in 1998 after twenty-four years in California public schools.[7]

5.3. Home to Bolivia

Escalante moved back home to Bolivia in 2001, supposedly in retirement. But, unable to give up the teaching he loved, he was soon in front of a classroom again at Universidad del Valle in his wife's hometown of Cochabamba. In addition to teaching part-time there, he returned frequently to the United States to speak. He was honored with membership in the National Teachers Hall of Fame in 1999 and became an education advisor to Arnold Schwarzenegger in 2003 during his campaign for governor of California.

After he was diagnosed with bladder cancer, Escalante traveled regularly to the US for treatment. In March 2010 a seriously ill Jaime Escalante underwent an alternative cancer care program at a clinic in Reno, Nevada. Once word of his condition spread among his friends and admirers, former students reached out to him with messages of encouragement and thanks for the way he had shaped their lives. They were now lawyers, doctors, architects, engineers, and professors. Though many of them never used calculus after leaving Garfield High, they were convinced that the mental agility, study skills, self-confidence, and *ganas* that Escalante had instilled in them were decisive in their success.

One student, a mechanical engineer, remembered that Escalante pressured him to quit his job in a liquor store to be a math tutor. He now worked at the NASA Jet Propulsion Laboratory. Cases like his were typical among Escalante's students.

Escalante's old friend and colleague Angelo Villavicencio came to visit. Actor Edward James Olmos did likewise. When he saw Escalante's frail condition and learned that insurance would not pay the full cost of his treatment there, he persuaded the family to let him appeal for donations. Former students organized a weekend rally on the Garfield campus to raise money.

The stocky figure that had once been so vibrant and full of energy was now emaciated and confined to a wheelchair, though his eyes still sparkled behind his glasses. His rakish newsboy cap was replaced with a knit stocking cap to keep him warm. His voice was reduced to a raspy whisper. He ate slowly, and scheduled his day around doses of more than twenty medications. Though he could barely speak, he answered a question about his former students by writing, "They understood the significance of *ganas*, the giant step to success. I had many opportunities in this country, but the best I found in East LA. I am proudest of my brilliant students."

5.4. Escalante's Legacy

After three weeks of treatment he went to his son's home in Roseville, California. Doctors had given him a few months at most to live. On March 30, 2010, Edward James Olmos announced to the press that Jaime Escalante had passed away.

In his *Los Angeles Times* obituary published the next day, Elaine Woo, who had written numerous times about Escalante over the years, noted, "Escalante was a maverick who did not get along with many of his public school colleagues, but he mesmerized students with his entertaining style and deep understanding of math."

She quoted College Board president Gaston Caperton who said, "Jaime Escalante has left a deep and enduring legacy in the struggle for academic equity in American education ... Because of him, educators everywhere have been forced to revise long-held notions of who can succeed."[8]

Edward James Olmos called Escalante "the most stylized man I've ever come across. He had three basic personalities— teacher, father-friend, and street-gang equal ..."

President Barack Obama released a statement that said in part, "While most of us got to know him through the movie that depicted his work teaching inner-city kids calculus, the students whose lives he changed remain the true testament to his life's work. Throughout his career, Jaime ... proved that where a person came from did not have to determine how far they could go. He instilled knowledge in his students, but more importantly he helped them find the passion and the will to fulfill their potential."

At his death, the only remnant of Escalante's seventeen historic years at Garfield High was his old classroom with a sign by the door reading, "Jaime A. Escalante Math Center GANAS." It was scheduled for demolition that summer to build a new auditorium. The assistant principal said there were plans to put a plaque on the site honoring Escalante.

Olmos helped organize a wake for Escalante, whose casket rested in a Garfield lecture hall decorated to resemble his classroom from the 1980s, complete with sports posters on the walls and equations on the blackboard. A photo showed the teacher in his prime, complete with big glasses and the trademark newsboy cap he would be buried in.

The funeral service the next day was at the sports stadium of East Los Angeles Community College, where Escalante had started his summer program decades ago, and where thousands of middle and high school students have gone in the years since to prepare for advanced studies in a range of subjects. The Jaime Escalante Math Program thrives today at ELAC, open as space permits to any student who has graduated from sixth grade. The only requirements are that they promise to come to class and do the homework. Escalante would have required no less.

Jaime's legacy endures, though his teaching methods and standards have yet to be widely adopted or adapted. Explicit support among educators for his methods is spotty at best, in spite of his phenomenal track record. If he were an athlete, he would be in the league of Wayne Gretzky, Michael Jordan, and Usain Bolt. Yet his astounding legacy is obscured by infighting in an educational community riven with competing political agendas and violent social forces (factors if not less evident in sports then at least less detrimental to athletes). During his life, Escalante was simultaneously celebrated and criticized— honored by students, presidents, and Hollywood filmmakers, yet impeded and condemned by administrators, union representatives, jealous colleagues, and disaffected parents. Those opposing viewpoints still define the debate today.

Reducing Escalante's example down to its essence, two foundational lessons emerge from the life of this dedicated and visionary teacher: 1) The prime objective of a teacher is to set high goals and give students every tool possible to reach them; 2) Teachers must maintain a laser focus on this objective and do whatever is necessary to achieve and sustain it.

The only thing easy about these lessons is writing them on paper. Escalante's story tells us they are very hard to implement and that the personal and professional cost of doing so will be high. Considered on a wider scale, these lessons unleash a torrent of questions. What should the goals be? Who sets them? How is progress in achieving them measured? How are the needs and abilities of various student populations taken into account? (Even during Escalante's heyday at Garfield High, the school ranked overall near the bottom of Los Angeles high schools.)

What we do know is that Jaime Escalante achieved historic results. Yet in order to do so, he had to go outside the educational mainstream. The system was ultimately the opponent of this great educator, not his supporter. Today more than ever, parents, students, and taxpayers fed up with the poor performance of traditional American educational institutions are going outside the system to get results in the Escalante mold, and taking their money and support with them.

Is the chasm between traditional educational systems and educational excellence inevitable? Is there a way forward that brings them together? Can the system change or be changed to do the job it is supposed to do? Can and should stakeholders establish a separate system apart from the traditional bureaucracy that has failed?

What does the story of Jaime Escalante teach about prospects for the future of American education? How do we go up against the conflicting agendas, turf wars, political and financial battles, entrenched positions, hype, half-truths, misinformation, and apathy surrounding American education?

Great teachers are also great students: they're always eager to learn and improve. Escalante's colleague and friend Henry Gradillas took a year off in mid-career to finish his doctorate in part, he said, to show students at Garfield High that you're never too old to learn. Escalante agreed. Even after he became a celebrity, he often spoke of how important it was for him to keep learning how to teach. When he left Los Angeles for Sacramento at age 60, he worked to tailor his famous classroom style to a new student body and a new community.

Were he still with us, Jaime would likely insist that in order to set American education on the right track, it's time for educators and everyone else involved to do some learning of their own. He would get the attention of the warring parties by throwing a sock monkey at them and exclaim, "You *burros* are giving me a heart attack! Break it down. Work it out. Don't give up until you've got it."

It's time to break it down. Work it out. Don't give up until we've got it. One place to begin is with a look at who's driving the school bus—who is in charge of mainstream education in America and where they have taken us.

6. Teaching from the Top Down

For Escalante, inspiring and equipping students to excel depended on taking charge of the teaching environment: schedule, curriculum, teaching technique, discipline, testing, everything. Ever analyzing what he sensed around him both as teacher and as department head, and with the support of principal Henry Gradillas, Escalante constantly fine-tuned his teaching approach to make the most of the time available. He could re-explain something a different way, add another help session, or move on to a new topic depending on the needs of a particular class on a specific day.

During Escalante's tenure in the 1970s and 80s, Garfield High was a three-year school—the youngest students were in the tenth grade. Almost none of them had any higher-level math in middle school that would have prepared them for calculus. To ready them for the AP exam, Jaime had to cram five or six years' worth of math into three. That meant blazing his own trail, fighting for new textbooks, carving out extra time, and dealing with endless complaints from the bureaucracy for not doing what he was expected to do. He was expected to meet expectations, not to vastly exceed them!

Escalante's success stemmed in large part from the rapport he established with students and the attention he gave to them. He took time with his students and challenged them to make time to learn even when it meant giving up other activities. He talked with parents when necessary, bought the kids meals, gave them rewards, and otherwise became part of their lives outside the classroom. He resisted the ever-present interference and control from above that was almost always an impediment to success, seldom a benefit.

6.1. Decision-Making Taken out of the Classroom

Great teaching originates in the classroom. It has to. That's the only place where all the variables in a class of students can be clearly seen and assessed. It is the point of engagement where teachers take the initiative to apply their unique skills and interests in the best way possible. Everything else is generalizations and assumptions.

Yet for more than sixty years, the trend in American education has been to transfer decision-making and control of the classroom out of teachers' hands and into the higher rungs of the national educational bureaucracy. Rather than encouraging local oversight and equipping teachers for the task, the process has become increasingly centralized to the detriment of students, teachers, parents, and taxpayers who have seen breathtaking sums of money disappear into the endless gray buildings of Washington. The farther decision-making gets from the classroom, the less effective it is, the more frustrated teachers become, the more money is wasted, the more cheated America's schoolchildren and their parents are, and the farther we drift from solutions to restore an educational system that everybody agrees is broken.

It isn't supposed to be this way. According to the Act of Congress that authorized the Department of Education in 1979, "The primary responsibility for education resides with

States, localities, and private institutions; ... No provision of law relating to a program administered by the Secretary [of Education] or any other officer or agency of the executive branch of the Federal Government shall be construed to authorize the Secretary or any such officer or agency to exercise any direction, supervision, or control over the curriculum, program of instruction, administration, or personnel of any educational institution, school or school system."

From the outset, then, the federal government promised to leave education in local hands, declaring that the purpose of the new Department of Education was, instead, to ensure "access to equal educational opportunity for every American" and "to support more effectively States, localities and public and private institutions in carrying out their responsibilities for education." Equality of access and effective support—full stop.[1]

6.2. The Department of Education

Despite these noble and limited objectives, the idea of a full-fledged federal Department of Education was controversial. Republicans believed it was unconstitutional since the Constitution says nothing about education; Democrats believed it was constitutional under the Commerce Clause (which gives Congress the right to regulate interstate commerce) and that it would raise the level of education overall. Professional educators were divided: the National Education Association supported the legislation while the American Federation of Teachers opposed it.

The Department was one of a series of steps that brought federal control into neighborhood schools. The process unfolded slowly at first, picked up speed in the 1960s and again in the 1980s, and has rushed headlong since the first decade of this century. Over that time the federal role expanded from gathering and distributing information; to targeted spending on the poor, minorities, and other student groups; to effective oversight of curriculum, testing, teaching technique, and more. With regard to each of these educational variables, Jaime Escalante insisted on controlling them from the front of his classroom.

America's interest in education at a national level is older than America itself. The Massachusetts Bay Colony decreed in 1647 that every town of fifty families or more had to have a school. The first federal educational organization, in 1867, was under the Department of the Interior and was assigned to collect and share nationwide "such statistics and facts as shall show the condition and progress of education in the several States and territories." Sponsoring legislation for the education bureau was submitted in the House of Representatives by former Civil War general and college president James Garfield, later the twentieth President of the United States and namesake of Escalante's Garfield High.

The first attempt at setting up a Cabinet-level department of education occurred in 1924, when it was derailed by strong national opposition to federal interference in educational policy. After being folded into a New Deal agency during the Depression, the education bureau became part of the new Department of Health, Education, and Welfare in 1953. This national agency used its power over education sparingly at first. One early step into the politics of curriculum occurred four years after HEW began when the Soviet Union launched Sputnik, the world's first artificial satellite. The American government was shocked and stunned to be beaten to this milestone in the space race. To promote math, science, and engineering education, Congress passed the National Defense Education Act the following year, which offered incentives to students of these fields (and some others, including foreign language) in order to fill positions in government and academia that would enable

America to pull ahead of the Soviets in space exploration and national defense.

Beginning in the 1960s, the federal government used educational programs and legislation to battle racial discrimination, address economic inequality, grant direct financial assistance on a vast new scale, and give greater freedom and opportunity to disabled students. The biggest changes came as part of President Lyndon Johnson's Great Society legislation. This included a flood of new laws that gave Congress unprecedented power to disburse billions of dollars directly to public schools. Of course, such funding came with strings attached: for the first time Congress was able to set requirements for public schools to receive these funds. For example, the Elementary and Secondary Education Act of 1965 awarded money for books and supplies to districts with concentrations of low-income students.

In imposing such top-down conditions on local schools, the federal government largely ignored what teachers taught in the classroom or how they taught it. The focus was not on methods, curriculum, or results, but on equal access.

The next major step toward extending government control over schools was signing the new Department of Education (DoED) into law in 1980. The creation of the DoED set off a classic Washington turf battle when newly appointed members of the Department replaced workers who had been doing the same jobs in the education bureau of HEW. Arriving at their offices on the first day, some of the new hires discovered that the workers they replaced had nailed their office doors shut.

The Department has survived numerous efforts to shut it down. Republican presidential candidates have promised to defund or otherwise dismantle the Department. Under President Donald Trump, in his second term, the Department has seen a greater than 50 percent downsizing. Ronald Reagan promised, as a presidential candidate, to eliminate it. After his election in 1980, however, President Reagan reduced the Department's budget but still kept it. He assigned his Secretary of Education, Terrel Bell, the job of closing down the Department. Convinced that many of the education programs were good ones—it was the Department bureaucracy that was bad—Secretary Bell commissioned detailed studies on where programs could be relocated when the Education Department was shuttered.[2]

6.3. A Nation at Risk

One of the commissions formed by Secretary Bell produced a report that shocked the American public. Released in the spring of 1983 by Bell's National Commission on Excellence in Education and published by the US Department of Education, the report was titled *A Nation at Risk: The Imperative for Educational Reform*. The most famous passage from that report reads like the opening of a spy novel: "If an unfriendly foreign power had attempted to impose on America the mediocre educational performance that exists today, we might well have viewed it as an act of war: As it stands, we have allowed this to happen to ourselves. We have even squandered the gains in student achievement made in the wake of the Sputnik challenge. Moreover, we have dismantled essential support systems that helped make those gains possible. We have, in effect, been committing an act of unthinking, unilateral educational disarmament."[3]

The report delivered a scorching criticism of American education, claiming America's "once unchallenged preeminence" was being "overtaken" by foreign competitors and that "the educational foundations of our society are presently being eroded by a rising tide of mediocrity," having "lost sight of the basic purposes of schooling and of the high expectations and disciplined effort needed to attain them."

The Soviets, Japanese, South Koreans, and Germans were all outshining us in world educational achievement. American employers and military leaders spent millions on remedial education because the educational system churned out graduates unqualified for the work they were supposedly trained to do. The study warned of dire consequences in world competitiveness because American education was failing and justified historic involvement by the federal government in education, even though the results of the study were controversial and in some cases hotly contested.

According to Gerald Holton, a member of the Bell committee and author of the famous introductory paragraph, the study found that 23 million Americans were illiterate and 80 percent of seventeen-year-olds could not write a persuasive essay. There was also evidence that schools on the whole were run more as social welfare institutions than academic ones. He later wrote, "We also heard that 'too many teachers are being drawn from the bottom quarter of graduating high-school and college students' with low levels of preparation, little retraining in the subject matter, and low pay."

To right these wrongs, the committee made specific recommendations, as described by Holton: "Four years of English; three years each of math, science, and social studies; and a semester of computer science ... two years of foreign language for the college-bound ... We called for more-rigorous, measurable standards; higher expectations for academic performance and conduct; more time to learn the basics; heightened admissions requirements at four-year colleges and universities; and the recognition of, and rewards for, teaching as a profession. Finally, in italics, we urged citizens to 'hold educators and elected officials responsible for providing the leadership necessary to achieve these reforms,' and to 'provide fiscal support and stability.'"

He added, "Our concern, however, goes well beyond matters such as industry and commerce. It also includes the intellectual, moral, and spiritual strengths of our people which knit together the very fabric of our society ... A high level of shared education is essential to a free, democratic society."

Holton also touched on a critical point that most education debates ignore completely. He identified "the basic flaw in the structure on which the educational system in this country is built: that apart from their own parents' sympathy and the politicians' sentimental pronouncements, the children of America are the most disenfranchised members of society. They do not vote, they do not contribute to election funds, they have no ownership in the media, they do not count when budget wars are waged against their schools."[4]

For all the headlines it generated and its prominent place in the history of American education, the Bell report produced few results at the time. Holton and others believe President Reagan used the report as a tool to win reelection in 1984 by taking the education issue away from the Democrats. After the Reagan victory, Holton writes, "the Education Department's budget was again sharply cut, and educational improvement disappeared from the administration's agenda." As control of education became more concentrated in Washington, the educational system got ever more relentlessly enmeshed with the world of national politics. Presidential elections were now influencing America's educational policy, and education reform became just another political football.

Thus, in 1991 another government report cast doubt on statistics used to support the dire predictions in *A Nation at Risk*.[5] Prepared by the data crunchers at the Department of Energy's Sandia National Laboratories, the new report showed that while overall test scores had declined as *A Nation at Risk* had claimed, scores in each subgroup of students had actually improved. The overall decline was because the relative size of the subgroups changed, a statistical condition known as Simpson's Paradox. Educationally relevant but politically sensitive, the follow-up study was never released by the government. The report itself correctly predicted, "Administration officials will use a lengthy review process to bury the report." Only when it appeared two years later in the *Journal of Education Research* did its conclusions get a public hearing.

Education reform, its control reassigned to Washington, has increasingly been at the mercy of political winds. The result is lots of talk, lots of money being spent, lots of posturing and finger pointing, and little action. In 2008, an advocacy group called Strong American Schools suggested that there was no shortage of "commonsense ideas, backed by decades of research, to significantly improve American schools." The missing ingredient, the group believed, was political, not educational. Reformers have been "stymied by organized special interests and political inertia." Unless educational reform finds strong national leaders, it is doomed to be eternally discussed but never implemented.

Keying off of *A Nation at Risk*, a report published by Edutopia[6] and sponsored by the George Lucas Educational Foundation concluded, "Only on-site teachers can really make a broad ongoing assessment that gets at a range of achievements and takes the individual into account. By contrast, uniform standardized testing whose outcomes can be expressed as simple numbers allows someone far away to compare whole schools without ever seeing or speaking to an actual student. It facilitates the bureaucratization of education and enables politicians, not educators, to control schools more effectively."

By the time this report was written in 2007, America was spending about $500 billion per year on K-12 education (the 2025 figure is $800 billion). How many governmental bureaucrats and elected officials in Washington would be willing to give up their share of that pie in order to return control of education to the teachers, taxpayers, and local districts—and possibly put themselves out of a job? Self-interest and self-preservation being what they are, such government workers are more likely to try to add to their responsibilities rather than reduce them. The resulting bureaucracy is massive, unresponsive, and unyielding.

Edutopia goes on to quote James Harvey, a member of the commission that produced *A Nation at Risk*, who expressed concern about how the report was interpreted and the direction it has given to school reform today: "... educational decisions have been moved as far as possible from the classroom. Federal officials are now in a position to make decisions that would have been unimaginable even two years ago. They've established the criteria for disciplining schools, removing principals and teachers, and even defining appropriate curriculum for American classrooms.'"

6.4. The No Child Left Behind Act

While *A Nation at Risk* identified shortcomings in American education, the No Child Left Behind Act of 2002 had far more impact on the role of the federal government in the nation's schools. Passed by overwhelming majorities in both houses and supported by politicians as diverse as John Boehner and Edward Kennedy, the NCLB granted the federal government "unprecedented sweeping oversight" of education in America, requiring states to test its students every year or lose federal education funding.[7] It set goals for improving below-average schools and sanctions for failure to improve up to and including shutting schools that repeatedly underperformed. Critics would later call it "rigid and overly ambitious and punitive," with too much emphasis on testing.

Introduced as an update of the Elementary and Secondary Education Act of 1965, which helped fund education of disadvantaged students, NCLB was promoted by civil rights and business groups to improve American competitiveness and close the achievement gap between poor or minority students and the rest. A retrospective look at the law in Education Week noted that it was changed several times over the years, and that "for the most part, each new iteration has sought to expand the federal role in education."[8]

The law set procedures for judging teacher standards and required schools to demonstrate adequate yearly progress. If a school failed to meet improvement targets two years in a row, it had to let students transfer to another school in the district. If it missed three years in a row, it had to offer free tutoring. Further failure could lead to state intervention—shutting down the school, turning it into a charter school (which almost happened to Garfield at the beginning of Escalante's tenure), taking it under state control, or other remedies. Failing schools had to set aside ten percent of their federal Title I grants for low-income students to pay for tutoring and school choice.

States had to test reading and math in grades three through eight and once in high school. Each state had to demonstrate progress in student test performance and reach the state definition of proficiency by 2014. Not a single state made it.

6.5. The Race to the Top

In the intervening years, lawmakers debated legislation to make NCLB more flexible and return more oversight to the states. At the same time lawmakers were trying to reshape the unpopular NCLB, President Barack Obama, in 2009, signed into law Race to the Top, a competition among States for federal funding. Awards would be distributed in "a competitive grant program designed to encourage and reward States that are creating the conditions for education innovation and reform."[9] Winning programs were supposed to be ambitious and achievable. Other states would then adopt winning programs for their own districts.

Critics wondered how competition among states for money would create equity. Furthermore, their chances of winning were enhanced by adopting the controversial Common Core standards. To some, the program was yet another unwelcome federal intrusion into local education, though participation was optional.

Texas was one of the states declining to compete in the Race to the Top. According to Governor Rick Perry, "We would be foolish and irresponsible to place our children's future in the hands of unelected bureaucrats and special interest groups thousands of miles away in Washington."[10]

Common Core requirements were developed by the National Governors Association and the Council of Chief State School Officers. (Their names notwithstanding, these are both Washington-based trade associations.) The federal government encouraged states to adopt Common Core standards while allowing some leeway in those standards and how they are measured. By the end of 2015, 42 states and the District of Columbia used Common Core as a basis for their educational assessment. Yet Common Core was itself criticized for being overly rigid and focused on math and English to the exclusion of other equally important subjects.

Meanwhile, NCLB led to a 160 percent increase in spending by the states by 2008 while student performance declined. Between 2002 and 2009, the US ranking in math on the Programme for International Student Assessment (PISA) fell from 18th place to 31st. By 2022, it was down to 34th. The question became whether the NCLB concept should be salvaged at all. Political expedience required it to be salvaged because to end it would be to admit defeat. On the other hand, taking the side of academic integrity, *Education Review* criticized the policy for "growing the federal footprint in K-12 education, and for relying too heavily on standardized tests." It added that "emphasis on math and reading has narrowed the curriculum, forcing schools to spend less time on subjects that aren't explicitly tested, like social studies, foreign language, and the arts. Also the law has been chronically underfunded."

6.6. Are States Regaining Control?

In the summer of 2015, the US Senate and the House of Representatives approved separate legislation that, in the words of Senate Education Chairman and former Secretary of Education Lamar Alexander (R-Tenn), "restores to states, local school districts, teachers and parents the responsibility for deciding what to do" about student education. A summary of the bill stated, "The federal government may not mandate or incentivize states to adopt or maintain any particular set of standards, including Common Core. States will be free to decide what academic standard they will maintain."[11]

The National Education Association hoped the new law would "bring real teaching and learning back to the classroom" and take "a major step in closing the door on the disastrous 'test, blame, and punish' legacy of No Child Left Behind." NEA president Lily Eskelsen García praised evidence of a shift in Washington "away from the one-size-fits-all assessments that educators know hurt students, diminish learning, [and] narrow the curriculum ..."[12] House Speaker John Boehner commented that the law would replace "top-down mandates with conservative reforms that empower the parents, teachers and administrators at the heart of our education system."[13]

In December 2015, the Every Student Succeeds Act (ESSA) replaced NCLB, restoring educational accountability to the states. Critics of top-down control of education were cautiously optimistic about the new law, even though annual standardized testing would still be required. Since ESSA's passage, federal policy through 2025 has continued to reaffirm state responsibility for academic standards and accountability systems, with states submitting consolidated plans to the US Department of Education while retaining annual statewide assessments. Although no major overhaul has replaced ESSA, the past decade has brought smaller regulatory adjustments and ongoing debates about federal oversight, state flexibility, and how education law intersects with issues such as equity monitoring, early-childhood programs, and post-secondary aid.

Yet even with the retreat of federal micromanagement, many states have filled the vacuum with their own layers of prescriptive rules, accountability metrics, and mandated instructional frameworks that can be just as constricting. State legislatures and state boards increasingly dictate curriculum details, pacing guides, intervention protocols, and teacher evaluation formulas tied to test scores, leaving master teachers with little room to exercise professional judgment or adapt instruction to students' needs. In practice, this state-level centralization can replicate the very top-down dynamics ESSA was designed to undo, producing uniformity without excellence and reducing teachers to implementers of policy rather than inspirers of learning.

Are decisions that define what happens in America's classrooms therefore moving back home? The lack of support for Race to the Top and the successful bipartisan effort to overhaul NCLB are signs that this may be the trend. Teachers everywhere celebrate the chance to take charge of their classrooms again rather than carrying out orders from policymakers who never met the students involved and probably never spent a day as a classroom teacher. The general consensus among teachers and local administrators is that the farther from the classroom decisions are made, the less likely they are to be in the best interests of students, teachers, and the learning enterprise.

Terry Beasley, a middle school teacher in Missouri, speaks for many of his colleagues when he says, "So much has gone wrong since NCLB." He cites, "over-testing," "educators not having any flexibility to do what is needed in the classroom," as well as a "terrible business model approach to education." He concludes, "Students don't enjoy school like they used to, because they're not treated as individuals. They're just this group that we're supposed to whip into shape. That's not what education should be about."[14]

Jaime Escalante, by contrast, refused to let bureaucrats take charge of his teaching environment. That was for him to control. Not only did he leave us his own example, we have other successful educators who followed in his footsteps. Ray Mayoral began his career at Garfield under Escalante. He retired after a distinguished career as a principal in Oregon and Nevada. His observations on the struggle for control in America's classrooms could have come straight from Jaime himself.

"The district, state, and feds dictate what you do," Ray says. "They shove mandates down your throat—Expeditionary Learning, Common Core—constant monitoring and dictating. They take away the principal's ability to run the school. They keep adding mandates and not asking what's best for the kids. As a principal, my worst enemy was all the mandates. It forced teachers to do things I philosophically didn't believe in."

"When people move to the district office they lose sight of what's important. They get caught up in the bubble of politics and policies and lose sight of the classroom. They become policy peddlers and rule mongers." In the Escalante mold, Mayoral believes that money should be spent directly on improving the classroom experience. "The system should be changed so that the majority of resources go to support the schools. Cut back on administration. Cut the bureaucracy in half and transfer that money to the school site."[15]

Ray in turn passed the Escalante philosophy down to his colleague and friend, teacher Mark Peabody at Novato High School in Marin County, California. "Education is a political football," Mark says. "Everybody is allowed to beat up on it." Politicians and administrators anxious to make their mark replace the existing curriculum and assessment system with their own. "Every three to five years, new reforms are led by legislators and handed to us to implement. The problem is that many of them don't work. Older teachers know reform will fail because it always fails. Teachers in the classroom don't have the techniques or materials required by top-down planning. By the time an administration brings in its program, new textbooks and curriculum guides are in hand, and teachers learn the material and the standards for proficiency, a new regime brings in a new set of materials and standards and the process begins all over again."[16]

To sum up the preceding arguments and statistics, teaching from the top-down is destined to fail because students are not data points. Every young person is different, unique, exhibiting distinctive skills and experiences, and needing specifically adapted tools to succeed. Not only do blanket bureaucratic rules fail to apply successfully to everyone but they can't even benefit anyone in particular. The bigger the blanket, the more encompassing its bureaucratic rules, and consequently the more the actual teaching environment get shortchanged, smothering creativity and achievement through irrelevant and counter-productive rules.

Just as students are not data points, teachers are not soldiers simply following orders. The best teachers are creative, innovative professionals with their own special talents and classroom skills. They have to have control and flexibility, like Escalante occasionally even tossing a pillow at a distracted sophomore. To the extent that a top-down system takes away these freedoms, it takes away from great teachers the very things that make them great.

7. The Testing Juggernaut

A test made Jaime Escalante famous. As a teacher he focused on preparing his students for a particular high-stakes exam he believed was the ticket to a better career and a better life for everyone who passed it. As chairman of the math department at Garfield High, he structured courses and assigned students throughout the school in a way that fed the most promising kids into his AP calculus program.

Tests are a familiar and necessary tool for evaluating what students know, but as the educational landscape has been transformed over the last decades, testing has become a contentious point of policy. The purpose of the national AP calculus exam that Escalante's fourteen students prepared for so diligently in 1982 was specific, narrow, and clearly defined. These fourteen represented a tiny, statistically insignificant sliver of the student population at Garfield.

7.1. Standardized Testing

By contrast, No Child Left Behind Act (NCLB) and Race to the Top (R2T) imposed uniform standards and high-stakes testing on all students, regardless of their interests or abilities. Today, standardized testing remains deeply embedded in US K–12 education: state-mandated assessments are still taken annually in almost every state, and many teachers report that "teaching to the test" continues to drive classroom practices. Originally forty-five states adopted the Common Core State

Standards (CCSS). As of 2025 thirty-five states, along with the District of Columbia and some territories, still adhere to the Common Core. But the shadow of Common Core falls even on states that have formally rejected it. Florida, for instance, replaced Common Core with its B.E.S.T. (Benchmarks for Excellent Student Thinking) standard in 2020, whose overlap with Common Core is substantial.

Once a high-stakes testing program is launched, tens of thousands of careers and budgets suddenly depend on the outcome of a single exam. Many educators, parents, and students would agree with the college admissions officers who said of the Scholastic Aptitude Test, "What students do over four years in high school is more important than what they do on a Saturday morning."[1] Yet the push toward high-stakes testing has continued. Rather than thoroughly assessing student progress over time, these tests have become infamous for producing misapplied results, bringing stress and anxiety to educators and students alike, and encouraging a raft of tricks and deceits to improve test data.

One study after another agrees that nationwide testing has become a runaway train. Iris C. Rotberg, research professor of education policy at George Washington University writes, "Accountability has become the centerpiece of political rhetoric on education reform. The underlying assumption is straightforward: hold teachers and students accountable for students' scores on standardized tests, and academic standards will rise. Sounds good. But it doesn't work."[2] In 2015, UCLA research professor Mike Rose concluded that the assumptions of NCLB "reveal a pretty simplified notion of what motivates a teacher: raise your expectations or you'll be punished—what a friend of mine calls the cave man theory of motivation."[3]

In the decade since, little has changed: as of 2025, state accountability systems still rely heavily on standardized tests, ensuring that test-driven instruction and high-stakes pressures remain entrenched in American K–12 education. Under ESSA (Every Student Succeeds Act), states must still administer annual statewide tests in grades 3–8 and once in high school in reading/language arts and mathematics, with similar requirements for science. States use test results to identify struggling schools, monitor subgroup performance, and inform funding and intervention decisions. States see themselves as held hostage to testing because significantly reducing testing would undermine their ability to track performance and meet federal reporting obligations.

To many of Escalante's colleagues and successors, national standards testing is the poster child for educational bureaucracy run amok. In reflecting on the prospects for repeating Escalante's success today, educators have more to say about this than any other topic. Asked what one change in the educational landscape it would take to repeat Escalante's results, a veteran of more than thirty years in California public schools exclaimed, "Get rid of Common Core testing!"[4]

Mary Poplin, emerita professor of education at Claremont Graduate University in California and an admirer of Jaime Escalante, notes that testing has its place but that it has to be correctly used and interpreted. "We will never improve the education of the poor without holding educators accountable for standardized test scores," she says. "They are simply the most reliable and cost and time efficient form of measuring academic progress." Yet while standardized tests help insure equality "for students like those Escalante cared about, they're not going to give the teacher a lot of useful information like the smaller periodic assessments of particular knowledge and skill acquisition will."[5]

National testing programs generally emphasize math and language. Because so much is at stake, teachers and schools are under immense pressure to spend all the time they can on tested subjects to the exclusion of everything else. In pursuit of the golden carrot of test results that yield money and professional approval in place of criticism and ridicule, schools are tempted to throw everything else overboard: physical education, community service, music, art, theater, history, geography, foreign languages, literature, creative writing—so much of what enriches education by appealing to children's individuality, their talents, interests, and strengths. Children who do not know the history of their country have no reference point for how to make it better. Arts and humanities can enrich a student's life experience remarkably and may be the path to a fulfilling career. Yet because the tests don't address these disciplines, teachers increasingly downplay them or don't teach them at all.

Nashville teacher Houston Sarratt notes, "Standardized testing has severely narrowed the curriculum, to the students' tremendous detriment, especially K-8. What you've learned the entire year is assessed in two or three hours, and these scores are used to determine student growth. The kids don't really get taught literature or writing. The whole focus is choosing the right answer on a test. Students do fine on the test, but they can't write."[6]

So much of education these days focuses on skills and methods: Can you solve a particular equation? Can you read and make sense of a difficult grammatical construction? But procedural capabilities like this also need content—to be filled with particulars that are relevant to life. What does that equation say about your bank account and what you can afford to buy? How does your ability to read help you learn things that excite your imagination and therefore make you want to read? Numeracy and literacy need to be applied. The sciences and the humanities fill out these procedural capabilities, giving students the sense that they are learning important things about this fascinating world that we inhabit.

7.2. Important Content Left Untaught

Henry Gradillas, Escalante's principal and friend, writes in his book *Standing and Delivering* that the district administration once pressured him to accept low test scores and high dropout rates because his pupils could not be expected to do any better. Later they applied pressure to score high in order to meet NCLB requirements. "Too often important content is left untaught because standardized tests do not include it," he observes. To hit their numbers, some states seem to be watering down their exams.

"Even though scores on state tests keep rising, SAT and National Assessment of Educational Progress (NAEP) scores are stagnant, and colleges are complaining about the academic skills of the students the high schools send them. In this age of data-driven education, positive statistics are the Holy Grail," Gradillas continues. "Our top priority [at Garfield in the 1980s] was not to produce positive statistics, but rather to give our kids the best education that we could offer them. The higher test scores and lower dropout rates were fortunate by-products of improved education."[7]

Mark Peabody, whose principal Ray Mayoral worked and learned under Escalante, believes school should be "training people to enjoy life and do what they're skilled to do. School is the time and place where kids find their identities—'This is who I am!' versus 'This is what the school told me to be.'"[8]

Lucy Romero began her career in education as an intern at Garfield during the Escalante years, where she then also subsequently taught biology at Garfield's School for Advanced

Studies. Her experience is that national standards do not accurately measure a student's ability or a school's progress. "Classes are uneven from year to year," she says. "Some are exceptional, some are not as good. Yet there's unrelenting pressure to keep going higher. The success of the school is based on a number. Students know a lot about a little."[9]

Escalante's former colleague Angelo Villavicencio believes that standardized test results are especially misleading in poor and minority schools where expectations have always been low. Moreover, "testing has taken away the beauty of teaching math, taken away how wonderful the subject can be."[10]

Molly Slack, a seasoned middle school drama teacher on the outskirts of Houston, heartily agrees. "Standardized testing will be the downfall of this country," she declares, adding that children have different abilities and different learning styles that standardized tests don't take into account.

Teaching to the test robs teachers as well as students, Slack observes. "The testing craze takes so much time that teachers never have time to think about how to bring their personal strengths to the job."[11] Administrators focused on test results pressure teachers to abandon lessons or methods they are expert in or have a passion for in order to focus on the test-based curriculum. Teachers who have collected illustrations or study aids for decades and developed innovative ways of presenting them have to leave them untouched in the storage closet.

Besides bureaucratic requirements that narrow the curriculum and misapply results, teachers chafe at government-mandated paperwork that takes time away from classroom teaching, preparation, and professional development. "Teachers are pressed for time because they do so much administrative work that doesn't add to education," Houston Sarratt says. "The big culprit is standardized testing—level assessment, intervention, and so forth. This decreases the time for creative thinking and collaboration."

Another challenge to educators is when their curriculum standards shift in order to chase after better test results. Tennessee 2015 Teacher of the Year Karen Vogelsang began her career as a banker, so she was used to "standards, benchmarks, and expectations" before she stood in front of a classroom for the first time. Part of the frustration in today's world of education, she says, is having a test that measures old standards. Her experience recalls what Mark Peabody said about new administrative regimes throwing out everything that preceded them. She says, "It takes five to seven years to get a textbook through the approval process. By then somebody wants to do something different. What are we measuring? We can't teach to the new standard until we have the resources and materials."[12]

And while Vogelsang likes the idea of a nationwide standard "because I can talk to a teacher anywhere," she believes there is misunderstanding and confusion about "the relationship between testing and Common Core. I don't think one test is an accurate measure of what a kid does." She adds that Common Core "has nothing to do with a teacher's evaluation ... Holding me accountable for how another human being's brain takes in information really is not fair."

Houston Sarratt echoes Vogelsang's and Peabody's concerns about curriculum as a moving target. "The powers that be keep changing the requirements, which means changing the curriculum and changing the test. Then by the time all the changes are in place, there's someone else in charge and they want to put their stamp on education and so come up with new requirements and testing methods. I have had to use the curriculum for one program to prepare classes to test under another one." The consequences of combining old material with a new test are reliably disappointing. One predictor of how well a school will test is how long they have used the curriculum being tested. The shorter the time, the lower the grade.

Some experts believe high-stakes testing does further damage by driving good teachers away from the profession. Weary and frustrated with all the extra work and pressure, the most talented and ambitious leave the classroom for more rewarding work. Professor Rotberg points out one of the unintended consequences of the national fixation on testing: "It weakens academic standards when it discourages the most qualified teachers and principals from remaining in the profession." The focus on test-based accountability "affects instructional practices, public image, salaries, school takeovers, and resource availability." It "leads to excessive demands on teachers and principals," which reduces job satisfaction, weakening the ability of the profession to attract and retain highly qualified educators. As far back as 2000, *The New York Times* reported that "a growing number of schools are rudderless, struggling to replace a graying corps of principals at a time when the pressure to raise test scores and other new demands have made an already difficult job an increasingly thankless one."[13] And that was before NCLB.

Parents don't like standardized tests either. According to a 2014 PDK/Gallup Poll, sixty percent of Americans oppose national Common Core standards and sixty-two percent of public school parents oppose them.[14] Sometimes one searing example puts a whole issue into perspective. One mother described the scene of her ten-year-old daughter who could not sleep for worrying over the fourth grade New York state English language arts exam. Tears streaming down her cheeks and onto her pillow, the girl asked, "Mom, why is one test so important?" Then, playing back what she has heard for days on end in the classroom, she answered her own question: If she doesn't get a good grade on the test she won't get into a good middle school, which means she won't get into a good high school, which means she won't get into a good college, which means she won't get a good job.[15]

Parents of minority children may have even more reason to be wary of high-stakes testing. "Four Effects of the High-Stakes Testing Movement on African American K-12 Students" published in 2012 found that "NCLB became equated with one ultimate objective: producing high test scores." This, the article concluded, has disproportionately harmed black students by initiating harsher discipline standards and other policy changes, "creating a narcissistic education system that strives to make schools 'look good,' even if students are not really learning information that will help them improve the quality of their lives." The study also found that black pupils suffer disproportionately from the elimination of music, art, and drama in the classroom.[16]

7.3. Inflating Test Results

With so much at stake, the temptation to tinker with test results is intense. Students with learning disabilities or limited English could be exempted from NCLB testing. This tendency to tinker with results led to instances of large numbers of children being labeled learning disabled even before NCLB in order to keep their scores out of the mix. A 1998 article in *Policy Review* noted that in a sampling of Houston schools with good test scores, ten of 22 schools in the sample tested fewer than half their students.[17]

Another tactic for inflating results is for schools to hold lower-scoring children back the year before, producing apparent test score gains but also higher dropout rates. As an assessment coordinator in Kentucky remarked, "It looks like it's to a school's advantage to get kids to drop out rather than to keep them on the rolls and have poor test scores at grade 12."[18]

A report in *The New York Times* makes a similar observation. "When we read that states have raised academic standards, all we know is that they have initiated a high-stakes testing program. We know nothing about whether the quality of the educational program has improved. For example, if 25 percent of students drop out of school because they fail the test, we have not improved our schools."[19]

Jaime Escalante made national headlines when his students were accused of sharing answers on their AP calculus exam. By retaking and passing the exam, his students vindicated themselves and put the charge of cheating to rest. But cheating scandals are endemic to standardized testing. Testing is a high-stakes game for everyone involved, not just students, but especially educators. With so much on the line, educators may be even more tempted to cheat than their students. In what is described as the biggest cheating scandal in American history, 178 employees of the Atlanta public school system, including thirty-eight principals, were accused of improperly raising test scores. Eleven teachers, testing coordinators, and administrators were convicted in 2015 of racketeering and sent to prison.

The defendants changed students' answer sheets, sometimes having "erasure parties" around one of the principals' backyard swimming pool, then falsely certifying the results. School employees who failed to go along were fired or threatened with termination. Teachers and administrators were rewarded with bonuses for the higher grades. Beverly Hall, the superintendent of Atlanta schools, was honored as the 2009 Superintendent of the Year by the American Association of School Administrators. (Hall died of cancer before her court case was decided.)[20] Bob Schaeffer, public education director for FairTest.org and an advocate of rolling back national testing, says that cheating "is a totally predictable response to policymakers who have created a system in which teachers are expected to boost test scores sharply by any means necessary."

7.4. High-Stakes Testing

So why does the political and educational establishment keep pushing these tests if they cause such a long list of problems, and a majority does not want them? Why commit so many resources to a system teachers say hurts students and schools more than it helps? Through these tests, federal and state government imposes its will at the local level, all in the name of accountability. But are such tests the best way to achieve accountability?

No Child Left Behind, Race to the Top, and Common Core standards have been powerful instruments of top-down Congressional and state control. History tells us that once a government bureaucracy gains mastery over anything, it is reluctant to let it go. Therefore standardized testing in one form or another is likely to be a major force on the national educational scene for the indefinite future.

"It's astounding to me that administrators and legislators don't see the severe defect in the system," says teacher Houston Sarratt. "These testing programs are around because districts have invested so much and they don't want to admit failure ... They're being wooed by publishers and test writers who are making bazillions of dollars on standardized testing."

Bazillion seems right. From companies who design and administer tests to test preparation services (sometimes they're one and the same), from thousand-dollar-a-day consultants (on the low end) to the teacher who gets free gifts for trying an online product, the testing juggernaut nurtures a long list of companies and educators whose financial and professional success depend on the industry continuing to expand.

In this field, Pearson is known as "the Godzilla of education," a London-based media conglomerate with an estimated 60 percent of the US testing market, including teacher qualification, curriculum, tests, and test grading. Writing in *Fortune* magazine, Jennifer Reingold reports that "today standardized testing seems to many to have become the goal of education ... rather than a means of implementing it. Add in the increasing use of technology to teach students, government cutbacks, and the private-sector-funded reform movement, and companies have more clout than ever when it comes to what and how kids are taught."[21]

Pearson leadership do not see their company as trying to control education. Rather they portray themselves as working to help students succeed, and giving legislators and educators always the final word. "It's inevitable in a field as important as education that feelings are strong," says former Pearson CEO John Fallon. "We are here to serve parents, governments, teachers, and most importantly, students."

The famous AP calculus exam at Garfield High in 1982 under Jaime Escalante was an optional test that fourteen students, out of an enrollment of more than two thousand at the time, chose to take because they had learned calculus and wanted the benefits of demonstrating their proficiency at it. Moreover, the test results were applied to a very specific purpose: to judge whether these students exhibited enough knowledge of calculus to deserve college credit for it. Students with other skills and interests didn't have to take the test and were not expected to. The success or failure of fourteen teenagers on a Saturday morning didn't pass judgment on the principal of Garfield or the Los Angeles superintendent of schools; it didn't affect their professional standing or their paycheck.

Linda Darling-Hammond, an emerita professor at Stanford's Graduate School of Education, sees a big difference between testing in the past compared to now. "Until about 2002, there was always an understanding that tests are prone to error, that they only measure a narrow slice, and that they should only be one piece of information among others. We've lost that perspective in policy."[22]

Most standardized testing poses questions that lay out a range of possible answers, only one of which is right, the others being wrong. Objecting to the artificiality of this approach, Bard College President Leon Botstein remarks: "How to do something in real life is never defined by being able to choose a 'right' answer from a set of possible answers (some of them intentionally misleading) ... No scientist, engineer, writer, psychologist, artist, or physician—and certainly no scholar, and therefore no serious university faculty member—pursues his or her vocation by getting right answers from a set of prescribed alternatives that trivialize complexity and ambiguity."[23]

In his 2015 study published in *The American Scholar*, UCLA education professor Mike Rose sees teachers as forced into lockstep to define learning "as a rise in a standardized test score ... with the curriculum tightly linked to the test." Despite its "bureaucratic neatness," the process fails. "A teacher can prep students for a standardized test, get a bump in scores, and yet not be providing a very good education ... But because tests are easy to use and have an aura of objectivity, they are likely to remain central in the reform agenda."[24]

The same arguments surface time and again: It is impossible to reduce the academic performance of a school or a child to a single number; one test score doesn't accurately assess a student's knowledge or ability to learn; the same tests and standards can't be usefully applied to every school; student test scores are not a fair measure of teacher skill or curriculum quality. High-stakes testing as practiced today generates untold stress for students, parents, and educators at an exorbitant cost. It withers support for history, geography, art, music, drama, and everything else not tested; it narrows and distorts students' grasp of math and English by forcing teachers to emphasize only the aspects students will be tested on.

Formal testing also ignores that some of a teacher's most valuable lessons can never be assessed with questions on a page. Though Jaime Escalante's AP students excelled in their subject, they insisted then and later that what Jaime really taught them was the value of hard work, tenacity, setting goals, and establishing priorities. Few of them went on to careers requiring calculus. For every one of the group who later joined the Jet Propulsion Laboratory, many others went into law, business, government service, academia, and other fields.

Garfield graduates who studied with Escalante were accepted at America's most prestigious universities including Harvard, Yale, and MIT. At times, Jaime had former students in all three places at once. Success on a test was part of their résumés, but only a part. More important was a characteristic no exam could measure: an unwavering resolve to learn. They absorbed this resolve from their single-minded teacher as he drilled them day after day in the principles of calculus. He convinced them they were not quitters but winners. They would do whatever it took to master calculus. And with the confidence so gained, they were in a better position to face all of life's challenges.

Such learning outcomes are beyond the reach of Common Core to measure.

8. Turn Back the Wheel

In any other field, practices as successful as Escalante's would be universally praised and widely copied. Surgeons or architects or plumbers or hairdressers, getting wind of such incredible results from their colleagues or competitors, would do all they could to deliver them to their own clients. Instead, Escalante was driven from his job and his celebrated methods summarily supplanted with the old status quo, which had proven itself a resounding failure. When questioned about the decision to discard Escalante's methods, the new school principal declared that her system was fine: "We don't need any help." This unfathomable fiction resisted effective challenge from students, parents, and the school administration. Garfield High dismantled a spectacular and historic program and replaced it with a dud.

Can other teachers in other schools achieve Escalante's results? If they can, why don't they? Given the top-down control, testing obsession, and societal difficulties that so undermine today's public schools, where is the pathway forward to a system that is effective, fair, and cost-efficient? One that students, parents, educators, and policymakers all agree does the job right and does it well?

The solution isn't money. Since the beginning of the Great Society programs of the 1960s, America has spent trillions of dollars on K-12 education. If money were the answer, the problem would have been solved. Several European countries spend more money per student than the US, but many countries spend far less and get far better results. Nor is the answer top-down control and policy management. All the political and administrative tinkering over the past decades seems to be doing more harm than good. A look back at Jaime Escalante's methods reveal a set of simple tools and techniques. Can any teacher be an Escalante? Can any educator or school replicate his results by adapting his practices?

To answer those questions we can start by recognizing that everything Escalante did, any teacher can do. When we look at what is working in education today—at schools that deliver the results students and parents are desperately desiring—Escalante's methods are front and center. There are variations, of course, depending on the many variables that differ from one school or classroom to another, but the essence of the Escalante way is the core around which everything else is built.

One of the roadblocks against widespread adoption of Escalante's methods is that despite their demonstrated success, they are not popular in the world of professional educators. As Mary Poplin of Claremont Graduate University observes, "Escalante's methods are not rocket science, so they are reproducible. His personality may not be, but anyone with his vision and passion for what students could become could implement his work within the context of their own personality."

"Nevertheless his methods are not reproduced because his pedagogy—direct, guided instruction or what we may call traditional education—is unpopular. The academically respected and trendy methods, dominant for about thirty years, are radical constructivism and critical theory. These encourage teaching practices such as 'inquiry based methods' which use a good deal of hands-on activities, cooperative learning, experimentation, and dialogue."[1]

Despite the academic preference for more progressive teaching styles, direct instruction, Poplin says, has "been shown in research over and over to be more successful in increasing achievement, particularly for students who come to school with less background knowledge (students of parents who are not college educated, students of color and students who live in poverty)."

Poplin supports the position advanced in "The Lost Tools of Learning,"[2] a 1947 essay by Oxford scholar Dorothy Leigh Sayers. In that essay, Sayers championed teaching students how to solve problems rather than filling them with rote facts. Problem solving, she believed, was a skill that would serve them well all their lives, while mere information was of little use in the short term and likely to be of no use at all in the long term. As timely as this debate is, it has been going on before most of today's students' grandparents were born.

"If we are to produce a society of educated people," Sayers wrote, "fitted to preserve their intellectual freedom amid the complex pressures of our modern society, we must turn back the wheel ... to the point at which education began to lose sight of its true object." The ultimate objective, she believes, is learning how to learn: "Do you ever find that young people, when they have left school, not only forget most of what they have learnt (that is only to be expected), but forget also, or betray that they have never really known, how to tackle a new subject for themselves?"

Sayers and Escalante could hardly have been two more different people. Sayers was a woman Oxford graduate (a rarity in the early 1900s), a writer of crime fiction, a translator of Dante's *Divine Comedy*, and an essayist. Escalante was a down-to-earth immigrant, a former short-order cook, self-taught in English, and a math teacher. Yet they both saw the essential value of consistent standards, high expectations, and a focus on problem solving.

Poplin notes, "Escalante was working in a system that, with the exception of his principal, Henry Gradillas, did not value his insights, his methods, or his virtue of hard work for himself and his students."

Proof of the power, validity, and continuing appeal of Escalante's methods is that innovative, maverick educators keep developing alternatives to failed public school programs using some version of the Escalante template, and students and parents keep flocking to them and away from the status quo in ever greater numbers. These trailblazers are not necessarily copying Escalante directly, but whether they know of his work or not, they arrive at the same remedies he used. What worked for him works everywhere. Much of it, as Sayers wrote, is a simple matter of turning back the wheel.

8.1. Whole Language

An instructive example of moving ahead by turning back comes from California's disastrous experiment with whole language teaching. Traditional direct instruction, like Escalante and his contemporaries used and Mary Poplin champions, is the time-tested method of teachers passing along knowledge by lecture, demonstration, and direct engagement. Whole language, its advocates claimed, lets children absorb knowledge in a more natural and "humane" way, giving them more control. It also de-emphasized spelling and grammar on the grounds that children should have the creativity to come up with their own solutions. It also supposedly helped level the playing field for poor students and those with limited English.

California adopted whole language instruction in 1987. Young children were encouraged to discover phonics, spelling, and grammar on their own. But by 1999 fewer than 40 percent of fourth graders were reading at grade level, with minority students fairing even worse. As one analysis put it, "Instead of being taught to read, they are encouraged to discover reading. It doesn't work ... Many people believe that a whole generation of youngsters has been lost in one of the most disastrous educational experiments on record."[3]

Even in the face of overwhelming evidence of failure, some educational researchers and policymakers continued to defend whole language instruction. This is the same blinkered institutional mindset that Escalante and his supporters faced when naysayers, seeing irrefutable proof that the low standards and expectations replacing Escalante's program got inferior results, insisted, "We don't need any help."

As Chico Marx, when caught with his hand in the cookie jar, put it in the film *Duck Soup*: "Who you gonna believe? Me or your own eyes?" Our eyes tell us that whole language instruction is a fraud and that traditional approaches to literacy work far better. And yet, the thrall of ideology can cause us to disregard what should be blazingly obvious for all to see. Thus Kenneth Goodman, a language professor at the University of Arizona and one of the founders of the whole language movement, calls criticism of the method "part of a whole attempt to privatize education in the name of phonics," a scheme by cultural conservatives to discredit public education and ramp up support for private school vouchers.[4]

Goodman is not alone in heedlessly supporting whole language instruction. Jerome C. Harste, professor of language education at Indiana University, vowed, "They're not scaring me into going back into direct teaching." Stephen Krashen, professor emeritus of education at USC, believes that lack of access to books in California schools had more to do with poor reading skills than whole language instruction.[5] Others have condemned phonics as a way to sneak the Bible back into public education. One of the founders of PERT, Parents for Education Reform Today, was accused of being a tool of the religious right. Ironically, she is a Jewish Democrat who founded the group because she saw children who did not know how to sound out words. Some teachers smuggled in their own phonics lessons out of desperation.[6]

Thousands of teachers across the country shared the experience of Ann Edwards, a 20-year veteran first grade teacher in California. For years her phonics lessons produced a class that was "excited, happy and engaged in discovery," she recalled. "Now my students are disaffected and unhappy ... With whole language you invite the child to learn to read. You don't give them any rules, you don't give them any guidelines. The students are in charge and, frankly, the students should not be in charge."[7]

Decades earlier, President Johnson's Project Follow Through spent $500 million to learn the most effective teaching method for disadvantaged students. It found that direct instruction was "the only method that even came close to elevating poor readers to the fiftieth percentile in achievement. Child-centered approaches that diminish the teacher's role in the classroom and reject the teaching of basic skills finished in the basement."[8]

California abandoned whole language and returned to phonics in 1999. Marion Joseph helped start the drive back to phonics when she realized her granddaughter couldn't sound out words. As a former member of the California State Board of Education, she declared, "Having been the nation's leader in the giant experiment into untested theoretical learning, it is now our obligation to climb out of the hole and have instructional programs based on real scientific evidence. And the evidence is that phonics works ... I'm one of the most liberal individuals around and this is not about a political ideology. It is about teaching children to read."

Changing to whole language required a fortune in teacher training and textbooks. At the time California, spent $2.6 billion a year on textbooks. Changing back required another fortune, with consultants charging exorbitant fees to retrain teachers.[9]

8.2. Achievement Despite Circumstances

Escalante's principles succeed in every place and time wherever a teacher is willing to uphold them. One educator who quietly and humbly applied these principles to students the system had passed over was Marva Collins. Born into the segregated culture of Alabama in the 1930s, Collins moved to Chicago in 1959 to work as a substitute teacher in inner-city schools. In 1975 she spent part of her retirement savings to start Westside Preparatory School. Her goal was to teach black children that the school system considered learning disabled. Her curriculum and approach followed the principles that Dorothy Sayers endorsed and that Jaime Escalante practiced in his classroom every day: a logical question-and-answer format with high and consistent standards for everyone. She charged $5,500 a year for tuition when Chicago public schools were spending $11,300 per pupil. President Ronald Reagan cited her achievements, and she was awarded the National Humanities Medal.[10]

Another educator who moved ahead by turning back the wheel is the late Thaddeus Lott (who sadly died as the 2016 edition of this book was in preparation). He transformed schools in Houston's poor Acres Homes neighborhood where he was born and lived. When Lott arrived as principal at Mabel B. Wesley Elementary in 1975, only 18 percent of third graders scored at grade level in reading on the Iowa Test of Basic Skills. Five years later, 85 percent were at grade level. In 1996 100 percent passed the Texas Assessment of Academic Skills (TAAS), compared with a state average of fewer than 70 percent. The school system had expected poor performance from their poor minority students and that is what they had produced. Lott had other expectations.

Policy Review's 1998 feature on Thaddeus Lott's success was titled, "No Excuses": "To achieve this astounding turn-around, Lott eschewed popular nostrums—computers, school-to-work initiatives, parental involvement—for the basics: a proven curriculum, rigorous teacher training, strict discipline, high expectations of teachers and students, and a fervent belief that any child can learn." The article continues: "'It's a myth,' says Lott, 'that if you're born in a poor community and your skin is a certain color that you can't achieve on a higher level.'"

Given his outstanding results at Wesley, Lott was invited by the Houston school district to manage his own mini-system of four charter schools, three elementary and one middle school. His first step was to create an environment that encouraged learning: clean classrooms and halls with cheerful colors, "a staff of professionals who treat students with respect, and students who understand what type of behavior is expected of them." In many cases this meant wholesale replacement of teachers and other staff members, which his contract allowed him to do.

He introduced the Direct Instructional System for Teaching and Remediation (DISTAR) in place of the whole language approach, even though it was not approved by the state, and non-charter schools had to buy it with precious discretionary funds. This curriculum was made up of "structured drills and sequential lessons, each building on the last," with a reading program based on phonics.

In violation of state standards—which he could do only as a charter school—he brought lower-level elementary textbooks to his M.C. Williams Middle School when students from other elementary districts could not do grade-appropriate work. (Lott's local students were snapped up by magnet and private schools looking for high-achieving minority children, treating Wesley as a feeder for their programs.) Also, like Henry Gradillas at Garfield High, Lott found that achievement builds self-esteem, not the other way around.

Lott imposed a strict behavior code requiring students to walk single file, with no fighting or class disruptions allowed. Said Lott, "We can't let one or two students disrupt the educational experience." Rod Paige, Lott's boss as superintendent of Houston schools, concluded, "If I had to choose any single foundation of his success, it is his intense desire to cause children to learn." Or as Escalante might have put, *ganas*.[11]

In 2011 Mary Poplin led a team that studied 31 highly effective teachers in "the most economically depressed neighborhoods in Los Angeles County."[12] Teacher effectiveness was based on student scores on the California Standards Test for two or more years. This group of 31 saw 51 percent of their students move up a level, 34 percent maintain their level, and 15 percent drop a level. Teachers were male and female, black, white, Latino, Asian-American, and Middle Eastern-American. Their ages ranged from 27 to 60; their years of experience from three to 33. What did these great teachers, seemingly so varied as a group, have in common that made them great?

The first characteristic they shared was strictness. But both teachers and students recognized that strictness was there for a reason. One student wrote, "I think Mrs. E. is such an effective teacher because of her discipline. People might think she is mean, but she is really not. She is strict. There is a difference. She believes every student can learn."

The study continued, "Teachers didn't use the students' backgrounds as an excuse for not learning, and yet they were not naïve about the challenges facing some students ... These teachers neither taught to the tests or ignored them; tests were simply another resource."

The study defined six common elements these teachers all shared. The list has a familiar ring:

- Strictness, for effective teaching and learning, safety, and respect.
- Instructional intensity, meaning they devoted concentrated energy and sufficient time to the tasks at hand.
- Frequent movement around the classroom, giving feedback, answering individual questions, checking students' progress. "We rarely knew which students were classified as special education or English language learners because teachers' personal assistance helped mask this," Poplin wrote. Teachers had the same high expectations for every student.
- Traditional, explicit, teacher-directed instruction. Teachers constantly pushing students. Few constructivist projects or group learning activities.
- Exhorting time-honored virtues: hard work, responsibility, tenacity, honesty.
- Strong and respectful relationships; teachers showed profound respect for students and were genuinely optimistic about their futures.

Where will teachers like this find the welcome and encouragement to practice their proven skills? One place they're likely to be received with open arms is charter schools.

8.3. Charter Schools

Charter schools loom large in the contemporary history of education. They have developed and prospered by offering parents and students the choice of traditional, consistent, high standards in the Escalante mold over the often lax and failing alternative offered by many public schools. If the ranks of public schools had been populated by thousands of Escalantes, it is possible that the charter school movement would never have launched—it would not have been necessary. Parents and students desperate for a quality education created the demand for charter schools; enterprising educators have gone to work to satisfy that demand.

Charter networks tout high, consistent standards for academics and behavior, support from administrators, lots of time for learning, individual attention, and local control and flexibility. They also typically include music and other arts, foreign language, and other life-enriching subjects that so many public districts have jettisoned in the quest for higher test scores. Escalante circumvented bureaucratic rules he thought got in the way of learning. In choosing charter schools, parents and students attempt to bypass counter-productive rules so that effective learning can take place.

When the earlier edition of this book appeared in 2016, there were over 6,000 charter schools serving over 2.5 million young people, about 5 percent of all public school students in America. Today, in 2025, there are about 7,800 charter schools serving over 3.7 million young people, about 6.6 percent of all public school students in America. An even more telling testament to their popularity is that more than half a million unique students are currently on charter school waiting lists. One of the highest profile charter networks in the country is KIPP (Knowledge is Power Program),[13] which began with classes in a single Houston school in 1994 and now in 2025 enrolls 125,000 students in 279 schools from coast to coast.

KIPP stresses core principles, known as the Five Pillars, as well as standards of excellence. These are all classic Escalante: high expectations, no excuses, a safe and disciplined learning environment, a commitment from parents and teachers to excellence, extra time for academic studies, local control, and a premium on results. According to KIPP, although approximately 95 percent of their students are minorities and about 87 percent are low-income network-wide, nearly 39 percent of students who attended both a KIPP middle school and high school have completed a four-year college degree within five years of entering college—placing their long-term success well above the national average for low-income students (which remains in the single digits).

Success Academies[14] was founded in New York by Eva Moskowitz, a former city councilwoman. She lost a bid for Manhattan borough president in part because the United Federation of Teachers was angry over hearings she held to question work rules embedded in the union contract. Her objective was to give poor and minority students the same college opportunities as children whose parents could afford tutors and private school.

Long days, strict discipline, and parental commitment are required at Success Academies. Kids get candy for correct answers, and can win Nerf guns and board games for high test scores. So incentivized, the students, who are overwhelmingly low-income and minority, have ranked in the top percentiles on Common Core tests in New York State for math and English language arts. Demand is high for places in Success Academies' thirty-two schools. In 2015 the company took in 22,000 applications for 2,668 openings. Today, in 2025, it has 48 schools in the New York area serving 17,000 students (a six-fold increase in number of students served over ten years). As with all charter schools, any student who lives in the district can attend. If there are more applicants than places, the vacancies are filled by lottery.

One attraction for administrators at Success Academies is that the company organization handles off campus a lot of the paperwork that inundates public schools. "Because so many administrative functions at Success are handled by the organization, principals have a lot of time to observe teachers." This allows for targeted coaching and teaching innovation.

Despite its impressive track record, Success Academies has remained controversial. A *New York Times* feature described a system "driven by the relentless pursuit of better results, one that can be exhilarating for teachers and students who keep up with its demands and agonizing for those who do not." For those who fall short, there's "effort academy," described as "part detention, part study hall."

Stringent rules of behavior lead to high suspension rates. Success Academy Harlem 1 and Public School 149 share the same building, yet 23 percent of Success students were suspended for at least a day in 2014 compared with three percent of public school students. By 2022, the suspension rate at Harlem 1 had come down to 12 percent (according to data.nysed.gov)—better but still high. Moskowitz explained, "Often the suspensions are really to get the parents and the school to be on the same team, that there's a serious issue. If we don't intervene when they're 13, that's going to be a bigger problem."

Moskowitz, like Escalante, Lott, and other successful educators, is confident that student performance and satisfaction depend on reaching high goals, not being coddled with low standards and expectations. "We believe self-esteem comes from mastery," she says.

8.4. Alternatives that Lead to a Quality Education

While charter schools are growing in popularity and influence as a way to improve American schools, alternatives exist that display refreshingly unorthodox thinking. Jacqueline Edelberg is a former political science professor who was dissatisfied with the elementary school choices she had in the Lake View neighborhood of Chicago. When she and a friend visited Nettlehorst Elementary,[15] the principal, Susan Kurland, asked them what it would take to get them to send their kids there. The two mothers returned with a five-page list; they and the principal immediately got to work.

Kurland and a core group of eight mothers removed signs about loitering and trespassing, put up posters, renovated the library with donated materials, and persuaded a muralist to paint one of the hallways. As Edleberg says, "We changed the climate first. It's hard to be disenfranchised in a climate of care." The women gave baskets of peaches and gift certificates to teachers. Some teachers were grateful while others, resentful of the mothers' intrusions, threw them away.

Working the neighborhood, the mothers lined up afterschool programs in music, dance, martial arts, and other enrichment activities. As parental involvement increased, poorly performing teachers left the school. The first year, 300 families came to an open house and 78 signed up for tuition-based preschool. Transforming the school's atmosphere and standards, Nettlehorst raised its profile in the community. In sum, significant positive educational outcomes resulted because dedicated and determined parents refused to settle for the status quo, and a perceptive principal was willing to listen and help.

At the same time that parents and students were striving to secure a quality education, some policymakers were making efforts to turn back the wheel themselves. Lamar Alexander is a former Secretary of Education (1991–1993). As US Senator, he endorsed a plan in 2013 to address some of the problems of No Child Left Behind. "By removing many of the federal, state and union rules and constraints placed on traditional public schools, charter schools liberate teachers and principals to use their own good judgment to help children learn what they need to know," he said. "I would think teachers would be knocking the door down to teach at charter schools, because the whole point is the magic word good educators always want; autonomy."

The next year he supported a bill to "invest more federal funds in the replication and expansion of high-quality charter schools with a proven record of success, while still giving states the flexibility to invest in innovative new models." Among other advantages, he noted that charter schools are "stripped of many federal, state and union rules and constraints placed on traditional public schools" and "make almost a year-and-a-half's worth of progress in a single school year" because there are more hours of instruction.[16]

In December 2015, Congress replaced NCLB with the Every Student Succeeds Act (ESSA). Though it retains standardized testing requirements, ESSA returns authority and accountability for educational progress back to the states. This was the first time since the 1960s that control of education has moved away from the federal bureaucracy. ESSA sets the stage for a new generation of educators and systems that can radically change and improve American education.

The sheer size and complexity of the American educational apparatus makes it hard to imagine changing it from the ground up. From a distance, it looks like a monolith that operates above and beyond the power of any any person to fathom. Its implied message is that it is unchanging and all-powerful, much as the sci-fi movie monsters from the 1950s: "Your weapons cannot harm me; I cannot be defeated!"

But looking closer, that monolith is made up of thousands of school districts controlled by local school boards. In many cases those school boards are elected. By supporting visionary and energetic board members, by voting for better people when they come along—or by serving on the school board yourself—you have access to one of the most important levers of educational influence. Within the districts are the schools themselves with their principals, assistant principals, counselors, and teachers. Most schools also have a Parent-Teacher Association staffed with volunteer parents and community members. PTA participants are in a position to guide or influence what goes on in the classroom.

Since the trend in American education has been increasingly top-down, the advocates of good education have to address the top of the chain as well. Important here is the ballot box. Bureaucrats exercise considerable control over education policy, but bureaucrats are ultimately beholden to elected officials, and voters vote for these officials. Not that change at the top is easy—inertia, bureaucratic red tape, and special interests have significantly undercut grassroots efforts at top-level change. But parents and educators need to use what leverage they have to change the government's approach to education. The big challenge is finding out where in the labyrinth of government a particular policy is spawned and protected, and how to go about ferreting it out and dismantling it.

Turning back the wheel always means letting teachers take the wheel. In every age, effective education has depended on effective teachers. While it won't work to copy Jaime Escalante's ebullient personality, we can copy his methods. His methods are not rocket science; they're common sense. But they take dedication, intelligence, and a passion for the teaching craft.

Too many high-caliber people are attracted to other fields besides teaching because of better pay and better treatment. One key ingredient for reproducing Escalante's success is making it easier for top people to choose teaching as a career.

The National Football League and Major League Baseball spend millions every year recruiting top players. They follow promising recruits, sometimes even before they enter high school, identifying high achievers, offering special training, bidding for their services, and paying them well. A good teacher is at least as important as a good running back. The realities about supply and demand, however, mean no teacher will ever earn an NFL salary.

But American education could take a valuable lesson from pro sports. Set up an organization to scout for promising teacher prospects and field inquiries from people interested in teaching. Nurture them, encourage them to follow a teaching track, help them with tuition in exchange for the chance to work it off later in the classroom. Set them up with mentors, pay them like the professionals they are, reward them for excellent performance and time in service, ease them out with dignity if they fail. Pay for it all from the vast sums currently misspent on high-stakes testing. Instead of spending to assess teaching outcomes, spend to improve actual teaching.

In 1979, Finland moved teacher preparation training out of teachers' colleges and into universities. Teacher training programs recruit from the top quarter of high school graduating classes; those who earn a master's degree in teaching are typically in the top 10 percent. All teachers complete a three-year master's program funded entirely by the government. According to a 2013 report in *The Guardian*, "Finnish teachers' starting salaries are lower than in the US, but high-school teachers with 15 years' experience make 102% of what other [Finnish] college graduates make. In the US, that figure is 62%."

Yet overall Finland at the time spent 30 percent less per pupil than the United States on education.[17]

A *New York Times* editorial later the same year quoted a report by the National Council on Teacher Quality, which found that American teacher training programs were by comparison "an industry of mediocrity." The report rated only 10 percent of more than 1,200 programs as high quality, adding, "Most have low or no academic standards for entry."[18]

Pay statistics for teachers in Finland and the US have largely held steady to the present (2025). According to EdNC.org (Education, North Carolina), Finland's rigorous recruitment standards have persisted, with the profession retaining its prestige—teachers earning 92% of salaries for similarly educated professionals (versus 58% in the US).[19]

Finland has over the years consistently outperformed the US in the Programme for International Student Assessment (PISA), a standardized test given every three years to 15-year-old students in countries around the world. Interestingly, in the most recent 2022 assessment, the US was slightly ahead of Finland in reading and in general scored closer to Finland than in the past. Perhaps this is because of all the alternatives to conventional public school education that are now available in the US.[20]

In any case, it is essential for American public educators to fill their ranks with the best teachers applying the best practices. Otherwise, students and parents will keep heading for the exits in ever increasing numbers. As Mary Poplin reminds us of teachers like Escalante, "Sometimes the stars make the rest of us look bad, and that's hard to take. But if we are smart, we will follow their lead."[21] Ann Davis, principal of Thaddeus Lott's Osborne Elementary, puts it more plainly. "I'm in the education business. If I'm not doing my job, I need to be put out of business."

9. The Point of Education

Imagine you learned that you were going to die soon and had to find a new home for your children. Imagine further that you had two choices. Your first choice was a wealthy family where your kids would have plenty of money and every material thing they wanted but where their happiness was of no real concern. They would live a regimented life doing what someone else directed them to do. Your second choice was a family of modest means who would love your children, spend lots of time with them, encourage them, and do all they could to make them happy. Virtually any parent would choose the second option: happiness and personal fulfillment over wealth.

9.1. A Shift in the Focus of Education

Yet when we talk about success in education, the focus is increasingly on students' earning potential: are they likely to land a job in a well-paying field? As one surveys the vast field of books and articles on the value of education, everything from presidential speeches to sales pitches from testing companies underscores that success in education is measured in terms of material gain. Few parents would turn their children over to a foster family that revered money above all else, yet that is frequently the stated goal of laws, educational directives, campaign promises, promoters of testing, admissions gatekeepers, and a host of other interests that shape education policy in America today. The higher goals of education thus get short-changed.

Future financial success is only the latest in a series of national educational objectives stretching back over decades. In the 1950s and 60s, the impetus was to move from behind to pass the Soviet Union in the space race. The plan worked: after sending the first artificial satellite and the first astronaut into outer space, the Soviets were swept aside as Americans traveled safely to the moon and back. Going on half a century later, the American lunar landings remain unmatched as a feat of engineering and national resolve.

During the Great Society years of the 1960s, extremely broad federal educational laws were enacted with the aim of educating all students more fairly. Unprecedented billions of dollars were directed to schools with poor or disadvantaged student populations to give those children the same education as well off students. Tens of thousands of students rode school buses from their own communities to other neighborhoods in order to satisfy prescribed racial quotas.

Another memorable goal of education has been to make American businesses more competitive in the world market-place. As the economy becomes more global, American workers are competing with those from Europe, Asia, and the developing world. In recent years this has led to increasing attention to international competition. Michael Barber, chief education advisor for Pearson, the world leader in educational testing materials and programs, is one who holds this wide view, saying, "Students are going to be part of a global labor market. Either the work moves or the people move ... We want to make sure when we say someone is good at math they are good at math anywhere in the world."[1]

Yet if parents honestly answered where their children would live in the event of their death, they would also have to admit that earning potential is not the only, or even the best, way to measure educational success. In private moments, policymakers of every stripe would likely admit as much. There is nothing wrong with financial success. All else being equal, most people would rather be wealthy than not. But is that a worthy goal for the American educational system? If not, what should the goal of education be?

This is a critical question. For if we don't know or can't agree on the objective of education, there is no way to judge whether any given educational policy is good or bad. Once an objective is clearly identified and articulated, it becomes far easier to determine whether any policy decision is right or wrong: if it takes us in the direction of our objective, it is right; if it doesn't, it is wrong.

Trying to build a national educational policy without a national consensus on clear objectives is like Alice's experience in the animated version of her story when she was lost in Wonderland. Coming to a fork in the road, she asks the caterpillar which way to go. In return, the caterpillar ask where she's headed. Alice admits that she doesn't know. The caterpillar then observes that if you don't know where you're going, any road will do. For all the talk and investment in the question of which road to take, the discussion of public education in America is very thin on where, exactly, we are going.

The notion that financial gain should be the ultimate objective of education begins to fade in the light of careful scrutiny. For starters, three-quarters of high school graduates will never earn a four-year college degree. Some of them will be cooks, tailors, hair stylists, mechanics, carpenters, plumbers, assembly line workers, and others who pursue a career that doesn't require a college diploma. They may want to move up the income ladder later on or be happy to remain where they are. They are not chasing after immense wealth; they just want to earn a decent living doing something they enjoy and find meaningful.

Students who step off the traditional college track may be as bright and ambitious as any college graduate at the head of the class. They may find their callings in traditionally blue-collar professions. Some may find their callings in explicitly creative professions, such as artists, musicians, film-makers, designers, poets, inventors, or any of the many other thought leaders in our culture whose artistic abilities aren't measured in terms of academic performance. Some will find their callings in entertainment or sports.

Among these non-academics, some will be rich, far out-earning their typical college-graduate contemporaries. Golfing legend Tiger Woods, celebrity chef Wolfgang Puck, actress Jennifer Lawrence, record executive David Geffin, and fashion icon and arbiter Anna Wintour are only a few examples of those who bypassed college and whose creativity and drive brought them success and wealth even without a degree.

There are also many college-bound students who are not driven by money. Librarians and nurses don't pursue their fields to get rich but to enrich others and to be enriched through their work. Soldiers and sailors could typically make more money in civilian life. The best example before us of people not driven by money is teachers, many of whom add graduate studies to their college experience and yet may earn barely enough to qualify as middle class.

9.2. What Is the Objective of Education in America?

What then is the objective of K-12 education in America, and what should it be? On the way to answering this question, we have to determine who is the client—the "customer"—of American education. Whose needs should be the focus of our educational objective, whatever it is?

According to the seminal 1983 US Depart of Education report *A Nation at Risk*, the client is multinational companies competing against the Japanese and other foreign business interests. The 1958 National Defense Education Act singled out as client the military and defense organizations needed to overtake the Soviets.

Under the No Child Left Behind Act, the apparent client of American education is the student, but in fact the real client is the federal government as it tracks accountability metrics. Schools are judged primarily by standardized-test performance and federally defined targets, which means that educators are effectively serving compliance requirements rather than the diverse needs of learners. In this arrangement, test scores became the deliverables, and students become the subjects of measurement rather than the clients whose growth and development guides the system.

A similar dynamic emerges with the Common Core State Standards. Although framed as a way to benefit students through higher and more consistent expectations, the real client of the system became state and federal accountability structures that demand uniform benchmarks and commensurable data. As with No Child Left Behind, the system's primary allegiance shifts toward meeting standardized outcomes rather than toward the unique needs, aspirations, and learning trajectories of individual students.

Yet there can be no doubt what Escalante's answer to the question would have been: The primary customer of education is the student! Students were at the center of everything Jaime did. Students are the ultimate recipients of education. In consequence, any assessment of their education will hinge on what difference it makes to their lives and, in particular, what they are able to accomplish because of their education. Because students don't exist in isolation but in families, Escalante saw also a secondary customer of education—the parents. He worked closely with parents to keep them on board with the education he was providing to their children.

Education professor Mary Poplin likewise sees education as serving these two customers, each with their own objectives. The first is the student, who "needs to have good general knowledge and the ability and practice of thinking critically." She adds, "It is the responsibility of each generation to pass on its knowledge, to educate students broadly in wide ranging theories of how things work, history, literature, the arts and sciences. It is also our responsibility to provide students the understanding of and opportunities to practice the virtues of intellectual and physical work and the ethics that lie behind creating and living a good life." This is a long list, none of which has anything to do with climbing the corporate ladder or building a big retirement account but everything to do with gaining a broad grasp of how the world works, how to appreciate it, and how to "practice the virtues" of "creating and living a good life."

The second customer of education, according to Poplin, is the parents "who want the best for their children; who want their children to be acquainted enough with the various possibilities and background knowledge to be able to choose their field of work and to have the skills and virtues necessary to apply this knowledge effectually." As she points out, "Escalante didn't just teach math; he taught the value of hard work and achievement. He taught virtues and mathematics."[2]

Escalante's former students seldom if ever needed to recall a the details of calculus that they learned from him. What he taught them about mathematics for the AP calculus test has over the years faded in their memories. Yet what he taught about perseverance, personal accountability, hard work, and striving for mastery became a foundation on which they built successful lives and careers.

A small but representative sampling of Garfield High alumni who studied mathematics under Escalante shows that while not all of them used math in their jobs, they all thrived by putting his larger lessons into practice. While some were doubtless more financially successful than others, every person listed here has had the satisfaction of a fulfilling, meaningful, accomplished career:[3]

- Jorge Samayoa, the first Garfield graduate ever accepted at MIT. Two of his brothers went to Harvard.
- Daniel Castro, who earned a bachelor's and master's in electrical engineering at MIT, then added a law degree from UC Berkeley. Today he runs his own patent law firm whose clients include Apple and Microsoft.
- Olga Reyes, who went on to get a master's degree in civil engineering and is currently a nationwide authority on bridge design and construction.
- Victor Mendez, a graduate of Cal State LA, who has led major product development projects at California Edison.
- Anthony Garcia, who received a degree in sports medicine from Cal Poly Pomona and is now a professional trainer.

- Ben Rodriguez, who won an internship at the NASA's Jet Propulsion Laboratory. Escalante kept him in class by failing him so he couldn't play on the football team.
- Erica Camacho, now a mathematics professor at Arizona State.
- Christopher Martinez, today an attorney with the US Security and Exchange Commission.
- Leticia Rodriguez, the basis for the character Ana Delgado in *Stand and Deliver*, earned a master's degree in electrical engineering and became an electronics design engineer for Xerox.

We noted previously that MIT professor Amar Bose, inventor of the popular speakers, became a great admirer of Escalante and his students. One year in the 1990s, fourteen of Escalante's students were attending Harvard, Yale, or MIT at the same time. Bose covered the cost for Escalante to spend Thanksgiving with them in Massachusetts. Bose also had a standing offer to any Escalante graduate: apply to MIT, get admitted, and he would pay all expenses.

Even students who didn't make it to MIT benefited greatly from Escalante's teaching. The most important lessons he taught went well beyond advanced high school math. In 1997 Wayne Bishop, an admissions advisor at Cal State LA observed, "We got literally hundreds [of Garfield applicants] who had scored two or less on the AP calculus test or had never even taken it but had worked hard at their pre-algebra, algebra, and geometry so they could take Jaime Escalante's calculus class but fell short of their goal. They were still better off, much better off, for having made that effort ... Their well-honed study skills allowed them to succeed in unprecedented numbers."[4]

Education researcher David Rose believes that chasing after personal economic achievement is a false god promoted by a misguided cultural and political system: "The primary goal of reform was always presented as an economic one: to prepare our young people for the world of work and to protect our nation's position in the global economy." However, he says, "If we think about education largely in relation to economic competitiveness, then we ignore the social, moral, and aesthetic dimensions of teaching and learning. You will be hard pressed to find in federal education policy discussions of achievement that include curiosity, reflection, creativity, aesthetics, pleasure, or a willingness to take a chance, to blunder."[5]

Writing in *The Tyranny of the Meritocracy*, the late Harvard law professor Lani Guinier reinforced Rose's argument. "Meaningful participation in a democratic society depends upon citizens who are willing to develop and utilize these three skills: collaborative problem solving, independent thinking, and creative leadership. But these skills bear no relationship to success in the testocracy. Aptitude tests do not predict leadership, emotional intelligence, or the capacity to work with others to contribute to society ... Success isn't about being the best test-taker in the room ... It's about being able to work with other people who have different strengths than you and who are also prepared to back you up when you make a mistake or when you feel vulnerable."[6]

Earlier we heard from Nashville teacher Houston Sarratt. His grandfather, Madison Sarratt, was a campus legend at Vanderbilt University, who arrived as a professor of mathematics in 1916 and stayed until his death sixty-two years later. He famously challenged a class about to take a math test with the following: "Today I am going to give you two examinations, one in trigonometry and one in honesty. I hope you will pass them both, but if you must fail one, let it be trigonometry, for there are many good men in this world today who cannot pass an examination in trigonometry, but there are no good men in the world who cannot pass an examination in honesty."[7]

In her classic essay "The Lost Tools of Learning," Dorothy Sayers articulates the critical difference between useful learning and the rote memorization of facts: "Although we often succeed in teaching our pupils 'subjects,' we fail lamentably on the whole in teaching them how to think: they learn everything, except the art of learning."[8] She uses the example of teaching a child to play one song by rote on the piano as opposed to teaching the child to read music. Rote teaching produces a very limited result—one piece of music learned—while teaching the method allows the one to play anything. It is the difference between giving a hungry person a fish and teaching one how to fish. Giving a fish staves off hunger only until the next meal, while teaching to fish provides the knowledge to feed oneself for a lifetime.

Sayers adds, "Modern education concentrates on 'teaching subjects,' leaving the method of thinking, arguing, and expressing one's conclusion to be picked up by the scholar as he goes along." Traditional education on the other hand "concentrated on first forging and learning to handle the tools of learning, using whatever subject came handy as a piece of material on which to doodle until the use of the tool became second nature."

Though her essay was written in the 1940s, her rallying cry resonates with many today who attribute the education system's failure to a narrow, fact-driven focus on a narrow range of subjects (often in order to pass a specific test). As an educational objective, learning rote facts is a misguided substitute for learning how to think and reason. "For we let our young men and women go out unarmed, in a day when armour was never so necessary," she writes. "By teaching them all to read, we have left them at the mercy of the printed word …

They do not know what the words mean; they do not know how to ward them off or blunt their edge or fling them back." All the "devoted effort is largely frustrated, because we have lost the tools of learning, and in their absence can only make a botched and piecemeal job of it."

Sayers concludes, "To learn six subjects without remembering how they were learnt does nothing to ease the approach to a seventh; to have learnt and remembered the art of learning makes the approach to every subject an open door ... The sole true end of education is simply this: to teach [people] how to learn for themselves; and whatever instruction fails to do this is effort spent in vain."

9.3. What *Should* Be Our Objective for Education?

James Barham, whose interviews with Henry Gradillas, Angelo Villvicencio, and Ben Carson are in the appendices of this book, has a straightforward and traditional answer to the question of what the objective of education should be. Barham holds a master's degree from Harvard as well as a doctorate from Notre Dame. Yet in place of worldly success or academic prowess, the objective of education, as Barham sees it, is happiness and virtue. "It pretty much translates into good, old-fashioned common sense in the Gradillas/Escalante tradition," he observes, adding that "emphasis in the elementary grades [should be] on character building and the three Rs, in the higher grades adding in the humanities, the sciences, and citizenship."[9]

All the hours students spend in class by the time they graduate from high school ought to make them expert in something. But what should they be expert in at the end of all that time in class? If we know the answer to that question, we are closer to articulating the purpose of education. Then we can plot the steps and shape the policies to achieve that objective.

Performance psychologists tell us that mastery in any field can be attained by 10,000 hours of work in that field (the caveat being that this time be spent not goofing off but in what's called "deliberate practice"). The average high school graduate will have spent around 16,000 hours in school. That's because K-12 represents about 180 days of school a year over 13 years at roughly 7 hours a day. Multiplying these numbers together yields roughly 16,000 hours.

How should all those hours be used so that students' education and lives are maximally benefited? Socialization, moral training, emotional intelligence, extracurricular activities, and athletic development certainly deserve some of those hours. But the bulk of those hours should go into developing two types of knowledge skills. First, the directly practical, including the three Rs as Barham mentions above. Second, the life-enhancing and affirming. These are the "learning to learn" skills that Dorothy Sayers and Mary Poplin highlight: reasoning, marshaling evidence, persuasion and rhetoric, critical and analytical reading, memorization techniques, etc. These make learning not just something we do in school but something we do as a matter of course to enrich our lives.

In all this it's important to realize that much of what students learn in school—especially in the details—is quickly forgotten. In math, for instance, proficiency with problem-solving techniques deteriorates rapidly without continued practice. Of course, getting back up to speed will be quicker the second time around. Even so, we forget so much of what we learn. That being the case, what is the value of 16,000 hours of learning if only, say, two percent of what was learned sticks over the long term?

Two percent of 16,000 is 320. Could a 16,000-hour education be compressed into 320 hours if everything learned in those hours could stick? In raising this question, the 1980s comedic character of Father Guido Sarducci comes to mind, of *Saturday Night Live* fame, whose Five Minute University promised to teach everything students would remember a year after they graduated. Similarly, and more seriously, the storied consulting firm of McKinsey, in hiring super-smart graduates from elite colleges, will condense entire curricula into short training periods—such as an entire two-year MBA into two weeks (a business essentials mini-MBA).

The point about education is not what sticks in active memory once one graduates (otherwise a McKinsey cheat sheet would do). It's about the valuable habits of mind that get honed in the educational process. It's about the day-to-day learning activities that broaden our vistas of the world. It's about becoming mature learners who on their own can figure out how to learn new things. And even though mastery often fades because memory is imperfect, it's about gaining the confidence that mastery can be recovered. Forgetting is not amnesia—in forgetting there is typically some remembrance of what was forgotten.

Henry Ford (1863–1947), one of the wealthiest and most successful people in American history, never went to high school. Yet he had an effective education. He taught himself the basics of machine construction by dismantling a pocket watch that his father gave him. At age 16 he left home to work as an apprentice in a factory that made railroad cars. At 28 he took a night job in one of the early electric generating plants; two years later he was its chief engineer.

Years afterward when his automobile company was building half of all the cars in the United States, Henry Ford faced a lawsuit. Attorneys on the other side tried to discredit him, attempting to show he was stupid by asking him questions about various matters of fact that presumably he should have known but did not. Ford told the opposing attorneys that he had a phone on his desk and employed people he could call to answer those questions if he ever needed them answered. He knew that having a library of facts at hand was far less advantageous, practical, and profitable than knowing how to obtain them as occasion required.

Emanuel Lasker (1868–1941), a close contemporary of Henry Ford, mirrored this view that education is more than merely a store of facts, and that chasing after rote knowledge is a waste of time. Lasker was a philosopher and mathematician, as well as world chess champion from 1894 to 1921. To him chess was a metaphor for life. Touching on educational themes prominent in this book, he wrote: "Our education, in all domains of endeavor, is frightfully wasteful of time and values. In mathematics and in physics the results arrived at are still worse than in chess. Is there a tendency to keep the bulk of the people stupid? For governments of an autocratic type the foolishness of the multitude has always been an asset. Possibly, also the mediocre who happen to be in authority follow the same policy."

Writing specifically with respect to chess, Lasker continues: "Education in chess has to be an education in independent thinking and judging. Chess must not be memorized, simply because it is not important enough. If you load your memory, you should know why. Memory is too valuable to be stocked with trifles." Lasker put a premium on methods over isolated facts: "You should keep in mind ... only methods. The method is plastic. It is applicable in every situation. The result, the isolated incident, is rigid, because bound to wholly individual conditions. The method produces numerous results; a few of those will remain in our memory, and as long as they remain few, they are useful to illustrate and keep alive the rules which order a thousand results."[10] There are fish; there is fishing.

After these remarks, Lasker offers a philosophy of chess education whose lessons for education generally may be summarized as follows: Anyone who wishes to be truly educated must avoid what is lifeless in learning—artificial theories propped up by scant evidence and clever rhetoric; the comfort of surrounding oneself only with easy challenges; the habit of steering clear of demanding intellectual work; the weakness of uncritically adopting ideas or methods simply because others have proposed them (Lasker was a friend of Albert Einstein, who always counseled that people should think for themselves); the vanity of believing oneself to be self-sufficient, requiring no correction or accountability; and the inability to acknowledge one's mistakes. According to Lasker, the truly educated person must shun everything that leads to stagnation or disorder in the pursuit of knowledge. Point for point, Escalante would have agreed.

K-12 education is obligated to prepare students to earn a living and have a career, and is therefore concerned with the practical. However, a key truth too often overlooked is that this preparation is not only—not even mostly—a matter of gathering up facts to be recited later. It is essential that we see the practicality in gaining knowledge and skills that are life affirming and not just those that are necessary for earning a paycheck. For our lives to be truly enriched and find happiness, we need goodness and beauty, and not as philosophical abstractions but as practical lived experiences, such as the joy of conversation or the appreciation of a work of art.

Education should empower us to enjoy the beautiful and good things of life, not as a form of self-indulgence, but for our mutual benefit—to make the world a better place for ourselves and others—to give life meaning and make it worth living. Yes, education is for many of us a key to financial security. But success in learning is more than money in the bank.

Success in learning is also a sense of contentment. It is a curiosity about the world we live in. It is the satisfaction of learning how to learn so that any knowledge is within reach. Above all, it is the confidence that whatever the world throws at us and however it changes, we have the nimbleness of mind and fortitude of spirit to deal with it. The ability to make money and a career thus becomes a byproduct of education, whose aim is to prepare students for a life in which no good thing need be withheld, in which all good things become possible.

That is the life parents would wish for their children if they knew they had to entrust them to someone else. That is the life so many of Escalante's alumni have enjoyed since they sat in his classroom. That is the life the educational community should strive to deliver to every student.

10. If We Know What Works

We have seen how parents, desperate for their children to get a good education, have found a variety of ways around the bloated, misguided, and myopic bureaucracy that controls so much of American public education. We have seen how visionary and dedicated educators have sidestepped this bureaucracy to craft alternatives to conventional public education, responding to the needs of the students and parents they serve. We have also considered various answers to the question of what the purpose of education should be because without knowing and agreeing on an objective, we can't begin to agree on how to get there.

In trying to uncover the path to a reliable, responsible, and accountable educational system, we find encouragement in the example of Jaime Escalante. He left us broad steps we can follow—even before all the specific details are nailed down—to an education model that immediately improves on the status quo and sets the stage for ongoing improvement.

In 2024, the US Department of Education spend $268 billion. Since its predecessor—the Department of Health, Education, and Welfare—was formed in 1953, it's safe to say the US has spent trillions of dollars at the national level, plus untold dollars at the state and local levels, on education. Many of these dollars have been misspent chasing the latest fad, from whole language to open classrooms to the new math to self-esteem. These fads, once they've been tried and found to fail, get retired, though with a tendency like zombies to come back to life. Yet at the end of the day, Escalante's legacy—simple, no-nonsense, and consistent—remains at the core of every successful educational program in the country.

Escalante's methods may not be replicated exactly or called the same thing in different school settings, but they are still the starting point for most of what works in America (and throughout the world) today. As Mary Poplin points out, education is not rocket science. A lot of it is common sense: observing what works and what does not, then building on the one and discarding the other. But it takes vision, courage, and will on the part of educators to buck the system or go around it in order to create a learning environment where students can then excel.

Let us therefore turn to the key features that define Escalante's teaching style, and which we see replicated nation-wide in the educational programs that work. These are the programs that parents are flocking to and successful educators are continuing to refine. With Escalante at Garfield High, these key features of successful educational programs were vividly on display.

10.1. High Expectations

According to Escalante, his colleagues, and his students, high expectations are the indispensable precondition of successful teaching. Without high expectations, nothing else matters. The assumption among policymakers at Garfield High had been that poor Latino students could not learn calculus. Their family lives were difficult, middle school had not prepared them, their English was shaky, they had none of the "cultural capital"—books in the home, trips to the museum—that more fortunate children enjoyed. Low expectations led to low standards: a tenth-grade math curriculum at Garfield was, when Escalante started there, what he had taught to fifth-graders in Bolivia.

Escalante would have none of it. He was convinced that his pupils had as much potential as children anywhere else, and he set his standards accordingly. Other teachers as well as administrators, parents, and the students themselves thought he was crazy. Department chairs denied him textbooks, and angry parents complained about low grades, too much homework, and their children missing work or babysitting duties.

Escalante held fast despite the harsh reaction, and eventually proved to everyone that Garfield students could excel on a national level. His most valuable gift to students was not a knowledge of calculus, but proof that they were capable of so much more than the world would grant them. They were not low achievers; they were high achievers who needed a catalyst. That catalyst was Escalante. The sample of Escalante alumni listed in the previous chapter, along with thousands more of his students, testifies to the value of Jaime's approach.

A glance at the expectation level of educational institutions most admired for their results—charter schools, parochial schools, private schools, even military-style "tough love" academies—shows that regardless of their location, demographics, or any other variable, they all set the performance bar very high. Students are expected to excel academically and meet strict guidelines of appearance and behavior. To achieve high standards, the standards have to be there in the first place. Those who fall short get special help and proper attention, but they don't get to make excuses or exempt themselves from the standards that apply to everyone else.

Well-meaning critics claimed that Escalante's way was hard on the kids' self-esteem. It was important for poor Mexican-American students to feel good about themselves, and high standards meant the likelihood of lower grades, exclusion from extra-curricular activities, diminished social life, and other consequences. Henry Gradillas wasn't buying: "Yes, if you fail a kid or keep him out of football because of his bad grades, it's hard on his self-esteem. But it's a lot harder on his self-esteem a couple of years later when he can't get a job and has to eat leftover pizza out of the dumpster. Self-esteem is fed by rising to a challenge, not by being excused from it."[1]

More opposition to the school's consistent high standards, notes Gradillas, came from members of the community who said calculus and higher math were "white" subjects and that Latinos faced the added challenge of a cultural divide. "Escalante reminded his kids that they had Inca and Mayan blood in their veins, and that those civilizations were advanced in math," he explains. "He said the concept of zero originated with the Mayan. Criticizing math because it's 'white' is an excuse not to participate in something because they're afraid to fail." Escalante was not making this up. Mathematics historian Georges Ifrah confirms that the Mayan conception of zero was indeed a phenomenal achievement.[2]

In the same spirit of defying low expectations and wanting the best for their students, Escalante and Gradillas also thought that students should discontinue English as a Second Language (ESL) and other targeted programs as soon as possible because they set those students apart and gave them another reason to fail. Gradillas believed two years of ESL was almost always enough, especially since many of the kids taking it were born in the United States.

Though only a small percentage of Garfield students were in advanced math and even fewer were AP prospects, all of them benefited from consistent high standards that encouraged them to stretch beyond what they and others thought they could do. As Angelo Villavicencio, Escalante's colleague who succeeded him as the AP calculus teacher at Garfield, put it, "The number one reason for success" at Garfield was that "teachers, counselors, and administrators believed in students' potential."[3] Faith makes all things possible.

10.2. A Safe, Encouraging Learning Environment

One of Escalante's first steps at Garfield was painting his classroom and putting up inspiring posters with pictures of sports stars and slogans like "Calculus Need Not Be Made Easy; It Is Easy Already." He played music in class. He got air-conditioning. He wore silly outfits—anything to make the learning experience as engaging and rewarding as possible.

However, the atmosphere in the classroom was only part of creating a safe, productive, inviting place to learn. When Escalante arrived, the principal had accommodated gangs at the school by giving each of them a place to gather and post their colors. After an accreditation crisis threatened Garfield with closure because of poor performance, that principal was transferred. His replacement painted over graffiti, removed gang symbols, banned non-students from campus, and locked latecomers out of their classrooms.

As dean of discipline and later as principal, Henry Gradillas had no patience with disruptive students. Previously, teachers had worked under conditions that made learning difficult at best, including students routinely talking and acting out in class, wearing provocative clothing, openly threatening each other and bragging about their gang affiliations, and scaring other students away from the cafeteria and restrooms that were marked as gang turf. All that changed overnight on Gradillas's watch. "There's something in children that craves order," he noted.[4]

Escalante and Gradillas demanded and got order in the classroom because they refused to accept anything less. Class clowns, troublemakers, and girls in low-cut tops were distractions Escalante dealt with quickly, decisively, and sometimes harshly. Gradillas backed him up. Students who repeatedly misbehaved or failed to do their homework were transferred out of his class. Discipline problems were assigned to other teachers and sometimes other schools. In return, other students were sometimes transferred to Garfield to make a fresh start or separate them from a gang.

When Escalante sent one disruptive student out the door, the boy insisted he needed a hall pass. "That's your problem," Escalante replied. We've seen how he once sent a girl to the principal for wearing inappropriate clothing. She returned saying the (pre-Gradillas) principal agreed with her that it was within the school dress code. "Fine," Escalante answered, "you can wear it, but you can't wear it in my class." He, not the principal or a dress code, would decide what was a distraction in his class and what was not.

When another math teacher despaired over the bad behavior of his students, Escalante offered to exchange classes with him for a couple of days. His opening remark as a visiting teacher was, "I am now the boss. Are you listening?" He then marched down the aisle and grabbed a car magazine away from one student. As described by Escalante biographer Jay Mathews,[5] the teacher then declared, "You are all going to do what I say. If you don't do what I say, you gonna fly [be sent out of class]! We got all kinds of places we can send you. You won't like them. Any questions?" Three students were ejected before the rest of them stopped talking.

The next morning Escalante gave a quiz. On grading it, he "gleefully distributed a fistful of D's and F's." He said they were lucky to have the regular teacher they had. "I would flunk all you *banditos*," Escalante declared. "You're wasting my time." The other teacher had coddled his students because they were underprivileged. Escalante saw them as rude and lazy. They would be quiet, they would study, they would do their homework, or they would be gone. In two days the atmosphere of the classroom was completely transformed. Then and only then could the students have a chance to learn.

10.3. A Strong, Supportive Principal

Escalante could not have done what he did without the help of principal Henry Gradillas. His most productive years, and the ones that cemented his reputation, coincided with Gradillas's tenure as principal from 1981 to 1987. When Escalante sent a student to the principal's office for some infraction, Gradillas backed him up. If he had not, and if a student knew that Escalante's warnings were only empty threats, Escalante's authority would have been undermined and his efforts to hold up high academic standards and maintain a productive learning environment in class would have been severely damaged.

Gradillas shielded Escalante from the criticism of other teachers who thought he was too intense and who accused him of claiming more than his share of students' time and school resources. When he needed money for more advanced textbooks, Gradillas came through. When he had the chance to set up a summer program for Garfield math students at a local community college, Gradillas supported the project. When he justified the need for any resources he needed to drive his students to succeed, Gradillas made it happen.

When he suspended students for gang activity or fighting, Henry says, "I got lots of pushback saying this was life in the *barrio*."[6] But it was not, he insists, life for students on a path to academic success and a good career. A school that mirrors a dysfunctional community will also duplicate its failure.

Gradillas was a bold administrator who never avoided confrontation or opposition of the status quo if he thought it would help his students. In his book *Standing and Delivering,*[7] co-written with Jerry Jesness, Gradillas makes a point that principals have to look beyond regulations and mandates, beyond what they think they are allowed to do to what they believe they ought to do.

"We cannot defy mandates, but we can work with them," he writes. "If something is written into law or terms of a contract are bad, we should work to change them, but work within the legal guidelines. Still, mandates are not straightjackets. Educators who think that their hands are tied when given a mandate probably have not explored all their possibilities. "When educators get a mandate, they need to decide what's best for the kids and then work from there … Whenever I was told that my hands were tied, I found ways to untie them."

Gradillas tells of the time non-students were parking across from the school and turning up their radios to a distracting level. When he called the police, they said there was nothing they could do because the kids were not breaking any law. Gradillas explained that his job description made him responsible for the learning environment of his students and that he had to stop the radios in order to fulfill his duties. The police agreed and forced the disruptive drivers to leave.

Whether facing down an angry parent or a stubborn school board, Gradillas maintained the same resolve and focus he had used in the Airborne infantry when training young soldiers to jump out of airplanes. He was a tireless advocate for his teachers, breaking down whatever administrative or bureaucratic barriers they faced to give them the tools and support they needed. Rather than concentrating on the tangle of impediments to his plans, he focused on results, then knocked down the obstacles to those results one by one.

10.4. Time To Learn

Aili Gardena, a Garfield graduate who retook the famous 1982 AP exam, believes the amount of time she spent learning math was the most important factor in her success. "We worked through lunch. We worked before school. Anybody who had marching band in the morning did that extra work another time. We worked sixth period when most seniors got off for the day. We studied over Christmas break and spring break. I'd be surprised if we had not done well after all this instruction."[8]

Garfield students entered high school poorly prepared for Escalante's program. Most of them had little or no math fundamentals in elementary or middle school because educators didn't think they were up to the challenge. As time went on they got further and further behind. By their tenth grade year, Escalante had to push them hard to make up enough lost ground to teach them AP calculus in the three years he had them.

Escalante's demand for time required tremendous sacrifices from the students and their families. They had to give up many outside interests and much of their free time. This demand met resistance at every level and inspired many complaints against Escalante. Yet Escalante's demand that students put in the time was necessary to achieve the objective of telescoping years of math instruction into the limited period he had to prepare his students for the calculus exam. Jaime waived off the criticism and moved ahead.

One way he helped his students compress more learning into a short amount of time was by "double blocking," enrolling them in two math classes in the same term. These students would take an advanced course while taking a basic prerequisite at the same time. Another effective tool was summer school. Jaime developed a summer program for his students and attracted corporate sponsors to pay for it. The Jaime Escalante Math Program is still thriving today. Coordinated through East Los Angeles College, it has a summer enrollment with thousands of students from dozens of area high schools in which they study pre-algebra, algebra 1, geometry, algebra 2, and precalculus.[9]

10.5. A Strong and Appealing Team Spirit

Adolescents are desperate to belong. They want to be accepted into a special group. For some it is the band or the basketball team or the debate club or the theater troupe that meets this powerful need. For others, especially those who don't belong to a loving and nurturing family, acceptance may come from cliques, gangs, stoners, or other destructive groups. Jaime Escalante saw the power of team spirit and used it to recruit and hold onto promising students.

"Students loved being part of Escalante's programs," Henry Gradillas recalls. "We had a rule that you had to put paper covers on your textbooks. One day I saw some girls at school without covers on their algebra books. I asked why they hadn't covered them. 'Oh, Mr. Gradillas, we want everybody to know we're taking algebra!' they said. So I bought them clear plastic covers for those books."[10]

We've seen that Jaime invented a special vocabulary to make learning calculus fun and interesting, and to build a sense of camaraderie for his math insiders. "Face mask," "Secret agent," "Give and go," and "Red light" were just some of the long list of code words that Escalante used and his students adopted.

Jaime had a hard time remembering names. His solution was to give students nicknames ranging from glamorous (Elizabeth Taylor) to less glamorous *(Gordita* or Little Fat Girl), all of which they took as symbols of acceptance. (Names like this were part of the Latino culture then but would be problematic in today's politically correct environment.) The students in turn famously christened Jaime "Kemo," as in Kemo Sabe, Tonto's nickname for the Lone Ranger.

Escalante organized group activities including early morning and afternoon study sessions. He brought fast-food hamburgers and other treats to share and sometimes took students out for a meal. He handed out candy in class for right answers. Some years calculus students got special T-shirts or team jackets. They held pep rallies. They sponsored car washes and sold chocolate to raise money for textbooks and test fees.

Not only did this sense of community keep their spirits high under the stress of learning hard material, but it also made them more likely to make other sacrifices to stay on the team. Faced with the prospect of giving up band or an after school job to keep up with the calculus team, students decided to stay with the team.

Best of all, as with any team, the members inspired and encouraged each other to keep going even when they felt like giving up because they did not want to let the others down or be left behind.

10.6. Flexibility

Escalante's results depended partly on his and Gradillas's ability to finesse, avoid, bend, and sometimes ignore rules from higher authorities. Their objective was to teach their students. Anything that got in the way of that objective was an obstacle to be overcome. They did not kick problems upstairs for solutions, nor did they allow themselves to be hamstrung by apparent restrictions in their job descriptions or by otherwise malleable district regulations. "If you are in command, command!" Gradillas says.[11] When Jaime needed to take action in order to pursue his objective in the classroom, he and his supporters assumed the authority to act on the spot.

Jaime's success at Garfield depended also in part on his ability to address a problem immediately and aggressively. If students continued to misbehave, Escalante had them transferred to other classes. If students repeatedly refused to do homework, Jaime forced them to step up their game or else sent them to a place where their laziness would be rewarded—which was never his classroom.

Escalante's success also came from holding extra, unauthorized study sessions before and after school, scrambling for textbooks and other resources not specifically designated to him, ignoring or getting rid of prerequisites for his courses so anyone interested could enroll, and teaching classes smaller or larger than were supposed to be allowed. In the absence of direct orders, Jaime took the steps he thought necessary and commandeered all the resources he could to achieve his objective of teaching calculus to kids from the *barrio*. Everything else was secondary.

10.7. Maintaining the Standard Under Fire

Throughout his career Jaime Escalante faced opposition from colleagues, administrators, parents, and students. Early on they insisted that his goals were unrealistic and even damaging. Later they criticized his uncompromising attitude and lack of cooperation in the single-minded pursuit of his objectives. Jaime never wavered. He was convinced that poor Latino students were just as smart as anyone else, and that held to the same standards and given the same classroom opportunities as others, they could do just as well or better.

Eventually he was proven right, his story became a Hollywood movie, and the public celebrated him. What summaries of his story often omit are the years of intermittent progress against a bureaucracy that sometimes did not support him and even opposed his methods. Even so, he never gave up, never veered from his belief that his students with the right encouragement could succeed and that what he was doing was right. He accepted opposition as part of the cost of doing business. When it comes to unsympathetic administrators, "You can work with them and stand up to them," notes Angelo Villavicencio, "but it helps to have an iron suit."[12]

Escalante's astonishing academic success sprang more than anything from applying these simple, low-tech principles. Except for completely dysfunctional schools that eschew safety and discipline, teachers can put these principles into practice. Failure to do so often reflects the vain hope that Escalante's results can be achieved on the cheap without paying the necessary costs. But there are no shortcuts to delivering a quality education, especially when till now students have never had to apply themselves and get serious about learning.

Many students, teachers, and parents recognize the problems in public education and want to make it better. Their heart is in the right place. Escalante showed us how to get to the right place.

11. You Can Do Anything

11.1. Unleashing Intellectual Firepower

Escalante's historic success at inner-city Garfield High shows that high intellectual achievement is not reserved for the select few but open to everyone. Even so, a malaise infects American education. Whenever critics begin to identify problems with education as a first step toward solving them, excuses abound for why the situation is and must stay the way it is. Cultural forces are blamed for preventing students from attaining their full potential. The system is said to be stacked against the underprivileged and cannot be changed. Money flows to one coffer and cannot be redirected to another.

Systemic flaws thus condemn young people to be poorly educated and live way below their potential. If only the system as a whole could be fundamentally changed, everything would be better. But systems, especially large ones, operate in the face of massive inertia, and getting large-scale change in these cases typically never happens. Escalante taught us instead to invest our time and energy in building something positive rather than battling fruitlessly against an entrenched opposition. He did his best work by creating a functional workspace within a dysfunctional system, adapting to the system rather than demanding its abolition.

But the malaise infecting American education runs still deeper. Would-be reformers who see the key to improving American education as transforming the system typically don't have a very high view of human intellectual potential. Even if the system could be revamped, the improvement in education that many reformers seek and anticipate would be unimpressive: it would constitute a small incremental change and not a massive breakthrough such as Escalante achieved. In at-risk neighborhoods, it is tragically common for high school seniors to be reading at or below a sixth grade level. Presumably, then, success would be to have twelfth graders reading at a twelfth grade level. But should we be satisfied with that? What prevents sixth graders from reading at what now is regarded as a twelfth grade level?

Jaime Escalante's life, work, and legacy provide two crucial lessons for all subsequent educators who would repeat his results:

1. *Students can learn a lot more than they think they can—they can surprise themselves with what they are capable of learning.*
2. *Students can do a lot more than most other people think they can—they can surprise others with what they are capable of learning.*

These were messages he drilled into his students every day, along with math concepts and warnings about staying out of trouble. Without someone like Escalante to spur us to unanticipated heights, we have little chance of reaching our true potential. Conversely, we can achieve unbelievable things if someone like Escalante is there to unleash all that untapped cognitive energy.

A few decades back, it was common to hear that people use only ten percent of their mental faculties. The science behind that number may not be too precise, but whatever the percentage, Escalante confirms this claim in two ways. On the one hand, people without the right teachers and incentives tend to display little of what we might call "intellectual firepower." On the other hand, the same people with a teacher like Escalante can attain remarkable heights of intellectual achievement.

11.2. Success Is Path Dependent

What then prevents teachers like Escalante from thriving, multiplying, and showing American education the way forward? This is not the first time our look at the Escalante legacy has brought us to this question. If Escalante was such a standout success, why doesn't the world rush to copy him? What is the key to notable academic achievement not just for those with all the advantages but also for those without them?

The answer begins by realizing that education, like everything else in life, is path dependent. If we want to get to point B and we are currently at point A, we need to chart a feasible path from point A to point B and then take it. Starting at A and then magically materializing at B is typically not an option. That would be a miracle. Escalante was a master teacher, not a miracle worker.

A big part of the problem in modern public education (a problem that also infects private education) is that we often have no clear conception of point B, and sometimes not even of point A (our starting point). As we saw in a previous chapter, we, as a nation, don't agree on what the goal of education is or should be. Part of the brilliance of Escalante was wisely choosing a point B that was at once easily identified and also extremely challenging.

Not only is everything in life path dependent, but value in life is determined by difficulty or hardship—how hard it is to achieve the object of striving, how much resistance and adversity must be overcome. There is no merit in doing the easy thing. It is the hard thing that commands respect, that engenders self-confidence and true self-esteem. It was by helping his students to accomplish something inherently difficult that Escalante distinguished not only his students but also himself.

A convenient feature about the difficulty or hardness of a task is that it tends to act transitively: if C is harder than B and B is harder than A, then C is harder than A. Thus, if a student starting at point A can master C and knows that C is more difficult than B, the student can be confident that he or she can also master B. Once a student masters extremely difficult material, that student is filled with confidence that he or she can understand and accomplish practically anything. In choosing calculus as the subject to master, Escalante tackled one of the toughest areas of study in high school. In getting his students to master it, he showed them that they could master practically anything.

Escalante's choice of calculus might not have been strictly speaking necessary. Some other subject might have served equally well as a litmus test for students to attain the highest level of academic achievement in high school. AP chemistry or physics are challenging enough that they might have taken that role. But mathematics is the universal language of science. In that sense, the appeal of calculus extends beyond that of particular natural sciences. It's perhaps worth noting in this connection that the inventor of calculus, Isaac Newton, is universally regarded as the greatest scientist of all time, and so to learn calculus is to get into the mind of Newton.

Of course, it's also the case that some subjects are inherently unchallenging and thus unsuitable as a litmus test for high academic achievement at the high school level. Henry Gradillas, Escalante's principal at Garfield, thus tried to discourage students from taking what he described as "Mickey Mouse courses," saying, for example, that his young daughter could bake the cookies high school girls learned to bake in home economics class. Such courses require no serious mental effort, either because the subject is inherently undemanding or because teachers allow students to fake their way through them.

Escalante clearly identified the starting point A and carefully selected the landing point B. But even more significant than his choice of landing point, Escalante showed how to get there. It is not enough to realize one is at point A and espy point B on the horizon. We need a feasible path from A to B. In other words, we must have a clearly defined step-by-step way, with each step readily doable, to get from point A to point B. How do we know when a path is feasible? By putting people on the path and showing that they can indeed get to B from A. This is what Escalante did, providing what engineers call a *proof of concept*. He didn't just put forward a goal, but he also showed, in practical terms, how to attain it.

This proof of concept is crucial. There are libraries full of books and reports about the problems of education in America today. There are histories, studies, analyses, opinions, policies, and conclusions running into the millions of pages. What's in overwhelmingly short supply are demonstrated, actionable solutions. Escalante didn't spend time analyzing data or fighting the system. He set up his own demonstration program and showed beyond any doubt that his methods worked far better than the alternatives. His most important contribution to American education was that rather than analyzing or complaining or posturing, he gave us a blueprint for effective action. Regarding what to do about education in America today, Jaime Escalante solved the problem in the 1980s.

It is impossible to overemphasize how important Escalante's proof of concept was. It should be a game-changer for American education. For all the talk about the US falling behind in STEM (Science, Technology, Engineering, and Mathematics), Escalante showed us how we could fill all the STEM jobs we could ever hope to fill with homegrown graduates.

To do that would answer the question posed by Angelo Villavicencio about why there aren't enough Americans today to support the technological foundation the country depends on. "When Americans landed on the moon, I was selling real estate in Nicaragua," he says. "America didn't have any trouble getting home-grown scientists and engineers then. With one of the biggest and most expensive school systems in the world, why do we have to get our scientists and engineers from India and Asia today?"[1]

Why indeed? Why has Escalante been ignored? Why, for all the praises sung about his accomplishments, do we see few if any Escalantes now? Indeed, why did the principal who replaced Henry Gradillas short-circuit Escalante's math program and drive him elsewhere? The answer is quite simple: few administrators and teachers are willing to pay the price.

11.3. Instructional Intensity

Escalante's approach requires an *instructional intensity* that most educators are unable or unwilling to provide. It requires competent teachers who are totally committed to achieving the desired outcome. It requires committed administrators who will loyally back their teachers. It requires students who won't bail when the going gets tough. It requires keeping parents from mutinying when their otherwise overprotected children get stressed out because of demanding work.

The problem with instructional intensity is that it is not easy for anyone involved. It requires a discipline that is painful, especially when students have never experienced instructional intensity before. Yet, as we have seen, every popular and successful educational program available today is challenging and requires extraordinary sacrifice from everyone involved: students, parents, teachers, and administrators. The solutions to the problems that bedevil American education are right in front of us in the shape of a stocky middle-aged Bolivian with a comb-over. Yet because his way is difficult, we brush it aside time and again for something easier yet ultimately inferior.

Athletics provides an insightful analogy to the principle of instructional intensity. To build a championship team in any sport requires that everyone, from coaches on down, displays a rigor and determination as well as a knowledge of the game that lesser teams lack. The harder they work, the more committed they are, the more carefully they study the game, the more often they win. Interestingly, young people from impoverished and underprivileged backgrounds are known to rise out of their circumstances by excelling at sports. They have experienced instructional intensity in athletics.

What these athletically successful students typically don't realize is that this same instructional intensity is precisely what they need to thrive academically. It is also noteworthy that Escalante peppered his instruction liberally with sports metaphors and always had posters of his favorite athletic stars on his classroom walls. They were a constant reminder of the rewards of hard work. He himself had once been a star handball player. It's easy to imagine him applying the lessons of the court to the discipline of the classroom.

Which is more important—instructional intensity on the athletic field or instructional intensity in the classroom? World renowned neurosurgeon Ben Carson answered this question beautifully: "One of the things that really began to happen in a big way in the 1960s, that hadn't been going on before, is that we began to really *idolize* sports stars and entertainers—lifestyles of the rich and famous. And those things became much more important to us than the scientist and the doctor and the professor and people who utilize intellect in order to achieve things. This is not to say that no one in sports or entertainment is intellectual, but that's not the aspect of their lives that's emphasized."

Carson continued: "Consequently, you've got so many of these young boys running around—for instance, in the inner city — thinking that they're going to be the next Michael Jordan, or the next Michael Jackson, or somebody. If you can do that, and people are paying you millions and millions of dollars, [you think,] 'Why do I need to bother with algebra, grammar, all this stuff? I don't need to do that. I can buy and sell any school that I want.'

"But what they don't realize is only seven in one million will make it as a starter in the NBA. One in ten thousand will have a successful career in entertainment. So, your odds are not very good. Less than one percent of people who go to college on an athletic scholarship end up playing professional sports —and if you do end up playing, your average career span is three and a half years. So, we need to reorient people in terms of what real success is all about."[2]

Ben Carson's point is that instructional intensity in sports is highly unlikely to result in a professional sports career whereas instructional intensity in academics is highly likely to result in the knowledge and skills needed for a productive, satisfying, and gainful career. True, we may miss out on the glory of being a rockstar, but at least we'll have a fulfilling life. Leaving aside the tiny minority who make it as professional athletes or successful entertainers, the alternative to never experiencing instructional intensity in the classroom is, for many, a life of dependency and frustration, lacking the skills to navigate a tough and competitive world.

Not only is instructional intensity crucial to both academics and sports, but so is team spirit. We typically think of academics as an isolated, individual activity in which students hole up in a corner with a book or laptop and get to work. But we are social beings and effective learning happens in a social setting. Henry Gradillas referred to establishing a "learning culture" at Garfield. Instructional intensity is hard to maintain if students are not encouraging and prodding their fellow students. An essential feature of Escalante's proof of concept was his calculus students working as and feeling part of a team. They had matching T-shirts. They ate meals together. They had their own group cheers and inside jokes. They put up banners in the classroom. They studied together and helped each other navigate and master the alien world of calculus.

We've said that success in life is path dependent, namely, finding and taking a path from point A to point B. But how do we know when we have actually arrived at point B? For Escalante, point B was proficiency at first-year college calculus. To verify that this proficiency had in fact been attained, it was necessary to test it; hence the Advanced Placement exam. By passing the calculus AP test, students demonstrated that they had in fact reached point B, achieving competence in calculus. And with this competence, they knew they could achieve competence in other demanding fields, and thereby gain for themselves successful lives and careers.

Escalante, the great teacher, gave us the key to great teaching. He showed how all American students—not just the privileged elite—could thrive at the highest levels of academic achievement. On the other hand, the failure of American education to repeat Escalante's success on a wide scale reveals an unwillingness to take his methods and requirements seriously. It is a human weakness to try to take the easy way out.

But there is no easy way to learning well, especially if you've been part of an educational system that has made a virtue out of avoiding instructional intensity. Thus Escalante shows us not only how to succeed by following his footsteps but also why we fail to follow in them. Fortunately, instructional intensity does not depend on which political party is in power, what the budget is, how test scores are analyzed, who is elected to the school board, or any of the other variables that command so much of the discussion in American education today.

11.4. Breaking Through the Inertia

Reinvigorating American K–12 education depends on people who are willing to defer gratification, play the long game, and refuse easy-way-out shortcuts. As Mary Poplin observes, even in underperforming schools there are dedicated teachers working diligently every day and making a huge difference in their students' lives. We as a nation have to find and uplift those teachers. We have to nurture and train more teachers in the Escalante mold and give them the freedom and incentives to succeed. If we refuse to do this, promising teachers will burn themselves out and look elsewhere to make a living. Escalante himself almost left teaching several times because the obstacles facing him seemed insurmountable.

This is not a call to have teachers play Bolivian folk music in class, or buy their students hamburgers, or give them silly nicknames. The solution is not in cloning Jaime Escalante, but rather in instilling and nurturing his passion for teaching and learning. All good teachers will find their own way of delivering high-powered instruction based on their personalities, experience, and interests. They will teach students not only what is in the textbooks but, more importantly, what they are capable of: the life-altering lesson that they can do more than they ever thought possible. All young students—regardless of race, income, disability, and all the other ways we've invented to separate and label them—need that same hope and assurance.

Escalante showed his students that they could do better than what they thought is their best. That is the legacy of Jaime Escalante. He leaves us with the realization that giving American school children the best education is possible. Failure to deliver that education is on us as parents, educators, and policy makers for being unwilling to take his example seriously and refusing go to the trouble of following where he led.

His life and career show us that, yes, there is a simple formula for success. And though we often lack the resolve to carry it out, it is worth the trouble to adopt his methods, and it is not too late to do so. Whatever it takes to break through the inertia, ineptitude, short-sightedness, and roadblocks needed to educate our children well is worth the effort. Escalante worked sixty-hour weeks and more, crossed swords with his professional peers, sacrificed time he would otherwise have spent with his family, and devoted everything to the goal of better instruction.

Great teachers would have a better chance of success in replicating Escalante's outcome, and would not have to work such punishing hours or sacrifice so heavily, if there were more of them. The late Thaddeus Lott in Houston, Eva Moskovitz in New York, KIPP schools, and others have been exemplary in empowering teachers. Great teaching begins and ends with great teachers. Find them, recruit them, train them; then get out of the way and let them practice their craft.

The example of Finland is instructive here. Its government decided to stop doing what was known not to work and to completely rebuild the system from the top down and the ground up. They quit trying to fix a broken system and started over. They awarded their best and brightest college students with three years of teacher training, a guaranteed career path, and professional-level wages. The results proved phenomenal. The plan worked. Yes, the United States is far bigger and more diverse, but what Finland did can be adapted, if not on a national scale, then on a local scale.

Escalante also leaves us with the essential lesson that great education means no excuses (leaving aside, of course, real injuries, such as crimes, tragedies, and traumas). As Henry Gradillas told his students, "I'm sorry you have problems, but I don't care."[3] Race, poverty, poor English, family crises— everybody can find an excuse for failure, for giving up. Anyone can be identified as the victim of some injustice. But as soon as we focus on victimhood, we turn victimhood into a job, and our job is no longer learning. Bewailing victimization does not overturn victimization. To overturn victimization, we need to get on with our education, turning ourselves into the type of people who can't be victimized.

Hearing the complaint that rich capitalists had all the power, Gradillas replied, "All the more reason for us to become rich capitalists." Hearing the complaint that disciplining a boy is bad for his self-esteem, Gradillas asked what will it do for his self-esteem later when he can't get a job without a high school diploma and goes dumpster diving for food. If we let students who come to us for an education use victimhood as an excuse for bad behavior in school, Gradillas, Escalante, and like-minded educators would say we are cheating them out of a chance to succeed.

"No excuses" extends not only to students but to teachers, parents, administrators, and lawmakers. Any of us can always hide behind an excuse; we are all victims of something. If we insist on wearing that label, we have very little chance of succeeding in life. Sure enough, some well-known television personalities have made a profession out of victimization, playing a blame game, identifying victimizers to attack and finding victims to defend. And yes of course, there are real victimizers and real victims in the world who need their champions. But when it comes to education, the real champions, like Escalante, are those who refocus people away from victimhood and toward the productive work they need to do to become educated and succeed in life.

Escalante's example proves that a great public school education is possible in America today. It can be done, and ordinary people with extraordinary drive and vision can do it. All their lives, Jaime's students had limited themselves because they heard they weren't cut out to excel in their studies. Kemo refused to give life to that lie. If students were poor, they could raise money for supplies and testing fees by washing cars and selling candy. If they had to work after school, they could study on Saturday, and he would be there to help them. If they had other disadvantages, he was there to lift their load.

Educators and stakeholders who want a better future for American education and are willing to do whatever it takes to get there will face impediments, disappointments, setbacks, sacrifices, hard choices, and difficult situations. Nevertheless, if they've got *ganas*—the burning drive, desire, and determination that fueled Escalante—they will either find a way or make a way.[4] We have all heard that the entrenched educational establishment is too big and too ossified to take on. Kemo refused to believe that lie and proved it to be a lie. And so must we.

Jaime Escalante arrived in Los Angeles unable to speak English and without any teaching credentials that the American educational establishment would accept. After twenty years he was a household name, with a movie about his triumphs in the classroom and his own television show. Moreover, he had proved to a generation of poor Latino students that they could compete with the best students in the country. Why were they able to compete with the best students in America? Because, by studying at Escalante's feet, they had become the best students in America!

Afterword by Mary Poplin

Mary Poplin earned her PhD from the University of Texas and is a professor emerita in the School of Educational Studies at Claremont Graduate University. Her work spans K–12 to higher education. Poplin, who began her career as a public-school teacher, has conducted research on the inside of schools and classrooms, especially focusing on highly effective teachers in poverty-ridden urban schools. Funded by the John and Dora Haynes Foundation, she and eight colleagues conducted extensive research from 2005 to 2009 with thirty highly effective teachers in nine low-performing urban K–12 schools in Los Angeles County. Her prior work included a study titled "Voices Inside the Classroom," funded by the John Kluge Foundation. She co-edited the book, Highly Effective Teachers of Vulnerable Students, *published by Peter Lang in 2019. Poplin has also worked as a university administrator, serving as dean and as director of teacher education. Her research has also explored contemporary intellectual trends dominant in the various academic disciplines—the natural sciences, humanities, and social sciences.*

In response to a long history of academic under-achievement for America's most vulnerable children and youth, the No Child Left Behind Act (NCLB) was authorized in 2001 with enthusiastic bipartisan support. The Act required states to develop curriculum standards and assessments and to report student achievement gains and losses by subgroups, such as by economic status or race. The goal of NCLB was to increase the achievement of students for whom achievement had historically been low (e.g., the poor, Black, Latino, English language learners, and Native Americans).

One of the advantages of NCLB was that teachers who increased their students' achievement could be acknowledged and others could be helped to improve. The results of the Act were that the nation did see small but consistent increases in achievement for all subgroups as documented on the sole national achievement measure in the US—National Assessment of Educational Progress (NAEP). At the same time, there was also a narrowing of the achievement gaps by race and class. A national conversation was revitalized regarding how to identify and increase the numbers of highly effective teachers and schools in low-income communities.

In the mid- to late 1980s, prior to NCLB, a group of urban educators in the US had led a similar initiative—the Effective Schools Movement. This handful of prominent educators was determined to demonstrate that students who live in poverty can reach high levels of achievement if provided with great schools and great teachers. Educator, author, and pioneer of effective schools research, Ronald Edmonds had been critical of desegregation because he felt that while desegregation would help middle-class Blacks, it would hurt the poorest, who needed instead to have their own neighborhood schools dramatically improved. So he began to study the characteristics of high-performing schools in the inner city. Edmonds, Albert Shanker, and Barbara Sizemore all promoted the idea that given great teachers with high expectations and strong instructional skills, poor students would excel.

During this same era, Ernest Boyer advocated making schools true communities with both coherent curricula and a productive, appealing school climate created by excellent teachers, administrators, and community leaders. James Comer, a child-development expert, also led a similar initiative focusing on child development and learning in low-income urban communities. All of these understood that great teachers were central to success. Others joined their enthusiasm and where they did, achievement scores rose and gaps lessened.

"What all good teachers have in common is that they set high standards for their students and do not settle for anything less." —Marva Collins

Henry Gradillas was one of the outstanding principals who understood what it took for a school to turn around and was lauded for his support of highly effective teachers. Gradillas has written the introduction to this important book and provided the authors with an interview in the Appendix.

Alongside these effective administrators and visionaries who sought to change policies, systems, and individual schools, there were a handful of classroom teachers who also made the news. These teachers began to demonstrate that the poverty of one's neighborhood or family did not destine poor youth to poor achievement. One of those teachers is the legendary subject of this book, Jaime Escalante. There always have been and still are many teachers like Escalante as well as inner-city educator and reformer Marva Collins—teachers who work in sometimes desperate communities with a hope, determination, and skill that does not disappoint.

In addition to these heroes of the classroom, there have been a number of studies of highly effective teachers done over the years. Two large research studies done from 2005 to 2009 and again from 2015 to 2016 were designed to define the characteristics of teachers who are highly effective with vulnerable groups. Two research teams of nineteen educators made year-long observations of over seventy teachers in low income urban classrooms. The teachers' student-achievement data demonstrates that their students made significantly greater gains in their classrooms than their peers teaching similar students. Much of what follows is drawn from the results of these two extensive studies.[1]

Two Keys to Achievement Gains for the Most Vulnerable

Two keys work in tandem to advance achievement and diminish the achievement gaps between subgroups.

The first key is school officials and teachers holding themselves accountable for the achievement of all their students— achievement increases overall and diminished achievement gaps for the most vulnerable. This requires a determined effort to create and maintain policies that use measures of achievement reported by groups—race, class, first language, and gender. The national data (National Assessment of Educational Progress —NAEP) shows that during periods when there are stronger policies requiring accountability for achievement, scores of vulnerable students rise and gaps lessen. During the Effective Schools Movement in the mid- to late 1980s, scores rose and gaps lessened. This happened again after the passage of NCLB in the scores between 2001 and 2012. However, since the relaxing of accountability in more recent years, NAEP scores have begun to decrease once again as they did in the 1990s after the Effective Schools Movement.

"We can, whenever and wherever we choose, successfully teach all children whose schooling is

of interest to us. We already know more than we need to do that. Whether or not we do it must finally depend on how we feel about the fact that we haven't so far." —Ron Edmonds

The second key to achievement for the most vulnerable students is to understand and increase the number of highly effective teachers working successfully in low-income neighborhoods. While these teachers vary widely in personality, age, and ethnicity, there are significant commonalities. There are six main factors by which their success can be understood:

1. Evidence of extraordinary student achievement
2. Optimistic vision of and commitment to students' potential
3. Establishment of warm, safe, orderly havens for building character and achievement
4. Strong relationships with students
5. Explicit instruction enveloped inside a big conversation
6. Personal integrity, humor, and physical fitness

Let's next examine these factors more closely.

Factor 1: Evidence of Extraordinary Student Achievement

To locate highly effective teachers in districts and schools where achievement was low and poverty levels were high as revealed in state data, district administrators examined the last three years of their teachers' achievement data by tracking student gains back to their teachers (rough estimate of value added). The teachers whose students had made the largest achievement gains over a period of three years were studied for one school year (2005–2009 and 2015–2016).

Just how different is the achievement of students in a highly effective classroom versus others? The first thirty highly effective teachers (2005–2009) had collectively moved 51% of their students up one entire level or more on the California Standards Test (CST) and 34% maintained their levels (thus had experienced one year's achievement growth), while only 16% fell back a level. An important measure of effectiveness is not just higher increases in achievement, but also fewer numbers of students dropping a level.

To understand the achievement gains and losses between highly effective and less effective teachers in low-performing schools, all the teachers in last three high schools were studied in 2009. Fifty percent (50%) of these English teachers and 60% of math teachers had 30–75% going down in one year; 65% of English teachers and 68% of math teachers had the same or more students going down a level as going up.

So who are these highly effective teachers with vulnerable students and what are they doing?

Factor 2: Optimistic Vision of and Commitment to Students' Potential

"My students have been under-performing compared to what I see as their potential; they have big gaps yet they are very smart. It's my job to turn this around, to fill the gaps and move them ahead. We are all going to have to work hard; I know we can do it!"

The collage of sentiments in this quote represents the basic disposition of highly effective teachers toward their students and their work. They know and accept that they will have to work smarter and harder, as will their students, in order to recapture lost time and make gains. This is their starting place;

they understand what it will take, and they have the desire and the determination to press ahead in extraordinary ways even under difficult conditions. They get to know their students' current abilities and first push to "fill in the gaps" and then move into the grade-level curriculum.

A fifth-grade teacher tells us, "Language arts is a bigger ball of yarn to figure out where their gaps are. Math, I can usually figure out their gaps within the first day or two at school."

Their optimism is not naïve. A high-school math teacher said, "I still remember that graph that every child will be proficient in Algebra II by 2014. It's not realistic, but yet I do know I can teach every student many things they do not know."

Teachers have various ways of expressing this optimism. "If I see someone struggling, I do my best. I do my best because it's rewarding to me. This kid didn't know anything about this, and now he knows something!" and "I'm running around the classroom, going from student to student, making sure everyone understands and is on task."

Highly effective teachers communicate to their students, collectively and individually, that the students *can* do the work and that they are there to help them do it. The teachers' sense of optimism and hope for their students' future lives pervades all they do and it is evident to their students.

One student wrote of his high-school math teacher's optimism, "One thing for sure, his attitude is always up, he never brings us down, but we all know he has faith in us to learn and succeed." None of their students is safe from their determination to get them to learn.

One middle-school teacher said to a student whose head was on the desk, "Why is your head down, Juan?"

The student replied, "I don't feel good."

"Are you ill?" asked the teacher, to which he replied, "No."

The teacher replied, "Then here [walking to his desk], let me help you; remember what I always say—you'll feel better when you get your work done!"

She stayed by his side helping. At the end of the session, he had revived and his work was done.

These highly effective teachers are also personally disciplined and responsible people with the same high expectations for themselves as for their students. When asked why he thought he was more effective than other middle-school English teachers, Mr. M. explained, "I think that my main trait is that I'm very self-critical. And so, it's hard for me to be satisfied with what I'm doing. I just re-self-evaluate and re-self-evaluate."

Another said, "When something doesn't work, or doesn't come out the way I wanted it to, I get very frustrated with myself. Now, what goes along with that is that I'm pretty strict with my students and I have really high expectations for them; if I have high expectations for myself, I have high expectations for them."

A high-school teacher, Ms. K. said, "When students don't do well, I take it personally. I know I shouldn't, but I think that that bothers me."

Factor 3: Establishing a Warm, Safe, Orderly Haven for Building Character and Achievement

The first day of school I'm introducing myself, getting them comfortable and familiar with me, setting up my rules and expectations, a lot of routines, a lot of repetition, having them redo it again correctly until it's done the right way as simple as lining up and sitting down, setting up comfortable learning environment for them but also being consistent ... with my rules, routines, and expectations.

On the first day I just establish those basic procedures. What does the student need to do if they need to go to the bathroom or get paper, or if they need a pencil. Then once again going back to, conveying the message to them that I'm going to have some expectations of you.

It's a balancing act, trying to balance that with not intimidating them. Making them feel welcomed.

Because the strong relationships between these teachers and their students are inextricably connected to the urgency for their students to achieve, the quotes above are appropriate. From the beginning of the school year, highly effective teachers exhibit a strong classroom presence uniquely fit to their personality that captivates children and adolescents' minds and hearts and establishes much needed order, safety, instruction, and encouragement.

On the very first day of school, observers note that highly effective teachers 1) genuinely and warmly welcome their students (individually and as a group), 2) tell students how happy they are that they are in their room and that it will be a good year together, 3) establish the rules and procedures they will all use to build a great class, 4) explain the purpose for each rule or procedure, and 5) establish their authority.

Welcoming

To expand on these points, teachers are enthusiastic about their new students; they report being both excited and nervous during the first days. They work to establish individual connections with students immediately. Some conduct individual interviews with their students in the first week; others have them complete a survey of their interests, hopes, and dreams, or write an essay on "what I want my teacher to know about me."

In terms of building a whole classroom community, some use the "family" metaphor, others a "team" or "community" metaphor—their plan is to build a classroom community that will be about individual and group learning.

Rules, Reasons, and Character

From the first day, the standards, procedures, and rules for the classroom operation are discussed and put into practice, from the way students should line up and enter the room to the appropriate times and processes for orderly pencil sharpening. While teachers often have limited times when students can sharpen pencils, they are also well stocked with sharpened pencils should someone need one at another time. Many of the rules are to increase concentration and attention and decrease distractions. Many of the rules are regarding the way members of the class will honor and help one another.

These non-negotiable procedures establish the orderly operation of a classroom that may have up to forty students. Sometimes teachers engage students in setting the rules and procedures, but more often than not these are simply introduced to the students with a clear explanation for why they are important for the creation of an orderly workable classroom where everybody can learn and enjoy themselves.

The rules are tied not only to academic achievement but also to the development of particular character qualities— respect, generosity, diligence, helpfulness, kindness, loyalty, and sensitivity. Teachers emphasize that the rules help the classroom become a good family (elementary) or work team just like adults at their jobs.

A Latinx sixth-grade teacher uses the Army motto, "leave no man behind," meaning that if you see a classmate struggling, it's your responsibility to help them out whether it be to borrow a pencil, calm down, catch up, or help start an academic task. Building character is inseparable from the teacher's vision of their students' academic potential and success.

"One of my biggest things is, and I tell them a lot, your grades are important and all that, but you've got value. Who you are as a person and your character, that's more important than anything else. Actually, I focus on character development quite a bit. These are little people we're going to release into the world. I just hope that they leave better people than when they came in." —Fifth-grade teacher

Establishing Authority, Relationships, and Strictness

All highly effective teachers are strict and their students recognize and report this as good thing. However, strictness is paired with being nice, fun, and helpful. They all establish their authority in the room as one of the first orders of business beginning on the first day. Whether the teacher is of slight or imposing build, even within the first few minutes an observer will notice that these teachers establish that they are in charge. One stout African American high-school teacher told us he makes sure students understand from the first day that "every square inch of the classroom belongs to me, including the doorways." How does he do this? He says, "From the first day,

I walk every square inch and stand in the doorways while I talk with them."

> *"Mr V. is fun when it's time to be fun and stubborn when it's time to be stubborn. I think Mrs. V. helps students learn so much because she wants us to be our best in the future. She is a very organized teacher. She is kind and strict, but a good strict and she likes everything a certain way and she expects a lot from us. She is strict, nice, hard, [and] helpful." —Three students of a fifth/sixth-grade science teacher*

There are often early challenges to a teachers' authority where one or more students will test the limits. For example, on the first day, Ms. B., a petite African American middle-school teacher introduced herself in a warm manner, telling them how grateful she was that they were in her class and telling them a little about herself. Then she taught students how to introduce themselves using her model. Since they had come from different elementary schools, they were to each present themselves by speaking in full sentences, standing up straight and tall, and speaking loudly so that everyone could hear. After each student's introduction she welcomed and encouraged them in some way. Immediately following this activity, she told the students that beginning tomorrow and every morning thereafter, she would begin the class by taking attendance. She would read each of their names and they were to answer, "I'm present, Ms. B."

The next day Ms. B. took her seat on a high stool with her attendance book on her small podium. As she began calling roll, the students did as she had instructed, each saying, "I'm present, Ms. B."

About midway through the list, a young man answered loudly, "Here."

She waited a few seconds and then called his name again, to which he answered, "I'm here!"

Then she slowly stood up and calmly and matter-of-factly repeated the instructions just as she had given in the beginning. She then slowly sat back down and called his name again. The class was silent and students were slinking down in their seats with their shoulders raised and tensed.

The young man waited a few seconds and then said, "I'm present, Ms. B." At which time there was an audible sigh of relief in the class. She had established her authority without any drama; her students were relieved. They were safe there. The teacher had both authority and warmth; she knew how to handle things. Immediately following the interaction, one preteen whispered to the one next to him, "This teacher is about business."

"Ms. D is very funny. She has a very nice personality. Sometimes she is very strict with her work, but we don't take that as a bad thing because that helps us stay focused on our work." —Student of a seventh-grade science teacher

Even in students' minds, their teachers' rules and strictness are linked with a grander vision or purpose, they often note that their teacher is strict or pushes them because they believe in them. A middle-school math student wrote, "She is very effective because she keeps us thinking. She doesn't let us play around in class. She sees what the students can become."

A fourth grader said, "When I was in first grade and second grade and third grade, when I cried my teachers coddled me.

When I got to Mrs. T.'s room, she said, 'Suck it up and get to work.' I think she's right. I need to work harder."

Other comments from students indicate their teacher is strict because he or she 1) does not want them to get ripped off in life, 2) wants them to go to college, 3) wants them to be at the top of the next grade, 4) wants them to have a good life, 5) wants them to be winners, 6) cares about them and their futures, or 7) simply "she's strict for a good reason."

A fourth grader writes, "She is nice, she don't play."

A seventh grader writes, "She wants us to have a great life. She wants us to the be the best and change the world."

Teachers often reference students' future lives as adults. Even first- and second-grade students told us, "She wants us to go to college." A teacher may say over and over, "Remember some day you will want to have a good job, a family, a house, and a car." A fourth grader wrote, "Mrs. T. wants us to learn so much because she wants us to have a good career. She is kind, sweet, caring, and beautiful. She thinks we can succeed in anything."

Frequently teachers inform students about their strengths, areas in which they excel. A fifth-grade teacher regularly makes efforts to inform each student regarding something in which they excelled. She tries to do this for every child every few weeks and marks it down in her grade book so that she will not miss encouraging anyone. She once leaned down and said to a young man, "Andrew, do you know how very good you are at math? It will be good to see how you will use this when you grow up." Now Andrew has heard from a respected adult outside his family that he is good at math and this could play a part in his future life.

These teachers' visions for students are long-term ones, which include teaching them to make good decisions. Some teachers even share mistakes they have made in their lives and the poor consequences that result. One student wrote, "She has passed through some troubles in her life and does not want that to happen to us. So she is preparing us for the troubles and telling us what is the best choice."

Factor 4: Strong Relationships with Students

Students know that their teachers care for them and take advantage of the fact that these teachers are there for them. Each teacher has open times, opportunities for individual students before or after school, or during lunch or nutrition. It all begins with their efforts to truly know each one of their students personally and, to the greatest extent possible, their parents as well. Every teacher was specially tending to particular students who were going through some crises—cutting, depression, divorce, or illness or death in their families.

They consistently encourage students about their situations, their schoolwork, and their great potential life they have ahead of them. One middle-school student wrote, "Because she cares and wants us to succeed 100% and be ready and prepared for high school and of course be ready in college. She always tries to guide us and stand by us. She has so much to offer and she has changed me 100% to the point that I never miss school. She's my role model. She's a great example."

A high-school teacher said he was honored when a student confided in him about abuse he was receiving at home. He handled it by first explaining to the student why he had to report it, to whom he would have to report it, and what would be the next steps. He told him he was available to talk when he needed. The teacher remarked with surprise, "I didn't even know he trusted me that much."

These relationships are not simple, superficial, or sweet; they are strong and unique to each individual teacher. An Asian elementary teacher described her attitude toward her students as being that of a strict parent, like her own mother. She said, "Tough love, that's what I was thinking. I feel like that's how I am with my kids."

On the other end of the spectrum, a Latina middle school teacher is teary-eyed when she tells us, "The part that I love about teaching is being in the position where I think, I hope, I'm wishing that I do change kids' lives. Oh my God, I think I'm crying or something. Sorry. I want to be that teacher that inspires kids that don't have much hope. I want to be that teacher that [students] say because of her, 'I'm doing something with my life; I did something with my life; I am somebody.'"

A high-school teacher and coach sees it more like the relationship of a good coach. He said having been fatherless himself, it was a coach who really helped him turn his life around and he does the same for his students. He calls his students by their last names using Mr. or Ms.

Even highly effective community-college developmental teachers specially reach out to encourage students who are troubled or struggling.

Factor 5: Explicit Instruction Enveloped Inside a Big Conversation

The first foundation of the instructional practices of these teachers is the mastery of their subject matter and knowledge of the state standards and curriculum. Highly effective teachers demonstrate an impressive ability to engage their students in high-level curricula conversations during explicit instruction on skills, concepts, and ideas.

In fact, observing them over the course of an entire year is much like following one big continuous conversation, where they often remind students of something they have discussed or experienced together before presenting new content—"Remember when we . . . ?" They naturally fold new topics, concepts, or instruction explicitly into prior experiences in the classroom, current topics in the media, contemporary media of their students, and events in the community. They also search for and use engaging short video pieces that might also aid students in understanding particular concepts or processes.

Highly effective teachers largely center instruction within this big conversation based on current district and state curriculum, as well as current texts and materials, or ones they have saved and used successfully in the past. They are masters of planning and pulling things together for the students so that they can easily understand; essentially they are entrepreneurs of classroom instruction. They know their content and if something is new to them, they study it until they know it well enough to explain it to students.

Effective teachers of vulnerable students constantly check in with students as the conversation continues, making certain they all understand. Some do this by show of hands or thumbs up if they get it, thumbs down if they don't, and thumbs sideways if they could use more explanation. One teacher asks, "On one through four, anything that is just like messing up your brain, you want me to answer it, you're not really sure you got it right, please answer that one. All right, I'm looking right here. Anything that's kind of throwing you off? Going once, going twice. Sold."

Intense Planning and Preparation

Students frequently note that their teachers are very organized. That might even be an understatement. A fourth-grade teacher puts it this way: "Having structure in the classroom, having a good discipline plan, and knowing my standards of what I need to teach the kids and being able to find the materials in order to teach them, I think is one of my strong points to being an effective teacher."

This is evident even the first day. One teacher says about her first days, "I have my checklist of what I want to do. The first day of school I'm introducing myself, getting them comfortable and familiar with me, setting up my rules and expectations, a lot of routines, a lot of repetition, having them redo it again correctly until it's done the right way; as simple as lining up and sitting down, setting up comfortable learning environment for them but also being consistent the first day, even the first month, being consistent with my rules, routines and expectations."

Students largely describe this planning and preparation as being "very organized."

Explicit Instruction

The sequence of the instruction used by highly effective teachers more or less mirrors the explicit practices described by Barak Rosenshine in his chapter, "The Empirical Support for Direct Instruction" of the book *Constructivist Instruction: Success or Failure?* edited by Sigmund Tobias and Thomas M. Duffy, or those practices earlier outlined in a number of books by Madeline Hunter, former head of the UCLA lab school.

Rosenshine lists the sequence of instruction as 1) beginning with daily review, 2) presenting new material, 3) guiding student practice in group discussions, 4) providing feedback and explaining corrections, 4) then moving to independent practice and finally, 5) reviewing the material periodically (weekly or monthly). However, the list does not convey the lively, engaging character of highly effective teachers' instructional sequences. All of these are done in the context of a conversation among friends who have a history together, with the teacher in the lead.

Fast Paced

The pace of instruction is brisk. There are rarely minutes not devoted to instruction and students seem to thrive on this fast pace. Teachers are in tune with student moods and dispositions. When students look tired, they stop and lead very brief stretch breaks where students take deep breaths and chat with friends. Two middle-school ELL (English Language Learner) teachers would lead a "Simon Says" game. Students were still getting language instruction as they "hopped on their left foot three times, then raised their right shoulder, then left shoulder." As the year progressed, the students were chosen to lead the game.

Enticing Introductions

"Today we are going to read possibly the most complex and brilliant passage ever written in the English language and I am so excited that we get to tackle it together." —High-school English teacher

Highly effective teachers generally begin new topics with an appealing and engaging introduction to the new content linking it to previous content and classroom or common student experiences—getting students hooked first. This often includes questions to check for prior understanding or familiarity, or to stimulate new thinking.

A fifth-grade teacher copied an *Atlantic* magazine article for his English learners. The article was on the first woman to pass the tests for Army Rangers. He began by asking them a number of questions—had anyone heard this in the news, did anyone know what the Army Rangers were, and what did they think about women serving in the military. After the discussion, he followed by their reading the article together with his copy on the document projector while he carefully circled the new vocabulary as they would also on their paper. They discussed all the words they had circled and the larger topic.

Lectures as Big Conversations

During their lectures and demonstrations, highly effective teachers keep students engaged in this big conversation, which is basically high-level explicit instruction. Generally a lecture or demonstration proceeds with teachers continuing to intersperse questions to increase student interest and to recall needed background knowledge and to think critically. Then they carefully and thoroughly explain or demonstrate the new content—facts, ideas, processes, and concepts—several times in multiple ways with varied examples.

These teachers may use their own stories to enliven content and ask students about their connections. They are masters of asking questions that cause students to relate content to previous knowledge, predict, explain, hypothesize, and critically evaluate. For example, a fourth-grade teacher after reviewing what an obtuse angle is, asked, "Let's think about whether a triangle could have two obtuse angles? Turn and talk with your partner (thirty-five seconds). Who can tell us?"

Classroom discussions are often interspersed with mini lectures escalating in intellectual demand, questions that escalate in cognitive demands while encouraging students to make connections to their lives. Teachers use the classroom discussions to assess the degree to which students understand the content and to determine how much re-teaching is necessary.

During instructional time, students are gently corrected for not paying attention or talking. Often a teacher just mentions a student's name, or physically moves nearer the student. One teacher will look at the group talking and say, "I'll wait on you but not for long."

To draw individual students back to attend to the task at hand, teachers generally mention the student's name as they talk.

"Sometimes a sentence has one word for the verb, Steven, and sometimes two words."

"Kelly, I know you are really smart. That is why it is so important that you and all of us are paying attention at every moment."

These comments become so frequent that students seem to take it as just a part of the sequence. Students do not seem particularly concerned or embarrassed; they simply turn their attention back to the teacher.

Explaining Over and Over

Students of highly effective teachers identify their teachers' willingness to explain things "over and over" as one of the major reasons their teacher helps them learn so much. A middle-school student wrote, "Mrs. M. helps us a lot by the way she explains the problem to us more than once. She doesn't just explain it once; she it explains it to the point where she makes sure we understand."

Repeating explanations is one of the major characteristics identified by students as to why their teacher helps them learn so much. Students described their teachers as explaining things "over and over" until they "get it in their heads."

A high-school teacher tried various technologies to demonstrate solutions to algebraic equations until the students told him they had rather he go back to writing it on the board while he explains it over and over.

An important caveat students make about their teacher explaining over and over is that when this happens, "they don't get mad if you don't understand—they just explain it again and again." Highly effective teachers are willing to patiently go over and over skills, concepts, structures, or examples, as well as return to them from time to time reinforcing connections. They are expert at finding multiple ways to explain concepts and remind students of the connections to previous learning.

Once most of the class appears to understand, they move on to check on particular students and explain again one-on-one or in a small group to those still struggling. They all make times available after school on some days of the week to help anyone who needs even more.

Highly effective teachers also employ mnemonics when possible. One highly effective African American first-grade elementary teacher had her students march to the playground each day counting by twos, threes, fours, or tens. One of the last days of school she showed her first graders that they already knew how to multiply, which elicited a good deal of jumping up and down and cheering.

A seventh-grade science teacher regularly has sequences with hand signals that allow students to memorize important facts, such as the stages of mitosis. She leads students in repeating this sequence using the signals at the beginning of class (before they walk in the room) and at the end when lining up to leave. Sometimes this repetition of a mnemonic device lasts for a week, sometimes periodically all year long.

Students of highly effective teachers also report that their teachers push them. Teachers also describe pushing their students to understand deeply. During classroom discussions, teachers often require students to answer in full sentences and use high-level vocabulary. For example, teachers may say in response to answers, "Excellent! Now can you put that into a sentence?" or as one teacher said, "Absolutely right! Now can you say that like a fifth grader?"

In some classes, students have to respond by first acknowledging the prior student's contribution, e.g., "Well, I agree with x but I'd like to add..." or, "I disagree with x because..."

One student writes, "She does not want us to fail so she pushes us to the limit, but thanks to her I learned a lot. She pushes us to be better, but she's not rude about it."

Teachers call on students randomly during these discussions (sometimes using "equity" sticks or phone apps) so that everyone stays alert and has an opportunity to participate. When a wrong answer is given, some teachers allow the student to choose "a friend" or someone to help them; they do not embarrass students for wrong answers but they do ultimately require all their students to participate. Some ask simpler questions to students who have less academic experience. Some reply to wrong answers or to students who suddenly don't remember what they were going to say by saying, "No problem, I'll come back to you," which indicates there is still an expectation of the student staying alert and ready to participate.

Moving from Desk to Desk

Highly effective teachers almost never sit down. Related to a teacher's ability and willingness to explain things over and over, possibly the single most effective and simple instructional strategy used by all the highly effective teachers is that during independent practice or group work, highly effective teachers moved constantly from desk to desk to deliver instruction one to one, or some may pull a small group to the side.

While students are working at their desks, teachers go desk by desk in order to 1) check their own instructional effectiveness, 2) help some students get started or keep focused, 3) re-teach individually and help students over hurdles, 4) see how "this kid's mind works," or "checking on how it's going," as well as 5) have brief personal interactions with the students.

One of Mr. R's high-school English students told us, "He's always there for you, just when you need him, he shows up at your desk."

Mr. R. always told students just before they started an activity following a period of his explicit instruction, "Remember I am here to help you; don't struggle; just raise your hand and I will be there." When a student would raise their hand while he was working with another, he would reply, "Mr./Ms. X [using their last names], I see your hand. Be there; got you covered."

Effective teachers expertly arrange the classroom to make it easier for them to wander through up and down aisles and rows or pods. One teacher requires students to put all their backpacks in the back of the room with their jackets; this way she can make her way easily up and down rows and aisles and help students with ease—"I can reach any student in three seconds."

They place particular students who are likely to need a little extra coaching in easy-to-access areas so they can better reach them while still staying alert to others. The teachers made changes in their rooms and student arrangements throughout the year as needs changed or as they noticed ways to make learning more likely. They often checked on students' preferences. Most report students prefer to be able to face the front and see the teacher.

Written Feedback on Student Work

There was also evidence of a good deal of teacher written feedback on assignments; some teachers had students during a period of independent work come to their desk where the teacher would read what they had written and discuss anything they needed to work on. Developmental students in the community college report this as one of the most effective strategies in helping them learn to write. One researcher found that community-college students said this was the biggest problem in their high-school classes—not getting real feedback on their writing.

Extensive Teacher Talk

Explanations, directions, focus, and reminders. While contemporary professional development specialists often suggest that teachers should talk less and students talk more with other students, these highly effective teachers are most frequently talking, either to the whole group, a small group, or an individual student. This appears to give students who struggle with language, especially those who are English-language learners, a clear and persistent language model, as well as provide much-needed explanations, reminders, and further directions. It also helps in keeping students on task.

Limited Well-Defined Group Work

While all the teachers use group work to some extent, very few use it extensively. When used, it follows instruction so that the groups have a small well-defined task. From an observer's perspective, the most effective seems to be pair-share. These quick interactions with a friend or partner generally last less than forty-five seconds. After that, teachers risk a loss of attention to the topic. Regarding groups of four, while there are a few that are successful, there are many that are not. From the back of the room, it can be noted that generally one or two of the four are completely disengaged or quickly disengage. One of the highly effective teachers described the most effective process for group work during her interview: her students are paired girls with girls and boys with boys.

Factor 6: Character, humor, and physical fitness

One would have to list emotional stability as one of the top character qualities of these highly effective teachers. These teachers are not only the authority in their classrooms, they also recognize and respect their authorities, as well as respect and reach out to parents. No matter their age, they appear to be physically fit for the grueling task of being on their feet and moving around the classroom most of the day. And they have a great sense of humor, able to make their students laugh.

> *"A coach (teacher) is someone who tells you what you don't want to hear and makes you do what you don't want to do so that you can become what you've always wanted to be." —Tom Landry, former Dallas Cowboys coach*

Emotional Stability

These teachers are emotionally stable; they rarely raise their voices. When things go awry, they stop everything immediately until order is resumed. Mr. R. would sometimes calmly have his high school students step back outside the classroom and come back in. He told us later, "It's not that they or I am in trouble, it's just that we are going to do things right in here." One teacher told us in the last week of school, she did the same thing. "It's like they came in like they didn't know any better, so we went back outside and started again." When instruction isn't working, teachers admitted it to the students and re-directed the class to another activity.

The highly effective teachers, unlike many novice or less effective teachers, do not need the students to love them; they need and want them to learn and to grow in character. Ms. B.

told us, "You've got to love what you do, but the students have to understand that you love them but you're not going to be in love with them. You've got to be firm, strict. You've got to be organized. You've got to tune into your students." Ms. K., who looks very young, told her students, "I have friends; I'm not your friend; I'm your teacher." Though single and childless, she always referred to her high-school students as "my kids," as do all the teachers. Ms. D. tells students they are her kids for the year and just like her triplets she wants them to have fun and to learn science and how to behave. She will treat them like she treats her own children because she loves them just as much. "So if I wouldn't let my kids do things, I won't let you do them either. If I want my kids to have fun, I want you to have fun too."

Humor

Each teacher has a unique sense of humor; students frequently use the words "fun" or "funny" to describe them. One high-school teacher said to her students on the first day, "There are only a very few reasons that are acceptable for not having your homework… and if you develop multiple personalities, you better make sure you assign one of those personalities to do your homework every night."

Appropriate student humor was also encouraged and appreciated. Ms. G., a second-grade teacher, stood on a chair whenever she spotted a spider; then some gallant young seven-year-old would promptly stomp it. Ms. N. regularly taught students using song and rhythm, clapping and dancing out math facts and phonics rules, such as "drop the y, and add i-e-s." A sixth-grade student writes, "She is nice when we are doing good, she loves teaching us about things; and she likes giving us compliments and adding humor to the lesson." Students of every teacher wrote about their teacher's humor—being funny, uses humor, or makes us laugh.

> *"Hey, if every time your cell divided you lost half your chromosomes, pretty soon you'd be a fruit fly." —Seventh-grade science teacher's lecture about mitosis*

Physically Fit

Toward the very end of the study while watching teachers move from desk to desk, something all of them do, with only two exceptions, these teachers were all fairly physically fit. While they were not always very thin, only two of over seventy highly effective teachers could be characterized as seriously overweight. Their fitness ensured the teachers could move around the room easily; they have the energy to motivate students, manage the classroom, almost never sit down, and endure long days.

When asked what kept them in shape, some said they worked out, ran, walked, ate well, or took vitamins. And yet most felt they should be doing more to stay healthy and fit. While there are studies of the relationship of student achievement to physical fitness, this is a relatively unexplored topic in teacher effectiveness and dispositions. Clearly this was a significant factor in the highly effective teachers having the energy to be so effective, providing immediate feedback and individual instruction, and going the extra mile for their students.

Reaching Out to Parents

All of the highly effective teachers believe parent communication is extremely critical and most have methods for regularly engaging them via journals and phone calls. They reach out in good times and then have a relationship built for other times as well. All of the teachers have ways of contacting parents in the first days of school with encouragement, introducing themselves, welcoming them to call on them as needed and complimenting their child as well.

Of course, all have some stories of when it may have been impossible to connect meaningfully parents. But these are rare, and in general their relationships with parents are quite good. They see these relationships as a partnership. One teacher explains how she describes herself to her students' parents, "I'm a helper. I'm just helping here. I always try to say that to the parents. I'm here to help. Tell me what you need from me. Yes, I have a 14-year-old and a 7-year-old, too."

The Making of a Highly Effective Teacher

Our observations of these highly effective teachers over the course of a decade lead us to conclude that teacher educators, teacher-development specialists, educational administrators, and novice and less effective teachers can learn from these highly effective peers in the following ways:

Observe Highly Effective Teachers in Action

Every novice and less effective teacher needs to watch some of these geniuses at work. A semester in one of these classrooms can inspire and instruct. During teacher education, it would be incredibly valuable for young teachers to spend at least a semester in a highly effective teacher's class just watching and working as the teacher directs. Many of these teachers may not want student teachers to take charge of their classes but all of them welcome observers.

Support the Proper Role of Testing

While many of the teachers believe students are over-tested, none of them dismiss testing for accountability or for instructional purposes. Generally they know how their students are doing in making progress in the curriculum they are teaching. Just given the latest decline in students scores [this was in 2016], especially for the most vulnerable since the relaxing of accountability programs set in place under NCLB, there needs to be a new push for accountability based on achievement.

While Common Core testing is still being worked out, eventually the tests should be useful for these purposes. But clearly, just looking at US educational history, the achievement gaps will not close, nor will the poorest students improve, without holding schools and teachers accountable for progress of their students. This is not to say everyone has to reach the same goal every year; but all students should be making progress.

Avoid Educational Trends

Avoid requiring teachers to use new educational trends without reliable research evidence. Teachers laugh a bit and grieve a bit about the newest latest trend with which they need to comply. These trends are not always well thought-out or truly researched before teachers are told to use them. Many of the trends, such as whole language, did not hurt the middle class, but they did hurt the lower-class students. Clearly, students can and do work together, but we need better understanding of how many minutes is optimal for groups, and with how much explicit direction.

Our study indicates that in highly effective classrooms the teacher is the major figure in instruction and that students can be engaged in a variety of ways and in a variety of settings from whole groups to small groups. *The issue is engagement and learning.* Too much unstructured or lengthy student interaction appears less effective. What is needed is engaging, explicit instruction by teachers devoted to student achievement and the enjoyment of learning. Before jumping on the latest professional development bandwagon, teacher educators and professional development experts need to make sure it works and will work for all students.

Engage in Explicit Instructions

Students construct knowledge when they have enough background and experience to apply to new situations. Students whose families have less background and experience with formal education need much more explicit instruction. If constructivism (the idea that students construct meanings from experiences) is true, then students will do this no matter what the instruction, because it is the way human beings' minds work. But the fuel for that construction appears to be superb explicit instruction.

In *Constructive Instruction*, Richard E Mayer wrote that it is not physical activity that is the goal (nor is it student cooperation). Instead, students should be active cognitively, and that can happen when a great teacher is standing in front of the room lecturing or when students are watching a well-ordered video. Paul A. Kirschner, John Sweller, and Richard E. Clark, in their paper, "Why Minimal Guidance During Instruction Does Not Work" (*Educational Psychologist* 41(2) (2006):75–86) noted that while constructivism may be the way children learn, the path to that learning needs to be through explicit instruction.

The Love of Seeing Students Learn

Lastly, much of what makes a highly effective teacher is their love of seeing their students learn and grow, and their instructional abilities to make it happen. Add to this their willingness to do the very hard work of instruction: knowing their academic content, being prepared, working tirelessly, and being willing to go out of their way to help their students.

Highly effective teachers love their students and their profession. This love is not a sweet love and many teachers do not call it love, but they are all convinced of their students' potential and determined to do what they can to see them thrive in their class and in life. It is their joy to see it, as one high-school English teacher says: "We love what we do and derive a purposeful life from our vocation." This is a strong, tough love as some refer to it—like a strong parent. This cannot be taught or measured, but it can be observed as a tough internal determination, unfailing diligence, and sheer joy in watching their students grow, learn, and laugh.

Often educators discuss the role of caring, high expectations, explicit versus constructivist instruction, and classroom management. What highly effective teachers do is all of these things. They are strict and fun-loving. They explicitly instruct while involving students in the large conversation. And they do all of this superbly because they respect and enjoy their students and want to do something big for them all. There is no separating these things out from one another.

Jaime Escalante's Secret to Inspired Learning

Jaime Escalante was a highly effective teacher in a time before there was such a label. He did it instinctively and with the support of Henry Gradillas, an outstanding principal who understood what it took for a school to turn around. I hope his story and techniques will inspire teachers and administrators to continue his legacy.

Appendix 1: Jaime Escalante in the 21st Century—Still Standing and Delivering

This article, written by Alex Thomas, appeared in 2015 at the same time as the interviews with Henry Gradillas and Angelo Villavicencio in Appendices 2 and 3. These three pieces kicked off a project to revisit and reclaim the legacy of Jaime Escalante. For this article, Alex interviewed many of the people cited in it. This book expands on and thus supersedes this article. Also, in places this book repeats portions of it verbatim. Even so, it seemed worth including this article here in an appendix as a convenient summary of Escalante's significance and continuing influence. In particular, it underscores what Escalante can still teach about teaching. Below is a slightly updated version of the original article.

1. The Legacy

1.1. Golden Age?

"Don't call it a 'Golden Age!'" Henry Gradillas declares with conviction. "That's the way it should have been all along."

To call the 1980s the Golden Age of East LA's Garfield High, he insists, implies that the school offered more during those years than students had a right to expect. Henry believes they were only getting the education they were entitled to.

He should know. Gradillas, born in 1934 and actively teaching into his 80s, remains passionate about education. He was principal there from 1981 until 1987 during a time of academic progress and achievement that has never been equaled.

In his first year as principal, accusations of Garfield High students cheating on the 1982 Educational Testing Service advanced placement calculus test made national headlines. Defenders claimed the ETS was merely prejudiced, unwilling to believe that Mexican-American kids whose parents were laborers and hotel maids could have scored so well on an exam aimed at high-achieving Anglos. When every student who retook the test passed a second time, a legend was born.

The 1988 film *Stand and Deliver* told the story of these students and their unorthodox calculus teacher, Jaime Escalante. The actor who portrayed Escalante, Edward James Olmos, received an Oscar nomination for his role in the film and made the teacher an international celebrity.

The movie also introduced millions to the philosophy of a focused, passionate, sometimes controversial teacher who, against impossible odds, led teenagers from the barrios of East LA to triumph in a demanding calculus test year after year. Escalante, assisted by teachers Angelo Villavicencio and Ben Jimenez and supported by principal Gradillas, masterminded the program that educators have held up as a shining example of excellence ever since.

The students in Jaime Escalante's math department were not stereotypical calculus nerds. Seventy percent of the children were poor and 95 percent were black or Hispanic. Many of their parents were undocumented aliens who spoke little or no English and had never finished high school themselves.

And yet Escalante became one of the most famous and most admired teachers of his time by inspiring and cajoling students to excel in spite of their poor preparation in junior high; difficult home situations; inadequate study habits; drugs, gangs, and other daunting obstacles. A passing grade on the calculus Advanced Placement (AP) test put them in an elite group of top academic performers, typically opening the door to prestigious colleges and earning college credit.

1.2. Building a Fast Track

Though Escalante started teaching at Garfield in 1974, it took four years to lay the groundwork, get the textbooks, and establish the curriculum before he reached his goal of offering AP calculus. He believed higher mathematics was the key to a good job, a promising student's ticket out of the barrio and into a successful career. Southern California was full of aerospace companies, aircraft makers, computer, engineering, and manufacturing businesses eager to hire qualified young Latinos. AP calculus, as the supreme test of a high school student's achievement and potential, became the ticket into these industries.

Escalante knew he had kids who were up to the challenge. But between the basic consumer math most Garfield students learned and a mastery of calculus was a minefield of geometry, algebra, trigonometry, and mathematical analysis. Students arrived at Garfield entering the tenth grade (it was a three-year high school) without the fundamentals needed to tackle higher math. Jaime and his colleagues had three years to teach five- or six-years' worth of material to reach the level of the AP test questions. And these were kids who needed help with basic arithmetic. Understanding the sine or cosine of x—much less the second derivative of f—was a long way off.

Jaime recruited students for his classes the way coaches recruited for sports. He got word of kids who seemed to have an aptitude for numbers and lobbied them to join him. Finally, in 1978 he persuaded 14 students to take his inaugural calculus class and sit for the AP calculus exam the following spring. He scrounged copies of old AP test questions and prepared handouts from other sources. He started his 8:00am class at 7:30 every morning, then tutored students after school. One by one students fell by the wayside, unwilling or unable to maintain Escalante's demanding pace, preferring instead to keep up with sports and other extra-curricular activities that meant more to them than mastering calculus. Five made it to the end of the academic year and took the test. Two passed.

The next year nine students made it all the way through the year; six passed the test. In 1981, 15 took the test and 14 passed, including one with a 5, the highest possible score. In 1982, the year of the famous retest, 18 Garfield students took the math test and for the first time everyone passed. In 1987, the year of peak participation in Escalante's fast-track program, 127 Garfield students took the AP calculus test, more students than at Beverly Hills High and more than all but four high schools in the entire country. Eighty-five Garfield students passed. This meant that 27 percent of all Mexican-American students in America who passed the AP calculus test that year were students in Escalante's program.

1.3. Shining Successes

Jaime and his team shepherded hundreds of students through calculus and other higher math courses at Garfield in numbers unequalled before or since. Many of them took and passed

Advanced Placement tests. Some made it through the best colleges in America and went on to high-profile careers in teaching, science, engineering and other fields.

The Escalante program launched many bright careers. Here's an incomplete list of some of the people for whom that program was the difference maker:

- Daniel Castro, who earned a bachelor's and master's in electrical engineering at MIT, then added a law degree from UC Berkeley; today, he is an attorney specializing in patent law and intellectual property.
- Jorge Samayoa, the first Garfield graduate ever accepted by MIT; two of his brothers went to Harvard.
- Olga Reyes, who went on to get a master's degree in civil engineering and is now a nationwide authority on bridge design and construction.
- Victor Mendez, a graduate of Cal State LA, who has led major product development projects at California Edison (a student of Villavicencio's at Don Lugo High after he left Garfield).
- Erika Camacho, now a mathematics professor at Arizona State University.
- Anthony Garcia, who received a degree in sports medicine from Cal Poly Pomona and is now a professional trainer.
- Ben Rodriguez, who won an internship at NASA's Jet Propulsion Laboratory; Escalante kept him in class by failing him so he couldn't play on the football team.
- Christopher Martinez, today an attorney with the US Security and Exchange Commission.
- Leticia Rodriguez, the basis for the character Ana Delgado in *Stand and Deliver*, earned a master's degree in

electrical engineering and became an electronics design engineer for Xerox and Honeywell.

MIT professor Amar Bose (1929–2013), inventor of the popular speakers, became a great admirer of Escalante's students. One year in the 1990s, 14 of them were attending Harvard, Yale, or MIT at the same time. Bose helped pay for Escalante to spend Thanksgiving with them in Massachusetts. Bose also had a standing offer to any Escalante graduate that he would pay all their expenses to attend MIT if they were admitted.

Even students who didn't pass the AP calculus exam benefited from their time in Jaime's program. In 1997, Wayne Bishop, an admissions advisor at Cal State LA observed, "We got literally hundreds [of Garfield applicants] who had scored two or less on the AP calculus test or had never even taken it but had worked hard at their prealgebra, algebra, and geometry so they could take Jaime Escalante's calculus class but fell short of their goal. They were still better off, much better off, for having made that effort... Their well-honed study skills allowed them to succeed in unprecedented numbers."

1.4. Endangered Dynasty

Yet in spite of universal praise for his results, Escalante's methods were not widely adopted. After his principal and key supporter, Henry Gradillas, departed Garfield at the end of the 1987 school year, the program lost its momentum. Following Escalante's move to another high school in 1991, the calculus dynasty he had built was never the same. The aggressive curriculum that prepared Garfield students for the AP test was modified to be less rigorous. Administration interest and support moved on to other things. At its peak, Escalante's program produced 85 passing grades. Nine years later, five years after Escalante left Garfield, 11 students passed AP calculus.

In a 2002 article, Jerry Jesness, who later collaborated with Gradillas on a book, wrote of Escalante's legacy at Garfield, "By 1996, the dynasty was not even a minor fiefdom." Reporting Escalante's death from cancer in 2010, the *Los Angeles Times* observed, "Without him, Garfield's calculus program withered." Angelo Villavicencio—"Mr. V." to his students— who took over Escalante's calculus classes after he left Garfield and who taught for decades in California, said in a 2014 interview, "The program fell apart" once Escalante transferred to another school.

What happened? Why was such an outstanding program allowed to decline? When asked why Garfield's nationally renowned calculus program was abandoned after he and Escalante left, Villavicencio stares thoughtfully into his coffee cup. "I have no idea," he says quietly at last, shaking his head. Then he adds, "There were some narrow-minded people there. They were jealous of his success."

1.5. It Takes *Ganas*

Jaime Escalante focused on results. His pupils had been told all their lives that they weren't good enough. Because they were poor Latinos, no one expected them to excel at advanced mathematics. Escalante believed that anyone with *ganas*, a Spanish term meaning "drive" or "desire," could grasp difficult mathematics and use the skills thus gained as the key to a well-paying career. He was dedicated to doing whatever it took to make that happen.

Such focus and dedication made Escalante enemies. Parents resented the high standards that at first tended to produce low grades for their children. They resented the long hours that took students away from after-school jobs and family duties. Some teachers were jealous of the extra resources he attracted from corporate sponsors who wanted to support his program, especially after the movie made him a pop celebrity. Faculty colleagues and union officials complained that his extra hours and large class sizes set unhealthy precedents for other teachers and violated existing work agreements. Some of them resented that after the film came out he was gone much of the time on speaking trips, leaving others scrambling to cover his classes.

Escalante's own personality magnified these points of contention. He was blunt in criticizing other teachers' performance. Elected chairman of the math department in 1981, he steadfastly ignored the administrative duties he wasn't interested in; he failed to answer calls and letters from district headquarters; he almost never came to department meetings. He was quick to reprimand colleagues when he caught them skipping out early on Friday or doing work for their second job in the teacher's lounge. "He wasn't a team player," Henry Gradillas admits.

Yet Gradillas strongly agreed with Escalante's approach of high standards, long hours, and relentless consistency. Gradillas saw it as the way to transform how students viewed their own abilities and to get them to believe in their potential to succeed. Gradillas himself was an East LA native who knew all about what he calls "the discrimination of low expectations." He wanted Garfield students with the *ganas* to make it through the higher math curriculum to have the chance to do so and go on to college.

Gradillas fended off angry parents, unhappy administrators, concerned union officials, and resentful teachers so Escalante could carry out his program. He also made sure Escalante had whatever resources and equipment he needed. When Jaime ramped up his summer program, he asked the school to air-condition his classroom. To the dismay of other teachers, he got his wish. When the janitor griped about Escalante's early hours, Gradillas gave the teacher a key of his own.

1.6. Down the Drain

The beginning of the end of the glory days came in 1987 when Gradillas took a leave of absence from Garfield to complete his doctoral dissertation in education, titled "Characteristics of Capable Teachers." "I wanted to show the kids you're never too old to learn," he says about his decision. His replacement at Garfield was Maria Tostado. "Mrs. Tostado had a different approach from mine," he says.

Others were more forthright about this changing of the guard. Angelo Villavicencio came to Garfield the year Henry Gradillas left and taught calculus alongside Escalante. In his view, Tostado "did not want any Escalante legacy at Garfield and brought in her own team of teachers she believed were better. She tried her best to get rid of any Escalante legacy, and she succeeded."

Lucy Romero, a faculty member at Garfield for more than 30 years, remembers Tostado as a "very, very insecure person" who "wanted to make her mark" as a principal. Three years into Tostado's tenure, the faculty petitioned the district unsuccessfully to have her removed. She left after nine years on the job.

Gradillas and Tostado differed radically in how they dealt with Escalante. Gradillas, an ex-instructor and officer in the elite Airborne infantry, protected Escalante from his critics because Gradillas believed the results were worth the effort and inconvenience on his part. Tostado, an ex-nun, had little patience for Escalante's unorthodox style and no desire to shield him at her own expense.

In 1990, Escalante was replaced as chairman of the math department by Ben Jimenez, a young teacher he had trained and who taught advanced math using Jaime's techniques. Escalante was stung by the slight, and by the role of the teacher's union in engineering this outcome. The change took away his power to assign teachers and students in a way that kept the math pipeline filled with promising young calculus hopefuls.

That year he decided to move to another school, then changed his mind in order to continue developing a summer program he had started at nearby East Los Angeles College (ELAC). When changes in administration policy kept him from teaching the courses he wanted in summer school at Garfield, Jaime arranged to teach his summer classes at the ELAC campus. Under sponsorship of the National Science Foundation and ARCO, the program had grown to 1,000 students a year from schools all across the district studying math, science, English, and teacher training in the Escalante method.

But at the end of the next academic term, in the spring of 1991, Escalante finally left Garfield High. He had been there 17 years. "Faculty politics and petty jealousies" were the reasons cited in the *Los Angeles Times* announcement of his resignation, even though publicly Principal Tostado had called him "an undisputed leader of his profession ... a master."

Ben Jimenez left at the same time, and Angelo Villavicencio took Escalante's place. A year later Mr. V. followed his mentor out the door. "I saw the writing on the wall and said, 'I'm not going to last,'" he says of those days. He was identified with the Escalante regime, and, he says, the new principal's attitude was, "My team is better than Escalante's team." Tostado declined his request to add a third class of calculus in order to reduce class size, and in fact threatened to make matters worse by taking away the large classroom Mr. V. had inherited.

She shied away from supporting Escalante's strict standards in the face of continuing complaints from parents and district officials. Don Mroscak, a counselor at Garfield from 1967 to 1994, remembers that "expectations fell off" during that time. "There was no more push." Concludes Mr. V., "It took four or five years for the whole thing to go down the drain."

1.7. Starting Over

Officials in Sacramento were "elated" to welcome the famous Jaime Escalante to Hiram Johnson High. They turned a shop room into his calculus classroom. It was air-conditioned at Jaime's insistence (sponsors paid for it). It even had observation mirrors to accommodate visitors from around the country who wanted to see their new star in action. The special treatment got him off to a bad start with his colleagues, as did the attention his arrival generated in the press. Some were jealous before the first day of class.

As he did at Garfield, Escalante began by teaching lower-level math courses. His third year he taught basic calculus; his fifth, he started teaching more advanced calculus. Yet during 10 years at Hiram Johnson, Escalante never approached the success he'd had at Garfield. When he moved to Sacramento in the fall of 1991, Jaime was 60 years old. He was 65 by the time he was able to lay the groundwork for AP calculus there. This was a challenging season of life to begin something from scratch.

But the main reason his program never gained the momentum it had at Garfield was that the administration and parents in Sacramento failed to back him up when it came to maintaining the standards necessary to achieve stellar results. Teachers and parents allowed students to drop his courses. They took exception to his heavy-handed classroom technique that included badgering and barking at students, giving them sometimes unflattering nicknames, and demanding long homework assignments.

As Don Mroscak recalls, "The families in Sacramento were less pliable." At Garfield, threatening to call a parent was often all Escalante had to do to make a student toe the line. He had a rapport with the Latino families there that he lost among the Asian, Anglo, Latino, and African-American mix at Hiram Johnson. Now the response to his threat might well be,

"Call anybody you want!" Without the family support he had counted on before, Escalante lost a lot of the leverage he had used to keep students in class when they wanted to give up.

By 1995, Escalante had reestablished his early morning and lunchtime help sessions, and was prepping 30 or so students for the AP calculus exam. But two years later the calculus program at Hiram Johnson was fading fast. In 1997, only 11 students took the AP test. The next year only seven signed up for advanced calculus and the class was deleted from the curriculum. Another teacher already had the beginning course, so that year Escalante taught no calculus at all. A third of his algebra students dropped during the school term, leaving twenty young teens rattling around in his giant showcase classroom by the spring of 1998. Three years later, Jaime Escalante retired and moved back to his native Bolivia.

1.8. A Class by Itself

After a rocky period for Garfield following the departure of Henry Gradillas and then Jaime Escalante, Garfield experienced an upswing. Though it has never repeated the calculus successes of the Escalante era, Garfield did emerge from the doldrums of the Tostado era. Counselor Don Mroscak notes, "Escalante was the catalyst for AP and more teachers got on the bandwagon." The very memory of Escalante's time there seems to have had an invigorating effect on Garfield.

Jay Mathews, Escalante's biographer, points out that Garfield in 2015 [when this article was written] had a healthy participation in Advanced Placement programs. In 2014 the students there took 650 AP tests in 10 subjects. Sixty-six students sat for the calculus test (47 took the AB level test, 19 took the harder BC test) and 34 passed (23, the AB; 11, the BC). Not quite Escalante's high of 85 passing marks, but also nowhere near the single digits. In the California Academic

Decathlon, open to all public and private schools in the state, Garfield has placed in the top 20 each year for the previous five years.

Still, the triumph of the Escalante years was in a class by itself. What made those historic results possible? What would it take for other schools to repeat that success today?

2. Why It Worked

Jaime Escalante's unorthodox teaching style and wacky classroom persona receive attention in any discussion of his legacy. Yet a closer look at his example tells us that style alone, or a teacher's passion for education alone, will not produce the results that made Escalante and his students famous. Along with Jaime's rare level of dedication and ability to inspire and motivate students, other factors were also essential. In exploring the history of Escalante's tenure at Garfield and talking with people who were there, a handful of policies and practices emerge consistently as the keys to Jaime's legendary achievement.

2.1. High Expectations

According to Jaime Escalante, his colleagues, and his students, high expectations lie at the root of all successful teaching. Without high expectations, nothing else matters. The assumption among policymakers at Garfield High had been that poor Latino students could not learn calculus. Their family lives were thought to be a disaster, middle school had not prepared them, their English was shaky, they had none of the "cultural capital"—books in the home, trips to the museum— that the privileged kids enjoyed. Low expectations led to low standards: the tenth-grade math curriculum at Garfield was what Escalante had taught to fifth-graders in Bolivia.

Escalante would have none of it. He was convinced that his students had as much potential as kids anywhere else, and he set his standards accordingly. Other teachers opposed him along with administrators, parents, and the students themselves. Department chairs denied him textbooks, and angry parents complained about low grades, too much homework, and their children missing work or babysitting duties. Escalante held fast despite the harsh reaction, and eventually proved to everyone that Garfield students could excel on a national stage. His most valuable gift to students wasn't a knowledge of calculus but proof that the world was wrong about them. They were not low achievers; they were the best students in America —especially when it came to making more with less.

A glance at the educational institutions most admired for their results shows that regardless of their location, demographics, or any other variable, they all set the performance bar very high. This includes charter schools, parochial schools, private schools, even military-style "tough love" academies. Students are expected to excel academically and to meet strict guidelines of grooming and behavior. To achieve high standards, the standards have to be there in the first place. Those who fall short get special help and attention, but not an exception.

Well-meaning critics claimed that Escalante's way was hard on the kids' self-esteem. It was important for poor Mexican-American students to feel good about themselves, and high standards meant they were likely to get lower grades and be excluded from extra-curricular activities. Henry Gradillas wasn't buying it: "Yes, if you fail a kid or keep him out of football because of his bad grades, it's hard on his self-esteem. But it's a lot harder on his self-esteem a couple of years later when he can't get a job and has to eat leftover pizza out of the dumpster. Self-esteem is fed by rising to a challenge, not by being excused from it."

More opposition to the school's consistent standards, notes Gradillas, came from members of the community who said calculus and higher math were "white" subjects and that Latinos faced the added challenge of a cultural divide. "Escalante reminded his kids that they had Inca and Mayan blood in their veins, and that those civilizations were advanced in math," he explains. "He said the concept of zero originated with the Mayans. Criticizing math because it's 'white' is an excuse not to participate in something because they're afraid to fail."

In the same vein, Escalante and Gradillas thought that students should discontinue ESL (English as a Second Language) and other targeted programs as soon as possible because they set those students apart and gave them another reason to fail. Gradillas believed two years of ESL were almost always enough, especially since many of the kids taking it were born in the US.

During the time of Garfield's flourishing under Escalante and Gradillas, only a modest percentage of Garfield students were in advanced math and even fewer took AP calculus. Yet all Garfield students benefitted from consistent high standards that encouraged them to stretch beyond what they and others thought they could do. As Mr. V. puts it, "The number one reason for success" at Garfield was that "teachers, counselors, and administrators believed in students' potential."

2.2. A Safe, Encouraging Learning Environment

One of Escalante's first steps at Garfield was painting his classroom and putting up inspiring posters with pictures of sports stars and slogans like "Calculus Need Not Be Made Easy; It Is Easy Already." He played music in class. He got air-conditioning. He wore silly outfits—anything to make the learning experience as rewarding and appealing as possible.

But the atmosphere in the classroom was only part of creating a safe, productive, inviting place to learn. When Escalante arrived, the principal had accommodated gangs at the school by giving each of them a place to gather and post their colors. After an accreditation crisis threatened Garfield with closure because of poor performance, that principal was transferred. His replacement painted over graffiti, removed gang symbols, banned non-students from campus, and locked latecomers out of their classrooms.

As dean of discipline and later as principal, Henry Gradillas had no patience with disruptive students. Previously, teachers had worked under conditions that made learning difficult at best, including students routinely talking and acting out in class, wearing provocative clothing, openly threatening each other and bragging about their gang affiliations, and scaring other students away from the cafeteria and restrooms that were marked as gang turf. All that changed overnight on Gradillas's watch. As he remarked, "There's something in children that craves order."

Escalante and Gradillas demanded, and got, order in the classroom because they refused to accept anything less. Class clowns, troublemakers, and girls in low-cut tops were distractions. Escalante dealt with quickly, decisively, and sometimes harshly. Gradillas backed him up. Students who repeatedly misbehaved or failed to do their homework were transferred out of his class. Discipline problems were assigned to other teachers, sometimes other schools. (In return, other students were sometimes transferred to Garfield to make a fresh start or separate them from a gang.)

When Escalante sent one disruptive student out the door, the boy insisted he needed a hall pass. "That's your problem," Escalante replied. He once sent a girl to the principal for wearing improper clothing. She returned saying the (pre-Gradillas) principal agreed with her that it was within the school dress code. "Fine," Escalante answered, "you can wear it, but you can't wear it in my class." He, not the principal or a dress code, would decide what was a distraction in his class and what was not.

When another math teacher despaired over the bad behavior of his students, Escalante offered to exchange classes with him for a couple of days. His opening remark as a visiting teacher was, "I am now the boss. Are you listening?" He then marched down the aisle and grabbed a car magazine away from one student. As described by Escalante biographer Jay Mathews, the teacher then declared, "You are all going to do what I say. If you don't do what I say, you gonna fly [be sent out of class]! We got all kinds of places we can send you. You won't like them. Any questions?" Three students were ejected before the rest of them stopped talking.

The next morning Escalante gave a quiz. After grading them, he "gleefully distributed a fistful of D's and F's." He said they were lucky to have the regular teacher they had. "I would flunk all you *banditos*," Escalante exclaimed. "You're wasting my time." The other teacher had coddled the students, seeing them as underprivileged and therefore needing to be indulged. Escalante saw them as rude and lazy. They would be quiet, they would study, they would do their homework—or they would be gone. In two days, the atmosphere of the classroom was completely transformed. Then and only then could the students have a chance to learn.

2.3. A Strong, Supportive Principal

Escalante could not have done what he did without the help of Garfield's principal, Henry Gradillas. Escalante's most productive years, and the ones that made his reputation, coincided with Gradillas's tenure as principal from 1981 to 1987. When Escalante sent a student to the principal's office for some infraction, Gradillas backed him up. If he hadn't, and if a student knew that Escalante's warnings were only empty threats, Escalante's authority would have been undercut. In turn, Escalante's efforts to maintain high academic standards and foster a learning environment in class would have been severely damaged.

Gradillas shielded Escalante from the criticism of other teachers who thought he was too intense, and who accused him of claiming more than his share of students' time and school resources. When he needed money for more advanced textbooks, Gradillas came through. When he had the chance to set up a summer program for Garfield math students at a local community college, Gradillas supported the project. When he justified the need for any resources he needed to motivate his students to succeed, Gradillas made it happen.

When he suspended students for gang activity or fighting, Henry says, "I got lots of pushback saying this was life in the barrio." But it was not, he insists, life for students on a path to academic success and a good career. A school that mirrors a dysfunctional community will also duplicate its failure.

Gradillas was a bold administrator who never avoided confronting and opposing the status quo if he thought it would help his students. In his book *Standing and Delivering*, co-written with Jerry Jesness, Gradillas makes a point that principals have to look beyond regulations and mandates, beyond what they think they are allowed to do to what they believe they ought to do.

"We cannot defy mandates, but we can work with them," he writes. "If something is written into law or the terms of a contract are bad, we should work to change them, but work within the legal guidelines. Still, mandates are not straitjackets.

Educators who think that their hands are tied when given a mandate probably have not explored all their possibilities... When educators get a mandate, they need to decide what's best for the kids and then work from there... Whenever I was told that my hands were tied, I found ways to untie them." (p. 116)

Gradillas tells of the time non-students were parking across from the school and turning up their radios to a distracting level. When he called the police, they said there was nothing they could do because the kids weren't breaking any law. Gradillas explained that his job description made him responsible for the learning environment of his students and that he had to stop the radios in order to fulfill his duties. The police agreed and forced the disruptive drivers to leave.

Whether facing down an angry parent or a stubborn school board, Gradillas maintained the same resolve and focus he'd used in the Airborne infantry training young soldiers to jump out of airplanes. As a tireless advocate for his teachers, he broke down whatever administrative or bureaucratic barriers they faced to give them the tools and support they needed. Rather than concentrating on the obstacles to his plans, he kept the focus on the results he wanted to achieve. He then knocked down the obstacles to those results one by one.

2.4. Time to Learn

Aili Gardena, a Garfield graduate who retook the famous 1982 AP exam and whose story was folded into the character of Ana Delgado in *Stand and Deliver*, believes the amount of time she spent learning math was the most important factor in her success. "We worked through lunch. We worked before school. Anybody who had marching band in the morning did that extra work another time. We worked sixth period when most seniors got off for the day. We studied over Christmas break and spring break. I'd be surprised if we had not done well after all this instruction."

Garfield students entered high school poorly prepared for Escalante's program. Most of them had little or no math fundamentals in elementary school because educators didn't think they were up to the challenge. As time went on, they got further and further behind. By their tenth-grade year, Escalante had to push them hard to make up enough lost ground to teach them AP calculus in the three years he had them.

Escalante's demand for time required a large sacrifice from the students and their families. They had to give up virtually all outside interests and free time. This demand met resistance at every level and was the cause of many of the complaints against Escalante. But it was necessary to achieve the objective of telescoping years of math instruction into the limited period he had to prepare his kids for the calculus exam. Jaime waived off the criticism and impediments and moved ahead.

One way he helped them to learn a lot in a short amount of time was "double blocking," enrolling them in two math classes in the same term. These students would take an advanced course while taking a basic prerequisite at the same time. Another effective tool was summer school. Jaime developed a summer program for his students and attracted corporate sponsors to pay for it. The Escalante program (theescalanteprogram.org) is still thriving today (2025) at East Lost Angeles College. In 2022, summer enrollment in this program came to roughly 4,000 from all across the city.

2.5. A Strong and Appealing Team Spirit

Adolescents need to belong. They want to be accepted into a special group. For some, it's the band or glee club. For others, it's the basketball or football team. Yet for those who lack a healthy support group, acceptance may come from social cliques, gangs, alcohol or drug abusers, or other destructive groups. Jaime Escalante saw the power of team spirit and used it to recruit and keep promising students.

"Students loved being part of Escalante's programs," Henry Gradillas recalls. "We had a rule that you had to put paper covers on your textbooks. One day I saw some girls as school without covers on their algebra books. I asked why they hadn't covered them. 'Oh, Mr. Gradillas, we want everybody to know we're taking algebra!' they said. So I bought them clear plastic covers for those books."

Jaime invented a special vocabulary to make learning calculus fun and interesting, and to build a sense of exclusivity for his math insiders. Leaning over a student deep in thought, Jaime would shout, "Face mask! Face mask!" meaning the student made a mistake at the beginning of the problem and needed to go back, just as a face mask call at the beginning of a run in football brings the ball back. "Secret agent" was an easy-to-miss minus sign outside the parenthesis that reversed the values of numbers. "Give and go" for absolute values and "Red light" for factoring were others in a long list of code words that Escalante used and his students picked up.

Jaime had a hard time remembering names. His solution was to give students nicknames ranging from glamorous ("Elizabeth Taylor") to less flattering ("Gordita," or "Little Fat Girl"), all of which they seemed to take good naturedly as symbols of acceptance. The students in turn christened Jaime "Kemo," as in Kemo Sabe, the nickname for the popular western hero the Lone Ranger coined by his sidekick, Tonto.

Escalante organized group activities including early morning and afternoon study sessions. He brought fast-food hamburgers and other treats to share and sometimes took students out for a meal. He handed out candy in class for right answers.

Some years, calculus students got special T-shirts or team
jackets. They held pep rallies. They sponsored car washes and
sold chocolate to raise money for textbooks and test fees.

This sense of community kept students' spirits up under
the stress of learning difficult material. But it also made them
more likely to make other sacrifices to stay on the team. Faced
with giving up band or an after-school job to keep up with the
calculus team, students preferred to stay with the team. Best
of all, as with any team, the members inspired and encouraged
each other to keep going even when they felt like giving up
because they didn't want to let the others down.

2.6. Flexibility

Escalante's results depended partly on his and Gradillas's
ability to finesse, avoid, bend, and sometimes ignore rules from
higher authorities. Their objective was to teach their students.
Anything that got in the way of that objective was an obstacle
to be overcome. They didn't kick problems upstairs for solutions. And they refused to be hamstrung by restrictions in their
job descriptions or district regulations. "If you are in command,
command!" Gradillas says. When Jaime needed to take action
in order to pursue his objective in the classroom, he and his
supporters assumed the authority to act on the spot.

Jaime's success at Garfield depended in part on his ability
to address a problem immediately and aggressively. If students
kept misbehaving, Escalante had them transferred to other
classes or even other schools. If students repeatedly refused to
do homework, Jaime removed them.

Escalante's success also came from holding extra, unauthorized study sessions before and after school, scrambling for
textbooks and other resources not specifically designated to
him, ignoring or getting rid of prerequisites for his courses so

anyone interested could enroll, and teaching classes smaller or larger than were supposed to be allowed. Apart from clear direct orders from above, Jaime took the steps he thought necessary and commandeered all the resources he could to achieve his objective of teaching kids calculus. Everything else was secondary.

2.7. Maintaining the Standard Under Fire

Throughout his career Jaime Escalante faced opposition from colleagues, administrators, parents, and students. Early on, they insisted that his goals were unrealistic and even damaging. Later, they criticized his uncompromising attitude and lack of cooperation in the single-minded pursuit of his objectives. Jaime never wavered. He was convinced that poor Latino students were just as smart as anyone else, and that held to the same standards and given the same classroom opportunities as other kids they could do just as well or better.

Eventually he proved he was right, his story became a Hollywood movie, and the public adored him. What accounts of his story often omit is the years of intermittent progress against a bureaucracy that sometimes did not support him and even opposed his methods. But he never gave up. He never wavered in his belief that his students could succeed and that what he was doing was right. He accepted the barbs of critics as the cost of doing business.

When it comes to unsympathetic administrators, "You can work with them and stand up to them," notes Angelo Villavicencio, "but it helps to have an iron suit."

Jaime Escalante's astonishing academic success came more than anything else from these simple, low-tech, old-school principles. Any school anywhere can put them into practice. So why don't they?

3. Why It Fails

Jaime Escalante's template for high achievement in public schools today is easy to state, but not easy to carry out. "The push for academic excellence," says Henry Gradillas, "will always be subject to certain criticisms." Angelo Villavicencio puts it less delicately: "As long as the fate of education is dictated by bureaucrats and politicians, the success of *Stand and Deliver* will be hard to repeat."

According to Escalante's former students, colleagues, and admirers, here are the main reasons why public schools today are unlikely to embrace Escalante's proven formula for high academic performance.

3.1. Failure to Set and Maintain High Standards for Academic Performance and Behavior

When asked why low-performing schools don't adopt Escalante's methods, biographer Jay Mathews ascribes the primary cause to "a DEEP and false assumption that low-income kids are not up to it." As high expectations are the essential first step to excellence in education, low expectations are at the root of the failure in American schools today, especially in poor and minority districts.

This failure is often credited to the best of intentions. Teachers and administrators are painfully aware of these children's shortcomings and social handicaps. They want them to feel comfortable and secure. They don't want to be accused of discrimination by trying to force unfamiliar standards of performance and behavior on underprivileged students. They don't want to crush a child's already-fragile self-esteem.

But what Escalante demonstrated throughout his career was that low expectations reinforce low self-esteem whereas high expectations produce high self-esteem. A child who meets a hard-won goal is empowered, successful, confident. Old assumptions and self-imposed limitations give way to new self-confidence and an expectation of achievement.

Even kids who don't make it all the way to the top of the academic ladder benefit from striving outside their comfort level. When Jaime insisted that his students could meet high standards, showed them the path, and gave them unflagging encouragement, they did just as well as their more privileged counterparts. The lives and careers of Escalante's students in the years after Garfield prove the lifelong value of his methods.

After the film *Stand and Deliver* was released, Gaston Caperton, then president of the College Board, which administers the Scholastic Aptitude Test (SAT), said of Escalante, "Because of him, educators everywhere have been forced to revise long-held notions of who can succeed."

Henry Gradillas remembers that Jaime was "always talking of the low expectations many had of our students mainly based on ethnic shortcomings, poverty, and little or no parental involvement with the school.

"The racism of low expectations is most damaging in the lower grades," Gradillas continues. "That's where the result of low expectations is most acute. Later, the problem is poor preparation. Kids can't learn because they haven't been prepared."

Yet when Escalante retired from teaching in 2001, the *Los Angeles Times* reported, "Poverty and parents' educational achievement are viewed as the best predictors of academic performance." Jaime, his supporters would argue, proved otherwise. But the notion that poor or minority children require separate, lower standards has been enshrined in American public education.

Standards of behavior were as important to Escalante's methods as standards of academic achievement. Students can't be expected to learn and teachers can't be expected to teach in a chaotic classroom where students don't respect authority and feel intimidated or threatened. Escalante insisted on quiet obedience. He sent disruptive kids to the principal. If they still failed to behave after a visit to Mr. Gradillas, they were suspended. Further misbehavior drew a transfer to another school or possible expulsion.

Some parents of undisciplined students were unsupportive of the principal until they learned that their AFDC checks required their children to be in school. An interruption in payments was usually enough to enlist their help.

As with poor academic performance, today's administrators excuse bad behavior because it's part of the community's culture. Escalante would argue that those policies set students on a pathway to failure, and that a school's responsibility is to reform bad behavior, not reinforce it.

A teacher in the Chicago public schools reports that recent [ca. 2015] changes in administrative policy mean that she cannot discipline a child for throwing something in class. This comes on top of policies that allow students to shout "F—— you!" to her face without consequences. Escalante and his colleagues would say that under these conditions learning is not only impossible and school a waste of time, but also the situation is dangerous for the teacher and other students.

According to this Chicago teacher, the rationale behind this permissive policy is that too many African-American boys were being suspended for throwing things and that this behavior is part of the surrounding culture. Jaime and his team at Garfield would have insisted that excusing African-American boys from disrespectful and dangerous conduct because they're African-American boys is discrimination at its worst.

The responsibility of a school is to equip students to make their way in the world. A student who goes through high school believing it's all right to insult teachers or throw objects in class is not likely to do well at a first job interview. If the world tells such students that they're exempt from respectful behavior because of their skin color, ethnicity, or surrounding violence, then the educational establishment that is supposedly looking out for their best interests has cheated and deceived them, making their prospects for the future dim.

3.2. Political and Educational Bureaucracy

When Escalante first announced his plans to leave Garfield, a teacher with 37 years of experience wrote to the *Los Angeles Times* that he was sad to see Escalante go, especially since the reported reason was bureaucratic squabbling and lack of support. It was unfathomable to him that administrators could allow policy matters and personal feelings to get in the way of holding onto a legendary teacher.

"You have to understand that most administrators want to move up the ranks," he wrote, "and hesitate to take risks to support teachers. The system protects them... My guess is that 15 percent of all administrators in LA are innovative, skillful, completely supportive of teachers and 85 percent are inept, mediocre, and afraid they won't move up the chain of command."

Jaime Escalante was willing to take on the bureaucracy. Today, America's educational establishment is bigger than ever, especially at the national level, and few teachers have the time, energy, or *ganas* to oppose it. For teachers trying to walk in Escalante's shoes, today's bureaucratic objectives are even more at odds with the goals he pursued.

Henry Gradillias, who even in his 80s continued to work with high schools and high school students, says, "Educators see the benefits of high standards, but most of them care less about supporting them than they do about keeping parents and administrators off their backs. They decide that stopping the complaints is more important than holding onto the standards. They're looking out for their careers, too. They don't want to be the squeaky wheel."

Angelo Villavicencio notes that administrators sometimes have "little or no teaching experience" and don't understand what teachers need in order to achieve their best in the classroom. Yet they're the ones in charge of rules and policies that dictate what teachers do. "Politicians and bureaucrats come and go," he says, "setting policies and making noise in an effort to justify their salaries. But it doesn't help the kids."

High-level policy decisions may focus on money, race, unions, technology, and a host of other issues that overshadow the classroom fundamentals on which Escalante and his peers built their reputations. The further from the classroom decisions are made, the less effective they tend to be and the more teachers chafe at being told what to do by boards and committees who've never met them and never met their students.

To many of Escalante's colleagues and successors, the poster child for educational bureaucracy run amok is national standards testing. In discussing prospects for repeating Escalante's success today, teachers had more to say about this than any other topic. Asked what change it would take to match Escalante's track record today, a faculty member with more than 30 years' experience in California schools immediately exclaimed, "Get rid of Common Core testing!"

Lucy Romero, who began as an intern at Garfield during the Escalante years and subsequently taught biology at its School for Advanced Studies, says national standards don't accurately measure a student's ability or a school's progress. "Classes are uneven from year to year. Some are exceptional, some are not as good. Yet there's unrelenting pressure to keep going higher. The success of the school is based on a number. Students know a lot about a little."

Angelo Villavicencio believes that standardized test results are especially misleading in poor and minority schools where expectations have always been low. "How can [the system] claim core standards are needed without having a foundation first? How can students understand without structure?... Testing has taken away the beauty of teaching math, taken away how wonderful the subject can be."

Molly Slack, a seasoned middle school drama teacher on the outskirts of Houston, heartily agrees. "Standardized testing will be the downfall of this country," she declares, adding that children have different abilities and different learning styles that standardized tests don't take into account. "The testing craze takes so much time that teachers never have time to think about how to bring their personal strengths to the job."

In *Standing and Delivering,* Henry Gradillas writes that when he was principal at Garfield, the district administration pressured him to accept low test scores and high dropout rates because his students couldn't be expected to do any better. Now the pressure is to score high on tests to conform to federal No Child Left Behind requirements.

"In this age of data-driven education, positive statistics are the Holy Grail," he writes. "Our top priority [at Garfield in the 1980s] was not to produce positive statistics, but rather to give our kids the best education that we could offer them. The higher test scores and lower dropout rates were fortunate by-products of improved education."

Today's teachers are pressured to teach to the test, whether or not their students learn the material as a result. Gradillas continues, "Too often important content is left untaught because standardized tests do not include it." To hit their numbers, some states seem to be watering down their exams. "Even though scores on state tests keep rising," Gradillas writes, "SAT and National Assessment of Educational Progress (NAEP) scores are stagnant, and colleges are complaining about the academic skills of the kids the high schools send them."

Catherine Holsen, who teaches ESL to foreign graduate students at Vanderbilt University, strongly agrees. "Teaching to the test does not teach the subject," she says. "Students can pass a standardized test and still have a very poor understanding of the material. Teaching to pass the test and teaching to learn and appreciate the subject are two different things."

Parents don't like standardized tests either. According to a PDK/Gallup Poll published in the *Wall Street Journal* in November 2014, 60 percent of Americans oppose national Common Core standards and 68 percent of public-school parents oppose them. So why does the political and educational establishment keep pushing these tests if a majority doesn't want them? Why commit so many resources to a system teachers say hurts students and schools more than it helps?

Some would suggest the current testing mania is one more manifestation of the Federal government imposing its will at the local level. Common Core in 2015 feds a $2.5 billion per year testing market and remains a powerful instrument of top-down Congressional control. Though some states have more recently opted out of it, Common Core is likely to remain a fixture on the national educational scene for the indefinite future.

3.3. The Assumption That More Money Is Always the Answer

Early in his career at Garfield, Jaime Escalante had to sponsor car washes and candy sales to pay for textbooks, worksheets, and testing fees. After he became a celebrity, corporate sponsors including Coca-Cola and the Foundation for Advancements in Science and Education gladly funded his programs. Still, Escalante scrambled for scarce resources at Garfield like everyone else, and in the process made adversaries of teachers who thought he kept taking more than his fair share.

Yet everything Jaime asked for was directly and specifically related to improving his students' performance. His supporters will point out that he never requested a dollar without a specific, student-oriented need in mind, and never used the lack of money as an excuse to veer from his path to excellence.

Rather than starting with a request for funds, Escalante started with the conviction that what he was doing worked and merited investment. After he demonstrated a need for advanced textbooks, administrators ferreted out a few dollars here and there to pay for them. After his students excelled year after year at the Ivy Leagues, Amar Bose paid the way for his future scholars. After his summer program began turning out math students ready for advanced college work, ARCO supported it because it put new engineering recruits in their employment pipeline.

The ARCO sponsorship highlights a difference in approaches to money between Escalante and the conventional educational bureaucracy. ARCO had been donating $100,000 a year to Escalante for his summer school at Garfield. The administration decided it was unfair to others to let Escalante control all this extra money, and insisted it be granted to the school for the administration to hand out as it wished.

When Jaime explained the new policy to his benefactor, ARCO replied that they weren't supporting the school. Instead, they were supporting his summer math enrichment program. If they couldn't donate to him directly, they wouldn't donate at all. Unwilling to let so generous a gift slip away, Escalante moved his summer program to the East Los Angeles College campus. ELAC was willing to accept the contribution on Escalante's behalf and pass it all through to him. In contrast, the administration at Garfield was willing to walk away from the gift rather than lose control of it.

Instead of being a means to an end, money has become an end in itself in the world of education. Policies are sometimes tailored more to financial considerations than to the welfare of students. For example, as Henry Gradillas and Angelo Villavicencio both note, principals today are afraid to suspend or expel a student not only because they don't want to face a parent's wrath or accusations of racism, but also because it costs the school money. An absence reduces the school's government grant for that day.

Money is also the reason behind some policies to keep students in ESL or other special learning classes longer than they need to be. Gradillas and Mr. V. insist that students who are able should be encouraged to catch up with their peers as quickly as possible. Yet transitioning out of those special classes means another cut in the school's government support. To the extent that educators put the amount of money they control over the welfare of their students, they fail the students, families, and taxpayers they're supposed to serve.

If money were the big problem in American public education, the hundreds of billions of dollars spent since Jaime Escalante started teaching so many decades ago would have long since solved it. Rather, the problem is that the waste and lack of focus in today's education system mean that no matter how much money goes into it, it's never enough. The more money there is, the more is wasted.

According to a worldwide study by the Organization for Economic Cooperation and Development in 2013, "The United States routinely trails its rival countries in performance on international exams despite being among the heaviest spenders on education." That year the US was number one worldwide in spending per student and around thirtieth in math literacy for 15-year-olds. Ten years later, in 2023, the US math literacy ranking was about five places lower. (The Wikipedia article on the Programme for International Student Assessment, or PISA, records all these rankings and performance scores.)

Angelo Villavicencio reminisced recently about watching American astronauts land on the moon in 1969. "I was selling real estate in Nicaragua," he recalls, "and saw Americans walking on the moon. All done with American technology. They were ahead of everybody! Now, despite spending billions on education, we have to import scientists and engineers from overseas."

3.4. A Deteriorating Home Environment

The final barrier to Escalante-style learning is something schools today can't control: the increase in households headed by a single parent, usually the mother, who is stretched to the breaking point with little time for nurturing her children. Students from these homes often come to school poorly prepared, and the parent may not support the administration in maintaining the standards they set.

Drama teacher Molly Slack says, "Most successful kids come from two parent families that have dinner together every night and enforce discipline." Single-parent children are far more likely to be poor than two-parent children, and more likely to struggle with schoolwork. According to the US Census, the percentage of students living in two-parent households when Escalante was teaching at Garfield in the 1980s dropped from about 80 percent to 70 percent in 2020.

Single-parent families turn to schools for services that families used to manage on their own. Millions of schoolchildren now get two free meals a day on campus. Millions remain at the end of the school day in aftercare. Gradually, the responsibility for raising children in America today has shifted away from parents to schools. Counselor Don Mroscak notes that at some point along the way, "the school became the parent figure."

But schools are not designed or equipped to replace parents in raising their children. These extra responsibilities mean teachers and administrators have to divide their time and resources between traditional learning programs and social services. Schools can do a lot to prepare children for success in life but they can't do it all.

As our cultural texture grows more complex, schools will have to partner even more closely with social services, law enforcement, churches, and—most important—parents and other family caregivers to equip children for success. We as a society have to decide how much responsibility to delegate to schools for raising our children, and then give them the resources to fulfill it.

4. Closing Thoughts

4.1. Recipe for Excellence

In any other field—business, manufacturing, medicine, invention—the people in charge, on seeing such a shining example of success, would scramble to copy it. But today's educational mainstream shows little tendency to embrace Escalante's approach. Most prefer other paths to solving the problems of

21st century public education. Yet time and again Escalante's simple recipe for educational excellence has proven its worth.

The dissatisfaction of parents with today's public schools has opened the door to a host of alternative programs promising better results. Their tools? High expectations, a positive learning environment, local control for teachers and principals, and more time in the classroom—the same ingredients Escalante championed at Garfield a generation ago.

One example is the Knowledge Is Power Program, or KIPP, which as of 2025 operates close to 280 public schools across the country as charter schools and serves over 120,000 students. In 2015, as this article was published, their fundamental approach could have been seen as coming directly from Escalante. According to their website at the time, "We believe that all students will learn and achieve at high levels if given the opportunity." To do that, KIPP "must create classrooms and schools that not only deliver rigorous academics but also help students develop their character." These are almost identical to Escalante's first two ingredients for success. Similarities continued on down the line.

A decade ago, KIPP maintained strict rules of conduct not only in class but in the hallways. Students regularly studied long hours, including some weekends. They had to stretch to meet high academic standards. Parents or guardians were expected to play their part. A decade ago, KIPP students outperformed national averages in all categories and by a wide margin, including math and English scores, high school and college graduation rates, and other indicators of academic progress.

Yet school reformer Steven Wilson, in his 2025 book *The Lost Decade: Returning to the Fight for Better Schools in America*, suggests that KIPP has drifted from academic rigor toward social-emotional learning and equity-focused initiatives. He argues that the "no-excuses" model, which drove KIPP's early success through extended instructional time, strict discipline, and high academic expectations, has been diluted since around 2020. He cites pressures, such as diversity, equity, and inclusion (DEI) initiatives and a new generation of educators questioning traditional practices, as leading to relaxed behavioral standards and a focus on student preferences over measurable academic outcomes. According to Wilson, "What we are beginning to see anecdotally is that very high-flying, no-excuses schools are starting to turn in results that have often plummeted to the level of the surrounding district." (SOURCE: https://www.edu cationnext.org/why-some-charters-care-less-about-learning/)

It remains to be seen whether the changes at KIPP parallel the changes at Garfield when Henry Gradillas's successor as principal, Elena Tostado, gutted Escalante's math program. Unfortunately, destruction is always easier than construction. If there is one lesson that Escalante taught us, it is that students rise to meet the standards set for them; and so lowered standards, whatever their justification, damages student learning. Leaving KIPP and its future aside, schools that follow the path that led to Escalante's success continue to exist. Eva Moskowitz's Success Academy seems to be a case in point (https://www.successacademies.org). Regardless of whether such schools draw inspiration directly from Garfield's Golden Age or have reinvented the wheel, Escalante would be pleased.

4.2. Where To?

Understanding the legacy of Jaime Escalante won't by itself solve the problem of education in America today. Yet this slice of American educational history is important and needs to stay part of the national conversation. Escalante provided the clearest proof of concept of how much could be accomplished to advance the education of young people against seemingly impossible odds.

But even though Escalante's methods worked wonders in their day, how effectively can we transfer them to the 21st century? Parents and administrators today would be unlikely to stand for Jaime's taunts and badgering. The legal landscape is different and far more treacherous. There are daunting new top-down Federal requirements that reflect the government's heavier hand in local issues.

Technology has plunged its two-edged sword deep into the classroom, with interactive whiteboards on one side, sexting on the other, and generative AI in between. Covid moved much education online, and even as Covid has receded, the push it gave to online education will persist.

American public education needs help. Everybody agrees on that. But where do we go from here? Has the definition of success in public education changed? Has the role of educators in our culture shifted? Do we want Escalante's level of achievement enough to pay the price he and his students paid? If we could wave our magic wand and reinstate his policies today, would we do it? How have the values Escalante and his methods reflected changed since the 1980s, and how might they continue to change in the future?

"We do not need to invent new rules," Henry Gradillas concludes. For Gradillas, the old rules have worked well and proven themselves. Yet history also teaches that while we must learn from the past, we must not slavishly try to repeat it. We need to keep moving forward, but with an eye on the basics that have proven themselves so indispensable in raising learning achievement: high expectations, consistent discipline, safe learning environment, etc. And of course, it takes *ganas*!

Appendix 2: Henry Gradillas Interview

A veteran educator and author, Henry Gradillas, now in his 90s, is nationally admired as the principal of Garfield High School in East Los Angeles from 1981 to 1987. There he took a struggling inner-city school with few academic accomplishments and turned it into an intellectual powerhouse.

Among the teachers who helped Gradillas turn Garfield around was Jaime Escalante. Escalante set up the outstandingly successful AP Calculus program depicted in the 1988 film Stand and Deliver. *Escalante was the best-known teacher during Garfield High's "Golden Age," but Gradillas hired and provided an effective base for many other outstanding teachers.*

Gradillas was born in Santa Barbara, California, in 1934. His father was a boxer in Southern Arizona and later worked as a finish carpenter in Southern California. His mother was a homemaker, originally from Chihuahua, Mexico. His family, in which only Spanish was spoken, moved to East LA when he was still a child, and he grew up in the same barrio where he later worked as an educational reformer.

Gradillas, who rose to the rank of captain during six years' service in the United States Army, received his B.S. in Agronomy from the University of California Davis, and his Ed.D. from Brigham Young University. In 2010, he authored (with Jerry Jesness) Standing and Delivering: What the Movie Didn't Tell *(Rowman & Littlefield). F*

In 2014, James Barham interviewed Henry Gradillas for an online forum. Even though that interview has long since disappeared from the live web and search engines, it contains a wealth of information and insights that complement this book. Below is a lightly edited version of the original interview.

The Interview:

James Barham

Thank you very much for agreeing to participate my ongoing series of interviews with public intellectuals who are making a positive difference to our national life and culture today, particularly through education.

All Americans are (or should be) concerned about the state of public education in our country. In your long experience as an educator, you have developed a set of principles that have proven highly effective. You have set out these principles for the benefit of us all in your inspiring and entertaining book, *Standing and Delivering*. Therefore, the main focus of this interview will be on your approach to education and how it has played out in practice. But first, we would like to ask you to share with our readers a little bit about your personal history.

We have supplied some of the basic facts in our brief introductory notes above, but we are especially curious about several points. To begin with, what was your own early experience like growing up in East LA? You were born in 1934. What was your sense back then of how you and your family fit into the life of the larger country? What, if anything, did the "American dream" mean to you back then? What sort of schools did you yourself attend? And how did you discover the power of education to transform your own life?

Henry Gradillas

As early as I can remember, plants and all types of animals interested me. I collected live specimens, planted various kinds of seeds, constructed a workable irrigation system for our huge garden, and played all sorts of games with my sister and neighborhood friends.

All this happened during my elementary school years. In junior high school I was exposed to agricultural techniques involving horticulture, landscape design, and some animal husbandry. At home, we raised chickens, ducks, rabbits, and sometimes a goat. We lived a block away from a big low-income housing project in a modest two-story house. Friends and relatives often lived with us or rented a small room. A great deal of violence and vandalism occurred in and around the housing project. Law enforcement activity was a part of life in the *barrio*. I never took part in any of the criminal activities that happened in the community.

I clearly remember an incident that occurred on my way home from school. Several gang boys attacked me and held a weapon to my head demanding that I join their gang. I refused. They knocked me to the ground and forced what I thought was weed into my mouth. I spat it out and fought back. Another boy appeared and ordered them to let me up. I recognized him as the son of the lady that my mother helped several times a week. He said that he was letting me go because his ailing mother needed my mother's help. He shouted that if he ever caught me with a girl from another gang or if I made friends with the enemy, he would kill me. I made it a point to stay away from him and his friends and found another way home.

We did not know about the so-called "American Dream." Our dreams were to keep our family healthy, safe, fed, and happy. For a child growing up in the *barrio*, that was our dream. No one had great aspirations to become or attain more than that.

I attended the local elementary school near my home. I flunked kindergarten because I did not know a word of English. Even then, I soon realized that the classes were geared to the slowest person in the class. It was not a very interesting or informative curriculum. Disciplinary problems of all sorts happened on a daily basis. I made it through grammar school and soon found myself in a school called Belvedere. This was another *barrio* school made up mostly of Hispanic students. The school was over three miles from my home. We had to be bussed because the closest junior high had no room for us. Oh well, new friends in a new community.

The teachers at Belvedere were more in tune with what the students needed. I joined several clubs and learned to play the violin. Now that I look back on my education at the school, I can honestly say that there wasn't much rigor to the skimpy curriculum. All of the courses were quite easy and very few were challenging. I became good friends with the agriculture teacher. I spent every minute I could working with him in the green houses. I also signed up for every class and field trip possible. In spite of the poor curriculum, I learned a lot.

I entered Roosevelt High School in the tenth grade. Like most high schools in those days, it was a three-year school. Roosevelt had a varied demographic make-up. There was a large Jewish population in the community. Many of the Japanese returned to the community after the war (World War II).

The majority of the student population was of Hispanic or Latino decent. The student population numbered around 3,000 students. My high school years were most productive. With the help of some educators I was able to acquire skills and attitudes about education in general that would help me in the years ahead.

Like most Hispanic students, I was placed in low-level academic classes and made to follow a vocational course of study. I received top grades in all of my subjects and was bored with the instruction given. Towards the end of my first year at Roosevelt I became a laboratory assistant for the science department. In this position I was able to work in the chemistry and physics labs, as well as in all of the life science and biology rooms. When I asked my counselor to sign me up for classes in chemistry and physics for the following semester, she laughed and said that those courses were college-level and that I did not have the prerequisites.

However, I would not give up, so I brought my mother to fight for me. I also used one of the ROTC instructors to vouch for me, as well as one of my favorite teachers. My dear mother just smiled at the counselor and said that whatever I wanted was all right with her. The two teachers made such a strong case for me that the counselor finally gave in and gave me the classes that I had requested. She made it quite clear that if I did not do well, I would be returned to my previous schedule. She also informed me that I had to finish my high school college requirements in two years instead of three, since I was behind a whole year.

A full year of algebra, geometry, chemistry, and physics was required. Two years of college-level English composition and literature were also needed. I was told that I also needed additional classes in fine arts and in advanced social studies classes. I had to have a full program and would be required to take full academic classes in both summer school sessions. No Mickey Mouse courses for me.

I agreed and thanked my supporting teachers. The curriculum was most challenging, but—with the help of my enthusiastic and strongly committed teachers—I was able to get through with outstanding marks. Upon graduation, I received a nice scholarship to attend the Davis campus of the University of California.

One incident that occurred during my junior year of high school gave me a wake-up call that students like me seldom get. I obtained a job working for my biology teacher on Saturdays and holidays at his home. He was remodeling his home and needed help with landscaping and outside painting. I would ride my bike, or sometimes take the trolley, to his home in the Hollywood area.

On one occasion, I was asked to wash up for lunch in the master restroom because the laundry room was fully occupied. As I traveled through the hallway into the master bedroom and on into the restroom, I was totally taken aback by the luxuriousness of the rooms. The bathroom was huge. There was an immense shower and a hot tub could be seen in one part of the room. I noticed a special out-of-the-way place for the toilet. There were double sinks with "his and "hers" purple towels in the racks. Why, a whole family could be in there at one time and not get in each other's way!

I quickly washed up and went down the hall. I passed a room and asked my teacher whose room it was. He said that the room belonged to his seven-year-old son. I asked if I could go in and he answered yes.

What a room! The closet had large, sliding, mirrored doors. Inside the closet, the kid had seven types of shoes. I only owned two: the work shoes I was wearing and my school shoes. I noticed that he had many types of athletic uniforms. This huge room was all for him, alone. I had to sleep in a room with others. In one corner of the room there was a model railroad set up on a raised platform. I looked at the massive set and was about to turn the power on when I was cautioned not to because his son did not allow anyone to touch his "toys."

As I was leaving, I noticed a second room. My teacher said that it was his three-year-old daughter's room. As I entered the room I noticed a full-sized crib by the beautiful poster canopy bed. I asked if they were expecting another child. He answered that they were not expecting. I then asked why the crib? He answered that the crib was for his daughter's dolls. For dolls! I remembered that when my sister was born, she had to sleep in the bottom drawer of a dresser in my mother's room. My parents had to use this drawer as a crib for her for many weeks, until they were able to find somewhere else for her to sleep.

When I returned home my father was waiting for me. He had outlined the work I had to do before the day was over. I asked my father why we had to live this way. I told him about the spacious rooms I had been in and the fact that each child had their own room. The restroom we had was so tiny that no more than one person could occupy it at any one time. The make-shift shower was made of cinder blocks and was never finished.

My father responded by saying that he never approved of me working in Hollywood. He told me that he did not like me working for rich white people. He warned me that if I continued to complain, he would make sure that I would never work there again. I kept silent from then on.

Back in school I was ashamed to go to my teacher's biology class. I cut his class until a few days later he summoned me out of another class. He asked me what was wrong. In as few words as possible, I told him what had happened. I asked him why there was such a difference between our ways of life. He responded by saying that education made all the difference. He pulled a piece of paper from his wallet and said that with this paper he could command many jobs in education.

He was authorized to teach, to be an athletic director, and even to work as an administrator. He said that his wife was a CPA and also had a real estate agent's license. This meant that both of them could earn a good salary. I listened intently and then asked him: "Where can I get such a piece of paper?" He answered slowly that I was on the right track and that if I finished college and earned a degree, I too could have whatever I wanted.

At that time I made a promise to myself: If I married and had children, the kids would each have their own room. I would have a pool and all of the amenities available. This all came to pass.

James Barham

Could you tell us something about your career in the US military? How did you come to join the armed forces and what were some of the highlights of your time there? How would you assess the impact of your military experience on your subsequent career as an educator?

Henry Gradillas

This question highlights one of my main themes in the book. I was introduced to the Junior ROTC program upon entering high school. All male students were required to take military classes their first year in high school. Physical education credit was given for the course. What did I know about military science and tactics? My friends and I had no clue about the military, nor did we wish to become soldiers. World War II was over when I was only 11 years of age.

War movies were my only contact with soldiering. However, I soon became very interested in command. Little by little,

I gained rank. I became a squad leader and joined the drill and rifle teams. We visited army military bases and I learned weaponry and what it takes to become an officer. In my senior year, I became a colonel, the top officer in my school's military program.

Before graduation I was able to compete with all the schools in the city and was awarded the title of "All City Colonel." This gave me command of all ROTC units in the city of Los Angeles. I participated in the ROTC program during my four years at the University of California Davis campus. During my college years, I joined the California National Guard for a three-year period until graduation in 1957. I was commissioned as a second lieutenant in the US Army. I accepted a regular army commission and was on my way to Fort Benning, Georgia, for intensive training.

I spent two years as a training officer and company commander and my men succeeded in achieving outstanding performances and were recognized for breaking gunnery and tactics records. I spent three years in Germany during the Berlin Wall and Cuban Missile Crises. It wasn't just the military science and tactics classes that I studied and taught that made me a strong instructor/teacher; it was the discipline, commitment, rigor, and understanding of youth that enabled me to demand and expect the best from all kids.

James Barham

You have had a long—and sometimes stormy—career as a classroom teacher and a principal in some our nation's toughest schools, as well as an administrator at the state level. In which of these roles do you believe you were able to make the most difference? Which of them has given you the greatest personal satisfaction? Please elaborate.

Henry Gradillas

I strongly believe that the role of principal gave me the opportunity to make the most significant difference in promoting student academic achievement, as well as promoting student belief in self-worth, a can-do-it attitude, and that there is no limit to what can be achieved.

As a teacher, I was able to accomplish many of the goals I had set for myself, but I was doing this class by class. There were too many obstacles from those in charge, involving conflicting and outdated regulations and curricular objectives, for me to be able to progress at the speed I needed to go. As principal, I was able to overcome many of these obstacles, and I moved faster than the rate at which new obstacles were being drawn up by administrators.

It is hard for anyone to stop a fast-moving target. All of us—staff, students, parents, community leaders—were moving fast, and achieving at great strides, with little time to reflect.

James Barham

The film *Stand and Deliver* centered on the immense achievement of one of your teachers at Garfield High in the early 1980s, Jaime Escalante (played by Edward James Olmos). In the film, as in real life, Escalante takes a failing inner-city high school math program and turns it around, in only a few years, into one of the largest and most successful such programs in the entire country as measured by the number of students with top scores on the AP Calculus exam. What was Escalante like in real life (he passed away in 2010)? What was your relationship with him (personal and professional)? What sort of impact has knowing Jaime Escalante had on your life?

Henry Gradillas

I met Escalante while I was a teacher of biological sciences and he was assigned to the mathematics department. We shared many interesting moments, always talking of the low expectations many had of our students mainly based on ethnic shortcomings, poverty, and little or no parental involvement with the school.

We discussed the fact that in other countries low expectations were not prevalent to the same degree and that socioeconomic status or ethnic compositions were not important in educating students. Curricular rigor, hard work, positive school climate, and student encouragement were the main themes in the overall education of kids. Both Escalante and I strongly felt this way.

Within a few years I was promoted to administrative dean of discipline. The boys were assigned to me, and a female administrator worked with the girls. In this position I was able to work with the youth of the school, just as I had done in the military when I was in charge. Also, in this capacity I was able to work much more closely with Escalante, assisting him with disciplinary situations as well as working on curricular issues such as homework, attendance, tardiness, and after-school projects.

Escalante was beginning to expand his pre-calculus class and was working with a few students in AP Calculus. I was promoted to assistant principal and left Garfield. Three years later, I readily accepted the offer to return as principal of Garfield. Escalante met with me before the school year began. He gave me a big hug and said, "Congratulations sir, now we can do it."

And we sure did!!!

James Barham

During the "Golden Age" of Garfield High School in the 1980s, you helped set up a culture of learning in which outstanding teachers impacted students not just in math but in many other fields. As the most visible face of Garfield's "Golden Age," Jaime Escalante has received most of the attention from that time. But tell us about some of the other teachers and programs that also had great success back then.

Henry Gradillas

The movie *Stand and Deliver* was an accurate portrayal of what was happening at Garfield at the time, with a few exceptions.

First, the garbage can was never thrown down from the bridge. We did not have a garbage can there. However, a garbage can incident did happen early in my tenure as principal. Several non-students jumped the fence during lunch and assaulted a Garfield student, dumping him into a large can.

Second, I do not recall a chair being thrown across Escalante's room. Though some of the students were rough, there was a respect for Escalante and for all teachers and staff. Kids messed with each other over turf, drugs, boy-girl dating, and gang affiliation, but not with staff.

Third, all of the main characters portrayed were authentic. Who they were and how they acted was all on the up and up. However, to make the film flow, some of the class incidents that happened showed students from one or two previous classes. The incidents really took place; however, some students in AP classes may have been from the previous year.

The movie had a strong effect on the students as well as on the community as a whole. The fact that students from the *barrio* scored well across the nation should have stimulated others in power to publicize our success formula and work to achieve similar results. Escalante and I knew that it would work, just as I knew that my army recruits would do well in rifle marksmanship.

It was little surprise to me when it was announced that my training company had broken all records in their final firing sequences. I trained all my men to shoot well. All would be well qualified. Yes, some would be Snipers. Others would qualify as Experts. Yes, some would be Sharp Shooters. But all would qualify and learn to fire their rifles accurately. It might just save them and their buddies lives. I would have taken any one of my men to be my security guard. They were all well trained and they knew it.

Applying the same principles in the classroom paid off. Escalante was the proudest of all. I simply gave him the "Green Light." This meant "Go for it!"—that I would support him all the way. And he did!

Escalante was the main catalyst in the initiation of a strong academic program with Advanced Placement courses leading the way. When I first was assigned as principal of Garfield, students took a total of 56 advanced placement exams. The Spanish department was responsible for about 20 exams and Escalante had 18. The remainder of the AP exams were divided among the English and social studies departments.

During my six-year tenure as principal at Garfield, the total number of AP exams taken per year at our school rose to 357. The chemistry classes grew from one class per year to 17 classes per year, including two AP classes. The teachers in every major academic department took part in increasing the overall AP program, as well as teaching more honors and academically intensive classes.

Here is the list of our AP courses at Garfield at the end of my time as principal there:

- AP Art
- AP Biology
- AP Calculus AB
- AP Calculus BC
- AP Chemistry

- AP English Language
- AP English Literature
- AP European History
- AP Physics
- AP Spanish Language
- AP Spanish Literature
- AP US History

James Barham

Please tell us about some of the real-life teachers at Garfield —especially how the teachers who were not a part of the mathematics department reacted to what you and Escalante were doing, and to all the publicity the AP Calculus program and the film generated for the school as a whole.

Henry Gradillas

Garfield High School could not have gone from one chemistry class per year to 17 full chemistry sections had we not had the qualified staff available to meet the growing demands, and the academically prepared students. As the mathematics department grew in size and in curricular offerings, so did Escalante's fame and success.

Since I had given the "green light" to Escalante—which meant to go all the way with the students—many of the department chairs felt left out. The mathematics department received up-to-date text books, new furnishings, an increased number of student field trips, and strong recognition among the Fortune 500 companies and community organizations.

The majority of the department chairs expressed strong concerns about not sharing in some of the recognition that Escalante and the mathematics department were receiving. Their concerns were well-grounded and my intentions were to fully involve all of the teaching staff in the school's academic growth.

I arranged for an important meeting with department chair-persons and key non-teaching staff personnel. The purpose of the meeting was to give those in attendance the opportunity to voice their concerns regarding the expansion and adminis-trative treatment of the mathematics department. A heated discussion ensued and everyone was able to contribute and make recommendations on how best to proceed.

After listening to all of the group's concerns, I assured them that I would take everything into account and have a workable plan ready for our next meeting. My plan was not complicated. I would give all of my support to the department chairs and their departments to the extent that the following conditions were met:

- Increase the student AP participation and initiate a re-quirement that all AP students take the college advanced placement examination at the end of each course.
- Establish an AP course that is available through the College Board, if such a course is not currently being offered by the department.
- Continue to promote curricular rigor in all academic classes. concentrating on prerequisite courses necessary for success in advanced offerings.

Had all of the departments taken advantage of my proposal at one time, I would have had a problem delivering what I had promised. However, in the first year, only the science and Eng-lish departments began to work on my proposal. The following year the social studies and the foreign language departments came on board. The computer science and art departments soon followed.

Overall, the growth of the AP program at Garfield was overwhelming. All of the departments began to take pride in their accomplishments. The entire school was recognized as one of the top schools in the District. Now we were all a strong, functioning team. Nothing was going to stop us from going all the way to the top.

Escalante led the way and the rest quickly followed, adding their expertise towards achieving academic excellence among all their students.

James Barham

Tell us also about some of the outstanding students that you had at Garfield in the 1980s. How many are you still in touch with? How many lives were turned around? How many were on track to a minimum wage job or a life of crime, but now are professionals with good careers, happy families, and children that are themselves thriving? What difference did Garfield's "Golden Age" make to these students?

Henry Gradillas

Some of the outstanding students from some of Escalante's classes are mentioned in the preface to *Standing and Delivering* under the title "Finding Great Minds to Lead America into a Bright Future." I have the names of many other students and will have to research to get them up to date. I am in contact with many of the students who took AP courses at Garfield.

James Barham

Your book, *Standing and Delivering*, published in 2010 and thus two decades removed from your time at Garfield, is a unique document. It develops a comprehensive approach to education. It does this through explicit precept and through numerous telling examples. And it is written throughout in an engaging and personal style. Your book is an important document with great potential to sway the debate over public education policy in this country for the good. So, let's review some of the main points with you.

To begin, you lay great stress on school "climate." The school climate, as you describe it, is more than just discipline. To have a productive school climate, discipline is a necessary condition. But the school climate that you developed at Garfield was not just about keeping students in line but about giving them a vision of what they could do academically, and the pride they could take in such accomplishments.

Here's our question, in two parts. First, why, in your view, is school climate so important? And, second, what does it take to turn a bad school climate into a good one? What is the key ingredient?

Henry Gradillas

School climate is one of the most important factors in fostering outstanding schools. After all, the conditions under which you work and take recreation must be conducive to strong job performances in whatever field of endeavor. Your day-to-day surroundings, the attitude of your co-workers, the leadership and respect of your superiors—all are a part of the conditions under which you function on a daily basis.

We all know the feelings we get when we walk into a messy and disorganized room. If schools are to continue to maintain a professional attitude in what they do, then the conditions under which students and staff work must be conducive to good teaching and learning practices. School climate not only revolves around a clean and safe environment, but also includes a cohesive staff working together to achieve a common educational goal.

All students must feel that they are important and should function as a united student body. Regular grade level assemblies were conducted by me four to five times a school year, followed by short weekly homeroom visitations. The entire school was kept up to date on all positive programs, student and staff achievements, and overall standings in academics, sports and the arts. No one was in the dark concerning Garfield's important role in the community and in the District.

Little by little, students were able to identify themselves as Garfieldians—this is what we were by the fact that we were named for James A Garfield (left), the 20th president of the United States.

We took pride in President Garfield's message when he said: "There is no American boy, however poor, however humble, orphan though he may be, that, if he have a clear head, a true heart, and a strong arm, he may not rise through all the grades of society, and become the crown, the glory, the pillar of the State."

A positive school climate is the starting point when one wishes to turn a poor school into a good one. All the things I have mentioned so far were steps taken to improve Garfield's school climate. However, several other very important steps had to be undertaken, as well, in order for us to continue enjoying a positive school climate—namely, delivery of instruction, the curriculum, and support groups and organizations.

James Barham

Another factor you emphasize in your book is curriculum. You firmly believe in challenging students, trusting that they will rise to the occasion, regardless of whatever socioeconomic disadvantages they may be laboring under. In several places in your book (for example, on p. 11) you go even further and discuss the harm done by a certain kind of "compassion," in which it is regarded as wrong to hold disadvantaged or minority kids to the same intellectual standards as kids from the mainstream or elite culture. This phenomenon is sometimes known as the "racism of low expectations" (our term, not yours).

Could you tell us a bit about the specifically ideological challenges you faced in implementing your ideas at Garfield High? In other words, we know you had to fight against vested interests and institutional inertia—that goes without saying. But we suspect you also had to fight against an entrenched and destructive mindset (stemming from John Dewey and ultimately from Jean-Jacques Rousseau), which views giving children unconstrained freedom as more important than teaching them virtue. In the final analysis, it is a deep disagreement about what constitutes a good life for a human being. Would you care to comment?

Henry Gradillas

Delivery of instruction, in my opinion, is a greater factor than the actual curriculum one is to deliver. Any teacher who delivers instruction in an uninspiring manner and fails to use all of the teaching modalities at hand, is ineffective. Students will not learn to their maximum capacities. If the curriculum is weak to begin with, then poor delivery of such curriculum will be disastrous. If the curriculum is strong, challenging, up-to-date, and rigorous, then poor delivery of instruction negates the power of an outstanding curriculum. Not much is gained if the instructional message is not presented properly. Only if the delivery of a strong outstanding curriculum is done in an outstanding manner will the students benefit from such instruction.

The curriculum that is to be presented to students at each grade level is determined by the board of education of each state. In addition, local, county, and city governing bodies, including school districts, adjust and add to curricular offerings. The master curricular plan lists the basic skills that students in each grade level are to be taught and required to learn. The problem begins when the curriculum is not followed. In many cases, administrators and teachers feel that the students are not ready for that level of instruction. As the students progress through the grade levels, the curriculum continues to be modified to fit what educators feel is an appropriate substitute.

Many reasons are given for watering down the curriculum. The cry that the students are not ready for the mandated level of instruction is heard throughout thousands of school districts in this country. In attempts to reinforce these negative beliefs, educators cite that the students do not have the basic skills to absorb the prescribed curriculum. Many use socioeconomic status, uneducated or uncaring parents, language barriers, and other minority issues as reasons for failing to follow the prescribed curriculum.

"Racism of low expectations" is most damaging in the lower grades. Early childhood education—preschool through second grade—must include a rigorous and challenging curriculum. At ages four through seven, young students are extremely receptive to a strong and motivating curriculum. Students of all nationalities, socioeconomic groups, and cultural backgrounds have not, as yet, acquired the basic skills that will be needed in future grades.

Most of the students at this early age should generally be in the same boat, as far as education goes. If students are singled out and placed in a watered-down, meaningless curriculum because of who they are, we are then promoting a terrible wrong that will forever make under-educated, second-class citizens of our youth.

However, when we look at high school students who were cheated out of obtaining a top-notch education in their formative years because of low expectations, then we see a different picture. Educators at the high school level definitely have a huge problem. There, we do not see the problem of low expectations as we see in the primary grades. Rather, the problem lies in the real fact that the level of student preparation is far below that which the mandated curriculum demands. Students with such poor academic skills make it impossible for teachers to adequately educate a student in algebra/geometry, chemistry/physics, or creative writing, let alone Advanced Placements subjects.

The challenge that my staff and I faced was simple: Educate the students in those basic skills that they should have mastered long before reaching high school. We accomplished this in various ways:

- Remedial math, Garfield style—Remedial math became pre-algebra in conjunction with algebra I.
- Remedial reading and English—We instituted remedial instruction in English, concentrating on reading comprehension, basic grammar, and writing, while a second class was added in 10th grade English.
- Low-level science classes were eliminated and standard required classes were established in the physical and biological sciences.
- Non-vocational shop and basic home economics classes were cut from the program, and 100 computers were added to our economics and computer departments.
- "Language across the curriculum" was instituted, and all teachers were required to participate.

The measures mentioned above, as well as others implemented later on in the school year, began to produce positive academic gains. However, objections to what we were doing hit the school from every direction. Students and parents were angry because it was hard work to follow the new rules. The biggest complaint was the loss of an elective course or a class in physical education. But these sacrifices on the part of the students had to be accepted if we were going to double their math and English classes.

The incentive for students was to pass the remedial classes as soon as possible, so they could return to a more normal academic program. The heat was on. There were a lot of rumblings from District administrators and community organizations about our new policies. However, we were in the right.

Since one of the main California goals was to graduate as many students as possible, the only way this could be done was to follow the mandated curriculum and obtain the proper amount of credits needed for graduation.

That we were doing. That we accomplished.

James Barham

You have said that teaching children academic subjects should be viewed in the same light as preparing young athletes who will someday participate in the Olympics. In other words, intellectual mastery is a matter of rigorous training, acquiring both factual knowledge and cognitive skills. Instead of the current mad scramble to "teach to the test," the focus needs to be on giving students the knowledge and expertise they need to succeed later in life. How do you get students to value intellectual mastery and make it part of their lives?

Henry Gradillas

Students have always had difficulty in appreciating the value of education. The more help students receive in their formative years, the better educated they will become. The confidence students get from successful early training will give them a true appreciation of the learning process and will lead them to a more productive future. This, in turn, will create a more positive attitude towards further education and lead to a greater level of intellectual mastery.

One strategy used by me at Garfield, and especially as principal of Birmingham High School in the Los Angeles District, was to require every student to be a member of a school-sponsored group, club, or organization. My insisting that students work and function together in groups gave them the opportunity to share experiences, contribute to the clubs' overall goals, and learn valuable traits. The students became very interested in their clubs and were more involved in the overall learning process. Students, to varying degrees, soon learned to appreciate their contributions to their organizations and began to have a better outlook toward the education they were getting.

This strategy allowed students to bond together for a common goal. They began to take pride in their organizations of choice. A canned-food drive pitted all clubs against each other and all worked very hard to be one of the top three winners.

This year's Winter Olympics [Sochi, Russia, 2014] clearly point out the critical importance of early training. Almost without exception, top medal contenders began their first experience on the ice or on the slopes at a very early age. When some of the top contenders were interviewed, all stated that their parents had introduced them to the sport when they were very young. Many athletes said that they began to skate when they were 4–6 years of age.

Can we not learn from this and be truly serious when it comes to educating our very young by providing a vigorous and challenging curriculum? Successes in educating children in their formative years will surely bring success in the education of young adults.

James Barham

In your book, you speak about the need for a principal to work with the teachers' unions. In the eyes of many observers today, the public employees unions are the main obstacle to reform in many different areas of our public life. This also raises the issue of charter schools, school vouchers, and the like.

What role do you see the unions playing in higher education in America today? How has that changed since your time at Garfield? What do you think of the charter school movement? How do you see the future of education in this country, and what would like to see as a blueprint for educating our population as a whole?

Henry Gradillas

Unions, as I understand them, were established to help the working classes. Unions negotiated, on behalf of the workers, with employers in regards to employee benefits, wages, and working conditions. The head of the teachers' union for the Los Angeles Unified School District was responsible for negotiations with the school board. The teachers' union at the local school level was primarily concerned with teacher working conditions and certain grievances.

I informed the union members that one of my main priorities was to promote a healthy and positive school climate and to work closely with the teachers on having optimum working conditions. I had to ensure that the school had a strong, happy, and committed teaching staff. This also held true for the non-teaching employees.

Many of my staff became troubled as I required more of them. The union was concerned that I was asking too much of the teaching staff. After all, most of the teachers were not used to the new policy of curricular rigor. I met with the teaching staff and asked what I could do for them in order to make their teaching job more effective. The most important assistance that I could give the teachers, if I was going to continue with the current policy, boiled down to three main requests:

- Lower the size of the classes.
- Improve classroom attendance.
- Enforce consequences resulting from student poor behavior, unfinished or late homework assignments, and failure to finish classroom work or non-participation in curricular tasks.

As one teacher put it: "If you are requiring me to go the extra mile with our students, you will have to help us get there."

In the end, I had a tremendous positive response to my rigorous educational policies. Of course, teachers needed some assistance if they were to get the job done following my lead. This is what I proposed for the following school year, which was not too far away:

- I will lower your class size by four to six students.
- Attendance will be of top priority; if students continue to absent themselves from school, drastic measures will be taken.
- Students misbehaving in class or not responding to classroom assignments, including homework, will be removed from the class after all efforts with counselors and parents have been exhausted.

Since all English teachers were required to give weekly assignments in composition writing, I obtained funds to hire college students as readers. This was another way that teachers were helped. The sheer exhaustion stemming from the time-consuming reading and grading of hundreds of papers every week prevented many English teachers from performing what I requested. The college readers were a great help in ensuring that compositions and written assignments were done on a weekly basis.

Today, unions and management are adversaries. Not much is accomplished because they refuse to sit down and find workable solutions to existing situations. Compromise seems to be a bad word because each side feels that it implies weakness. My vision and sort of blueprint for the future in education can be found on page 117 of my book, *Standing and Delivering*.

James Barham

A dominant theme in your book is that as a principal or school administrator, one does not need to make up a lot of new rules, but rather apply existing rules that guarantee a student's right to a safe and productive education. Could you please elaborate on this concept for our readers and give some examples of how you applied it?

Henry Gradillas

Rules, regulations, laws, mandates, and compliance issues can be found in every state in the USA and in every school district. We do not need to invent new rules.

I will attempt to show how we used existing regulations to promote a positive school climate. The delivery of instruction, important as it is, can be regulated and improved using existing rules. Curricular issues have sufficient mandates and regulations that there is no need to create new ones.

In every school district that I have visited, as well as in those districts that have sent me their standing operating procedures, the following goals have been recognized for their schools:

- A safe, clean, and orderly environment where learning is a priority.
- Nothing should be allowed to occur that will hinder, reduce, or stop the instructional process. Instruction is to be carried out by the teachers in an atmosphere conducive to learning. Administrators are bound to make

sure that nothing interferes with the process of educating students. All equipment, facilities, materials, and books will be made available to the teaching staff.

- All efforts will be made to move students from grade to grade with the ultimate goal of graduation. In other words, nothing must interfere with the process leading to graduating a student.

These three major goals, which are acknowledged by every school district, give administrators all the mandate they need, as well as the obligation to get the job done. Generally speaking, those are the only regulations I needed to turn Garfield into an academically well-rounded and recognized school.

The following are but a few examples of how the three goals played a part in achieving a top-rated school: If students are involved in breaking rules, appropriate action should be taken. Who or what agency should be involved in adjudicating the infraction is of great importance. If the infraction is a penal code violation, then the proper authorities must be involved. Police involvement should be mandatory, not just an option. The following infractions are considered to be penal code violations:

- Any type of weapon or items that could be used as weapons.
- The use, sale, or possession of a controlled substance, including drug paraphernalia.
- Assault and battery against a staff member or against another student.
- Theft of school property or personal property of an employee or student.
- Vandalism of school property, including graffiti.

All Garfield students, their parents, and the community knew and understood the offences that required police intervention.

One situation that faces many school administrators revolves around their attempts to deal with penal code violations. Administrators spend a lot of time working with the student and his parents, trying to find a suitable solution to the infraction. All too often, civic organizations, school-based union representatives, district supervisors, teachers, and school management teams all get into the act in an attempt to influence the decision of the administrator in charge of the case.

None of this happened at Garfield because law enforcement was in charge. When parents of the perpetrator, along with Hispanic organizations, came to the school to discuss the violation, guess what? They were referred to the law enforcement agency that was handling the case. The student was charged with a penal code violation and was held in custody for a period of time or released to the parents pending a court appearance. The student did not return to his home school but was transferred to another school for the remainder of the school year pending further review of the case.

The message to all was very clear and simple: Anyone committing a penal code violation will be referred to the proper authorities and will lose the privilege of attending Garfield.

Non–penal code violations were handled in school and were of two main types:

1. Some of the following violations were classified as school-wide violations:

- Dress code violations.
- Excessive absences, truancy, and tardiness.
- Loitering in hallways, restrooms, athletic areas, and in other places on campus.

- Littering and not picking up and properly disposing of garbage after meals.
- Wearing inappropriate items and displaying gang symbols.
- Using profanity.
- Non-violence bullying.

2. The following were classified as classroom violations and the teachers, counselors, and sometimes the parents were involved in solving the situation:

- Non-compliance with classroom rules.
- Sitting arrangement problems.
- Non-participation in certain classroom activities.
- Missing or incomplete homework and class assignments.
- Gum chewing.
- Minor classroom disturbances.
- (For today's youth, I should add cell phone use.)

Any of the above violations can be properly handled with current state, local and district regulations.

Let us use loitering in hallways, restrooms, athletic areas, and in other places on campus as an example of a violation of existing rules. All schools districts have a policy that students must be under the direct supervision of an adult with proper certification. When students roam the halls and congregate in restrooms, they are not under any supervision. Consequently, the students and the administration are both in violation of a district rule. Therefore, it is only proper to insist that students be where they are supposed to be—in order to be under supervision.

At Garfield, we instituted tardy sweeps to move students into their classrooms as quickly as possible in an effort to avoid students from being tardy to classes. Excessive absences, truancy, and tardiness were handled in the following way, which proved to be most unpopular: The Aid to Families with Dependent Children Act requires that school-aged children be enrolled and actively attending school in order for the family to receive welfare benefits. Since excessive absences and truancies violated the AFDC requirement, a note to the organization from the principal initiated a check of school records. A few students were removed from the welfare rolls. This resulted in severe criticism of my administration.

However, within weeks the students were returned to their normal welfare status. Absences and truancy dropped significantly soon after, and continued to drop until we reached 97.6% average daily attendance.

James Barham

You discuss the role of race and poverty in the poor educational outcomes we see in so many of our nation's public schools. People on the political left would attribute these outcomes to persistent racism—the existence of which it would be foolish to dismiss out of hand—and especially to disparities of spending between rich and poor schools districts, and even between rich and poor neighborhoods within a single school district.

You do not confront these issues head-on in your book, but instead emphasize throughout that educational outcomes can be improved even in spite of these types of problems. Indeed, one of the most moving passages in your book comes when you say (p. 43): "Our students had come to understand that Algebra I is not that hard, and that it certainly was not beyond their grasp. It was not a 'white' class anymore. It was a Garfield class."

Leftist critics might respond that this is too idealistic and lets the system—which in their mind is purposely skewed towards preserving the power and privilege of the rich—off the hook too easily. We would like to give you the opportunity of commenting further on this important issue, which it is not always easy for Americans to discuss frankly with one another.

What role, if any, do you feel that racism continues to play in the problems plaguing our public education system and our society at large? How about power politics? In short, how would you respond to a leftist critique of this sort?

Henry Gradillas

You are asking me about racism, leftist critics, rich and poor school districts and the role that they play in education. To be quite frank, I haven't the time to get too serious on any of these areas. When I do, nothing gets done and things bog down. Items of huge curricular importance and student achievement issues are referred to committee and a "we will let you know" attitude prevails. Had I asked permission to institute algebra as a mandatory course, I would still be waiting for approval.

One thing I learned in the military: If you are in command, command. If, in the minds of leftists, educational systems are purposely skewed towards preserving the power and privilege of the rich, then I say "So be it." This gives me and my follow- ers a great incentive to dramatically and drastically educate students so that the system will skew their successful future performances as they become rich and famous.

As previously mentioned, racism in any form—including the "racism of low expectations"—that is perpetrated on a student for whatever reason is hurtful because it denies the student his or her equal rights. If this action takes place in a child's formative years, it imposes severe learning disabilities that most kids will never overcome.

James Barham

You have stated that you were often viewed as a troublemaker by your administrative superiors during your time at Garfield

High. Could you tell us a little more about that? Looking back, why do you think it was so hard for your superiors to accept what you were trying to do?

Henry Gradillas

I was viewed as a "troublemaker" because I was helping Garfield to begin a growth spurt. The need for a variety of curricular materials, extended hours, summer school classes, field trips, professional speakers, etc. put a strain on the District as a whole. Take library books, for instance. The greatest pride that our library could claim was an extremely low rate of book loss or book damage.

When I asked for circulation numbers, I was amazed that the numbers were dismally low. No wonder little or no losses were reported—books were not being checked out! So, I began a campaign to order the latest books in print for high school students. Teachers were encouraged to start reading lists and make systematic use of the library with their students. More book orders, more student involvement, more money, etc.

Textbooks were a major concern. Since we only had a few algebra I classes, and fewer still in geometry, the number of books we had in these areas was not a problem. But those we had were outdated and in poor condition. As we grew in the number of students taking algebra and geometry, the need for more up-to-date books became apparent. As the physical and biological science classes grew in numbers and in advanced course offerings, so did the need for more up-to-date books increase.

In the beginning, 18 books for the AP Calculus class that Escalante fielded was an acceptable number. However, when his classes grew to over 80 students and he needed the books to be of the same caliber that the calculus students at MIT and Caltech were using, then money became a problem and

I was a "troublemaker." Imagine the horror when the number of chemistry classes rose from 1 to 17! Not only did I demand the latest chemistry books, but I also demanded up-to-date laboratory books and special laboratory equipment.

A main irritation to the District administrators was the crackdown on gang activity and severe student disciplinary problems. These actions by my school administrators caused a lot of unhappy students, parents, community activists, Latino organizations, even law enforcement officials. District officials were swamped with concerns about the methods I used in attempting to combat negative student behavior. One District administrator told me that my school was causing him more problems than any other 15 high schools combined out of the District's 49 regular high schools!

This negative reaction among many administrators to my crackdown stemmed from their belief that this was simply our students' "way of life." Poor minority kids living in the *barrio* must belong to gangs in order to survive. I should understand this and let up.

I didn't—and in 1986 both the District officials and law enforcement officers recognized Garfield High School as the school with the lowest number of expulsions, suspensions, and incidents of police intervention in the District.

Garfield had been in a coma for many years, and now it was waking up—becoming ready to learn and deliver.

James Barham

Today in 2014, Garfield High is stronger academically than when you took over—thanks largely to the foundation you and Escalante laid 30 years ago. Moreover, student participation in AP programs is reasonably high, especially in comparison with other public high schools with a similar demographic profile. However, Garfield's AP Calculus program today is only a shadow of what it used to be under your and Escalante's tenure. The sheer number of students currently taking AP calculus is about half of what it was at the height of Escalante's tenure, and the pass rate is much lower.

Specifically, in 1987, when Escalante's AP calculus courses were operating at full throttle, 127 Garfield students took the AP Calculus test. Of these, 73 passed the AB calculus advanced placement test and 12 passed the more rigorous BC advanced placement test. Yet in 2013, even though 72 took the AB test, only 20 passed, and of the 7 who took the BC test, only 2 passed. These numbers speak for themselves, suggesting that a once thriving program is now languishing. We regard this as a tragedy, and it is very hard to accept how it could happen. How did it happen?

Henry Gradillas

After six years as principal of Garfield, I found that I had accomplished most of what I wanted to do. I felt that 6 to 8 years at the helm was a sufficient amount of time to get the job done. I moved on because I needed to finish my doctorate, and also because the powers-that-be felt they would be better served if I were to troubleshoot somewhere else ... or maybe not.

Part of my reason for starting a doctoral program at that age was to show my students that education is ongoing. One should never stop learning and should continue to be a contributing individual. The following year after I had received my doctorate, I was afforded the privilege of addressing the graduating class at Garfield. I attended the ceremonies with much pride. Just prior to my opening remarks, I made the following statement to the graduating students: "It is never too late to learn. The education learned through the doctoral program will help me in the years ahead." Pointing to the stripes on the sleeves of my doctoral gown, I told them: "These stripes are for you. They should encourage you to continue your education, no matter what." A tremendous ovation ensued.

After I left, Escalante lost a lot of his support, which made it very difficult for him to remain at Garfield. He finally moved to another school district. To keep the ball of academic success rolling and even gathering speed, outstanding programs that are working well must be nurtured continually. The push for academic excellence will always create new challenges and be subject to certain criticisms. Successful programs are expensive to maintain and they can interfere with the daily operations of a school, no matter how hard one tries to avoid friction.

The word "elitism" has been used many times to point out that the special few are being treated in ways that offend or take away from the rest of the student body. Teachers who teach honors and AP programs are sometimes criticized for having it easy because of the high quality of the students in their classes. That is why I initially spread the gifted, high, and low achievers, as well as other students, among all teachers. That way, teachers could teach classes that ranged in academic levels.

If the push for academic excellence is not forthcoming, or maintained by administrators, then strong academic programs will fail to materialize and progress.

James Barham

After you and Escalante left Garfield, did you ever have an opportunity to recreate the success you had there? Or was everything you did after that a distant second? As you look at the last 30 years in America public education, is there any example that you can point to of disadvantaged kids at poorly performing schools seeing as dramatic a turn-around as the kids at Garfield saw in the 1980s? Is the "Golden Age" at Garfield a unique event? Does it need to be a unique event?

Henry Gradillas

After leaving Garfield, I had the opportunity of working with the State Superintendent of Schools in Sacramento. In this position I was able to assist those schools that were having problems in the very same areas as were found in Garfield. However, poor school climate, a mediocre method used for the delivery of instruction, and a curriculum that was ineffective made it difficult for me to be understood by school administrators and teachers. I did all I could to help the schools improve. In my two years as trouble-shooter for the state of California, I visited many schools, K–12, and managed to set up programs that became effective.

Two years later, I was offered the position as principal of Birmingham High School, part of the Los Angeles District. Birmingham was a school in transition. I did not waste any time in making an evaluation of the educational program at the school. I identified problems that had to be addressed. I held meetings with administrators, department heads, and teachers' union representatives. I addressed major concerns, established priorities, and assessed (and altered where appropriate) job responsibilities.

The school climate was in poor shape: Gangs had claimed territory and fights between gangs were prevalent. Students who were not in class roamed the campus. I made a statement in one of my meetings that if the bells signaling the start and end of classes were not being used for their intended purpose, we should stop ringing them and go on the clock.

What took me three years to accomplish at Garfield I did it in half the time at Birmingham. The school was located in an affluent, middle-class community. Most of the students were white with local Black and Hispanic students attending. However, as part of the District's integration program and because South Central schools in the District were at capacity,

Birmingham and other Valley schools began accepting minority students in a large busing program.

The student population at Birmingham grew very rapidly and so did the problems brought about by such an increase in the number of low-socioeconomic, minority students—nothing new to me! Algebra became a standard course. Campus violence decreased dramatically, giving way to a safe and orderly school climate.

Now, about the AP program. At one point, I asked the counselor in charge of the school's curriculum and AP programs to give me the total number of students taking AP classes and those planning on taking the AP college exams. I was surprised to learn that a school like Birmingham only had 256 students taking AP classes. When I asked how many students were taking AP Spanish language or AP Spanish literature, I was shocked to learn that only a handful of students were taking the class and that of those, only 10 were signed up to take the exam.

I then informed the counselor that she should immediately sign up 100 students to take the AP Spanish language exam. She became very defensive, letting me know that it would be difficult for her to find the students. I told her that it would not be that difficult, all she had to do was to interview the students with dark complexions and she would easily get the 100 students. All of the students she signed up took and passed the AP test with a maximum score of 5. During my tenure at Birmingham, the number of students taking AP exams increased from 256 to 550.

The formula that had worked so well at Garfield worked just as well at Birmingham in even less time.

James Barham

Finally, what is your parting advice for how concerned citizens can help you in your work and aspirations? How can we help to persuade fellow citizens who are stuck in old ways of thinking that your approach to education is the last best hope for this country? In short, what will it take to recreate your success at Garfield High in every public school system across this great land? Can the Gradillas-Escalante-Garfield Golden Age happen again?

Henry Gradillas

You ask: "What will it take to recreate your success at Garfield High in every public school system across this great land?"

In order to recreate previous successes in education, one must realize that the *status quo* is not acceptable and recognize that problems and shortcomings exist. I believe that America's relatively low standing in numerous global assessments is beginning to bring it home to many people that this country is falling behind in many academic subject areas. Recent published reports state that US high school students test far below the minimum standards of most industrialized nations. Even students in a few underdeveloped countries score higher in mathematics than US students.

Government officials, educators, and the public in general must recognize the severe problems our country faces in its failure to adequately educate its youth. Strong measures must be taken to ensure that all kids get the best possible education. We all must demand and push for academic excellence if our country is going to compete in global markets.

It is ironic that during the past 60 years this country has seen tremendous progress in the fields of medicine, electronics, communication and transportation, science and technology, and in space exploration, but has failed to adequately educate its youth. The so-called "Gradillas-Escalante-Garfield Golden Age" can and must happen again—*if* we have the *ganas* to do it, and do it right. [Editor's note: In Spanish, *ganas* means "burning desire" or "fire in the belly."]

James Barham

Thank you very much for sharing your valuable time and extraordinary insights with us.

Appendix 3: Angelo Villavicencio Interview

Angelo Villavicencio is a mathematics teacher who worked with Jaime Escalante in the famous AP Calculus program at Garfield High School in East Los Angeles during the late 1980s.

Escalante—together with colleagues Villavicencio and Ben Jimenez, as well as school principal, Henry Gradillas—created an AP Calculus program at Garfield High that enjoyed an unprecedented degree of success.

At the program's height in 1987, a total of 85 Garfield students passed the two AP Calculus exams—the best result of any high school in the state of California. The accomplishments of the Escalante team came to the attention of an international audience through the 1988 film Stand and Deliver.

Villavicencio went on to establish a similarly successful AP Calculus program at Don Antonio Lugo High School in Chino, California. Villavicencio has also taught calculus to barrio students at East Los Angeles College (ELAC) for many years.

Born in Nicaragua as Angel, his name was changed to Angelo when a teacher at the English-language prep school he attended thought "Angel" was a girl's name and insisted he go by "Angelo."

In 2015, James Barham interviewed Angelo Villavicencio for an online forum. Even though this interview has long since disappeared from the live web and search engines, it contains a wealth of information and insights that complement this book. Below is a lightly edited version of the original interview.

The Interview

James Barham

In this interview, we want to hear of your personal involvement with the famous AP Calculus program at Garfield High during the late 1980s that was so movingly depicted in the film *Stand and Deliver*. But we are even more interested in hearing about how you were then able to repeat that success at a different high school a few years afterwards. We believe it is critical that the educational approach that your team developed at Garfield High and that you implemented at Don Lugo High be more widely followed in America today.

However, before we ask you about those important matters, we would first like to hear about your own personal story. When and where were you born? What sort of family and wider social environment did you grow up in? How did you first become interested in mathematics? How did you become a teacher? Please share with us anything about your educational background and life story that you think readers will find helpful.

Angelo Villavicencio

I was born in Managua, Nicaragua, in 1950. I grew up in a single-parent family of six. My father left us when I was nine years of age and my mother took care of us until she abruptly died in an automobile accident when I was 16 years of age. Her sisters took us into their homes and took care of us. My oldest brother and two of my sisters were already living in California when this event took place.

From pre-Kindergarten through 2nd grade I attended public schools, and from 3rd grade until graduation I attended a private school, the La Salle Institute for Men, in Managua. At least 25 percent of its students were from the upper class, 50 percent from middle class and the remainder had scholarships. I was one of the ones with a scholarship.

I grew up in a barrio which offered a great variety of street-wise learning and personal freedom since my mother was a single mom and had to work hard to support us. Her whole family was well-off—upper middle class—a fact that enabled me and my other brothers to process and utilize the value of education very well.

In 1970, I came to California to live with my brother. I started working and attended California State University at Los Angeles. I have to admit that I have always loved learning and going to school. School was a playground for me. Even though my physics and calculus teacher in high school completely disliked me, to the point of bombarding me with insults and humiliations, I always preserved this love for knowledge. Thus my attraction, first to teaching philosophy, and then to mathematics.

My awakening as a teacher came during my first two years of teaching at Griffith Junior High School in East Los Angeles, beginning in 1979. I was making a big impact in my students' lives. My classes were scoring the highest at this school on the District test. I was enjoying the communion with these kids. I learned about the humanity involved in teaching poor and minority barrio youngsters. How much discrimination, apathy, and condemnation existed toward these adolescents!

True, they had all sorts of problems and educational deficiencies, but they all had a beautiful mind and the right to an education—a proper education, the one that was demanded from the District, and more. I worked with them regardless of their backgrounds and deficiencies. They needed my dedication and support, as well as discipline, tough love, and a structured learning environment.

I have been married for 40 years to Kerube and we have two sons, Ali and Adyr. The fact that my commitment and dedication to my teaching profession have been exemplary is due in no small part to my wife's patience, support, and love. As a side note, my sons were part of the Escalante Program, first as students and then as teacher's assistants. They indeed experienced the thrill and enthusiasm of participating in this program.

James Barham

How did you first become involved with Jaime Escalante and the AP Calculus program at Garfield High? How did you get to know Escalante and what gave you the confidence to come on board with him?

Angelo Villavicencio

As I have already mentioned, I was teaching at Griffith Junior High, which fed all its students to Garfield High. One day, one of my ex-students—a Garfield student named Sara Sanchez—came to see me after school. Sara talked to me about Jaime Escalante, whom everyone called "Kemo." Sara said she wished I could meet Kemo, since she claimed that he and I taught in a similar way. I accepted Sara's invitation, and she arranged for a meeting between us.

When I went to see Mr. Escalante, we chatted for half an hour. Right on the spot, he told me that I had to come to Garfield and be part of his program there. This was in 1983. My desire to be part of such a program was reinforced by the fact that I was developing my own at Griffith Junior High. At Griffith, we were about to start teaching Algebra II.

I finally moved to Garfield in 1987. My involvement with Mr. Escalante and his program enabled me to see a world containing a wealth of educational possibilities which were accessible to all barrio kids and youngsters, given that they internalized and believed the concept of *ganas* (meaning, in English, a burning desire to succeed).

Most of these students were not challenged and motivated. Stereotyping them as Latinos (or, in general, as "minorities") was the rule, not the exception. I truly and deeply believed, and still do, that everybody has a beautiful mind and that our moral responsibility as educators is to inspire students to develop their minds and not waste them. Furthermore, I believe that education is the answer to generate this development.

James Barham

What was it like to be a part of Garfield's AP calculus program? Did you realize at the time that you were involved in something historic—both highly unusual and potentially very important? Why do you think the program worked as well as it did?

Angelo Villavicencio

The movie *Stand and Deliver* was being edited when I arrived at Garfield in 1987. My association with Mr. Escalante, witnessing how much success he and his programs had achieved, instilled a sense of pride in me and I felt I belonged to the program. The students' achievements were tangible and their academic development reaffirmed in me, once and for all, what I had always believed: If the right educational environment is given to every child, his/her intelligence and world perception are going to blossom and the desire for learning will captivate their minds.

The students were motivated and inspired to believe in themselves and understand that success comes from hard work, discipline, and determination. I could sense the pride and joy the students had from being part of this program and from being part of Garfield High School. History was being made in the USA—the largest numbers of Hispanic barrio kids were enrolled in an AP Calculus Program and, best of all, many of them were going on to four-year universities, including Ivy League Schools.

The program worked well because:

- The teachers, counselors, and administrators believed in their students' potential.
- They were motivated and caring.
- The program was supported by most of Garfield's faculty and non-faculty staff.
- The program had a key sponsor for the summer and through the academic year: East Los Angeles College (ELAC), which provided the program with facilities and financial support.
- Success was breeding success, which is I believe why the program blossomed: Based on its own merits and recognition, it inspired more students to be a part of it and all of its members to be proud of it.

James Barham

Can you describe for our readers the difference between the calculus AB and the calculus BC advanced placement exam? Did you and the other AP calculus teachers at Garfield prepare the students who took the BC exam prepared differently those who took the AB exam? How did the students who took the two exams differ?

Angelo Villavicencio

Calculus AB deals with limits, derivatives, and its applications, such as finding global extrema, instantaneous rates of change, and motion along a line. Furthermore, it also deals with the definite integral and its applications, such as areas bounded by curves in the xy-plane, in the polar plane, solids of revolution, length of curves, net changes, and differential equations and their applications to growth and decay.

Calculus BC, besides including all the AB Calculus topics, also deals with improper integrals, l'Hôpital's Rule, infinite series, parametric equations, polar curves, and vectors. The students taking Calculus BC are subjected to a more rigid and faster pace than those in AB.

James Barham

According to Henry Gradillas, Garfield's principal from 1981 to 1987, not just AP calculus but also AP courses across the board were seeing increasing student interest and success. Could you describe the synergistic effect of having a spate of AP courses at Garfield that students got excited about and in which they strove to excel?

Angelo Villavicencio

You know the saying, "Success breeds success." This was totally confirmed and reinforced by how the AP Calculus programs induced and motivated students to take other AP classes at Garfield High School. Furthermore, this led the instructional staff to create brand-new AP classes, such as AP Physics, AP Biology, and AP Economics.

In fact, one of my students (Daniel Castro) went to ELAC to finish the calculus series (multivariable calculus), and while he was there, he decided to take a differential equations class.

From there, he moved on to MIT, where he got a B.S. and an M.S. in Electrical Engineering. Thereafter, he got a Law degree from UC Berkeley. Daniel now owns his own tech-patent firm.

James Barham

How much of a difference did it make in students' lives and career success that they took AP calculus with you and did well on the exam? Please give us some examples of success stories that you personally witnessed and speculate, if you would, about what might have happened to some of these students if they had not been given the opportunity to excel academically in your calculus program.

Angelo Villavicencio

The Escalante program, as well as the entire AP program at Garfield, created a deep sense of pride and belonging to the school and in East Los Angeles. In fact, until this day, all those students speak and identify themselves with pride and joy when they are asked about their high school. In my 32 years as a mathematics teacher , I never saw the kind of excitement and pride among students that I experienced at Garfield. Those students discovered that they had a beautiful mind, that they were intelligent, and that a new world was outside waiting to be explored using their educational skills.

I believe that most of them, for the first time, understood and accepted the value of education. They discovered that they possessed the greatest gift in life—a beautiful mind. This fact alone gave the students the hope for a better life. It allowed them to recreate new perspectives and different life goals. I truly believe that a majority of these students are now professionals and doing much better than they would have otherwise.

James Barham

When the film *Stand and Deliver* came out, how did that impact the program? How did it affect you personally? What did you like about the film? Is there anything in it that you would have changed?

Angelo Villavicencio

When the movie *Stand and Deliver* came out, there was a euphoric explosion at Garfield. I believe it brought a new hope and excitement to barrio and ghetto schools. It lifted the spirit of education and reaffirmed those who believed in what the students could accomplish—that they were on the right path.

Furthermore, to those teachers who were about to quit, it brought a new light, a new way to approach teaching, a new hope. All kinds of people—educators, politicians and civilians —came to Garfield to witness the miracle-worker, Jaime Escalante. They wanted to meet him, and talk about his story and the success of the program.

Some educators were serious about replicating the Escalante Program at their schools. Some were very successful, especially one school in Texas (though I do not recall its name). Our program grew sky high. Kids were inspired. Some teachers were astonished at how our AP Program grew and how much enthusiasm prevailed at Garfield. Yet, there was a certain amount of jealousy at Garfield about the program, too.

I had never, as an educator, been part of this type of phenomenon. It was euphoria. I was elated to see the students who enrolled in our summer program staying with it and finishing it. I was naturally high on it—so high that I became the biggest cheerleader of the program. I was recruiting most of my students to our summer program and going around all other math classes in my building, giving the students inspirational talks.

The movie *Stand and Deliver* meant a whole lot to me and made me feel proud of its message: Care about your students, inspire and motivate them, assume nothing, and work with them, be creative, improvise, and above all recognize their humanity. They deserve better, they deserve to have a chance to go after what this world has to offer, and education is the best way to allow them to have a taste of it.

If I had been a producer of the film, I would have included an interview with Mr. Escalante filled with relevant questions about his program. At the end of the movie, people needed to see the real "Kemo" and what it took to create a program like his.

James Barham

When and why did you leave Garfield? Did you regret leaving? Could you describe what was happening at Garfield between the time *Stand and Deliver* came out and when you finally left Garfield? In particular, what was happening to AP calculus at Garfield during that time? What has happened to that program since?

Angelo Villavicencio

I left Garfield High School in June of 1992. Maria Tostado, the principal, made clear to me that she did not want any Escalante legacy at Garfield. She had brought her own team of teachers and believed that they were better than any of Escalante's team.

I had 110 calculus AP students in two classes. I requested the opening of a third class, so I could have smaller classes and so achieve better connections with my students. Mrs. Tostado denied my request. I was fortunate that I took over Mr. Escalante's classroom, which had 65 desks. Hence, I was able to have 50+ students per class. In fact, since Garfield High School became a year-round school, Mrs. Tostado was going to take away my classroom and give it to the other Calculus teacher (the one she had hired).

She tried her best to get rid of any Escalante legacy and she succeeded. She had a new vision for the program. The years went by, the AP enrollment fell, and the euphoria vanished. The program became a shadow of what it once had been.

I went back in 1995, after much urging from Mr. Dallas Russell (a teacher who worked in our program), to see Mr. Diaz, the new principal at Garfield at that time who had replaced Mrs. Tostado. We offered our help and stated our desire to come to work at Garfield so the program could be regenerated. We had the whole-hearted support of ELAC teachers Mr. George Madrid and Mr. Paul Powers, who were in charge of the Escalante Program in that institution.

However, Mr. Diaz was quite clear with us. He stated that he did not want any part of Escalante's legacy and that Garfield was doing well.

I therefore closed the book on Garfield and decided to create my own program at Don Antonio Lugo High School, in Chino, California. The program at Don Lugo did great because the required pieces and elements were there: support from the principal and a teacher who believed in the program, plenty of communication among its members, and academic flexibility.

James Barham

What were the circumstances that led to your being given the chance to repeat the success of the Garfield AP Calculus program at Don Lugo High School?

Angelo Villavicencio

When I went to work at Don Lugo, a similar culture existed to the one that used to exist at Garfield. Fifty percent of the students at Lugo were Hispanic and most of them were in the lower math classes. In fact, the only calculus class that existed was a class of 24, with only two Latinos—the rest were Asian and whites.

My success at Don Lugo was due to many factors. First, when you are part of a successful program like the one at Garfield, you are either just a passive part of it or you internalize its success by learning the program components and what drives its success. I did that, and this enabled me to transfer my knowledge to the math program at Don Lugo.

But best of all, I had the benefit of working with one of the best partners I've ever had, Mr. Blair Bradfor, the chair of the math department at Don Lugo. During my teaching years at Ayala High School in the City of Chino Hills, Mr. Bradfor kept challenging me to come to Don Lugo and create a program like Mr. Escalante's at Garfield.

He believed in the Escalante program's success and identified me as the necessary ingredient to generate a successful math program at Don Lugo. Mr. Bradfor's frankness, honesty, willingness to cooperate, and care for the students were unbelievable.

Mr. Bradfor and I also had the approval and full support of Don Lugo's principal, Mr. Cisneros, and his team. Mr. Cisneros promised me all the support required to put this program in motion.

His word and Mr. Bradfor's sincerity prevailed. I transferred to Don Lugo in 1995.

James Barham

Please tell us some more details about the program you put together at Don Lugo and its achievements. In what ways did you alter and improve on the approach that you and your colleagues had previously used at Garfield?

Angelo Villavicencio

Don Lugo was considered the worst high school in Chino. To make matters worse, there were some bureaucrats in the District office who did not believe or approve of what we were doing. However, Mr. Rossi, the Interim Superintendent, was totally excited about our program and gave us his support.

I took over the ESL classes and the Calculus class. Mr. Bradfor taught Algebra II, both the regular and the honors course, as well as Trig/Pre-Calculus. We had the components, and a pipeline was created. Our students were inspired and the right teachers were there to make sure they were taught properly and were offered any after-school assistance. Then, ELAC began to make a summer school program available to us: Algebra I, Algebra II, Trigonometry, and Trig/Pre-Calculus. Calculus AB was added later on.

The first summer, in the year 1996, I decided to teach a Trig/Pre-Calculus class (without pay) during the afternoons at Don Lugo High. I had about 18 students willing to do it and 12 of them were ESL. I had to do it so I could have a second calculus class the following academic year.

Mr. Cisneros spoke to the District Superintendent, Mr. Mike Rossi so that I could use the facilities for six weeks, Monday through Friday, from 1:00 pm to 6:30 pm. I strongly believed that a second calculus class was going to persuade and inspire other students to study harder and be able to enroll in a Calculus class later on.

They came. By the year 2000, we had four Calculus AB classes and one Calculus BC. Almost 60 percent of the students were Hispanics and 60 percent of the students in the program were females. This achievement was obtained with the coordination of the Administration and my colleagues in the Math Department, especially Mr. Bradfor, who was the biggest cheerleader of the program.

Mr. Bradfor and I talked every day. We evaluated our needs and came up with solutions. The students' weaknesses were addressed—academic improvement was on the way. We were fused together and there was a great respect and admiration for each other. Mr. Bradfor was the best colleague I have ever worked with!

I involved every member of the Math Department, and I asked them for their opinions and praised their work. I asked Mr. Cisneros to come to our Department meeting from time to time and praise the teachers for their good work. Mr. Bradfor had been at Don Lugo for 20-plus years. He knew the District policies, structure, and politics we needed to work with. But best of all, we had Mr. Cisneros's full support. He went to bat for us all the time. We generated success year after year. The enthusiasm was there and, just like Garfield, the whole AP Program at Don Lugo grew and new classes were created.

The program at Don Lugo grew so fast that by 2000 we had 140 students enrolled. Yet, I left Don Lugo because the District refused to accredit me six extra years of experience which I brought from Los Angeles. I acknowledge this was the biggest mistake I made as a teacher; however, I was proud of the fact that 60 percent of the calculus program at Don Lugo was made up of females and that 40 percent of the students in the program overall were Hispanic.

In the year 2000, the College Board acknowledged the success of the program and honored me, through the Siemens Foundation, as an Outstanding Calculus Teacher in the Nation.

I left Don Lugo High School the following year because the Chino Valley District did not want to recognize the extra seven years of experience I had when I transferred from the Los Angeles Unified School District. The program took a nosedive.

When I returned, Mr. Cisneros and Mr. Bradfor had left the school. After that, the program never went over 100 students, even though it had three Calculus AB and one BC. My team was gone, my academic flexibility was repressed with new testing (STAR—Standardized Testing and Reporting), and there were forces in the District office which kept fighting the program.

James Barham

It is widely believed that Escalante's time at Garfield was a "golden age" that has never been, and perhaps never could be, repeated. Please speak to the possibility of not just repeating but extending the successes seen at Garfield in the 1980s. What would it take for Garfield's success to be not just an outlier event but something common? Indeed, for the benefit of high school students everywhere in the US, it would be great if were common!

Angelo Villavicencio

As long as the fate of education is dictated by bureaucrats and politicians, the success of *Stand and Deliver* will be hard to repeat. The purity, the tenacity, the caring, the commitment, the expertise, and hard work of those teachers who thrive and dream for the success of students, ultimately depended on the character of the teachers, students, and administrators. There was room to improvise, to be creative, and to follow a logical path with the curriculum in place; but also to exchange ideas and make adjustments, to promote education, and make the students true believers.

Teachers need to be preachers. Their message should be illustrated with examples of the successes of students from the barrio and the ghetto. The AP Program undoubtedly measures students' knowledge and intelligence. All throughout the nation, it is a common denominator.

Speaking for myself, the success achieved through this program justifies the amount of freedom and creativity needed to implement it. It showed that anybody could be part of it and succeed. Barrio and ghetto schools need this program. But it has to be legitimated with the right teachers: true believers and hard-core missionaries.

James Barham

Henry Gradillas, then-principal of Garfield High, played a crucial role in the success of Escalante's program. Indeed, the extraordinary thing that happened at Garfield was at least partly the result of a synergy between a remarkable group of teachers and a school administration that was willing to go out on a limb to give them institutional support.

If that is so, then we imagine the administration at Don Lugo supported your efforts in a similar way. Is that right? If it is, please tell us how the Don Lugo administration enabled you to be effective. What are the lessons here? What do you want to see from a school administration to help its teachers be as effective as possible?

Angelo Villavicencio

The administration needs to support new teachers, assist them in any way possible, and place them with a veteran partner to make sure they evolve into good teachers. The principal has to visit the new teacher's classroom unannounced many times to see the teacher's true character.

The principal should send master teachers, within the same field of study, to observe, assist, and coach the new teacher, and make sure he or she follows through on the master teacher's recommendations.

When there is good chemistry between students and a new teacher, the administration should do their very best to support these teachers and help them to develop their skills. Special teachers do not come in bundles!

James Barham

We would now like to give you the opportunity to summarize your educational philosophy for the benefit of our readers. We all know that something is very wrong with public education in this country, but there is little agreement about what needs to be done about it.

What, in your view, are the most important factors in your success at Garfield and at Don Lugo? Do you believe that these factors, if implemented on a large scale, could make a real difference in the real lives of disadvantaged people in this country?

Angelo Villavicencio

I taught in the barrios of East Los Angeles for 13 years, and in the suburbs of Chino, California—which has a little barrio (Chino Center, the oldest part of the city)—for 17-1/2 years. I also taught at Ayala High School in Chino Hills, where most of the students were white and Asian.

I was successful everywhere because I was, and still am, a true preacher of education. I believe that education invites the mind to explore, to discover, to understand, and to translate new knowledge into undiscovered and unimaginable frontiers. Through education, we discover a new self and a new world perspectives.

I believe that the greatest personal gift we possess is our minds—the greatest asset in our lives. I believe that it is our moral obligation as educators to deliver this message to our students, and to make sure they internalize it.

I challenged them to believe in a better life by educating themselves. I believe that the ingredients to achieve such success are based on determination, discipline, and hard work. I called it *ganas*, which to me means "THE DESIRE TO SUCCEED."

The most important factors that contributed to my success at Garfield and Don Lugo were:

- Academic flexibility with the curriculum;

- Complete support from the administrators and staff;
- A summer program in place to bring academic advancement;
- And, most essential of all, educators who have the passion to teach the required knowledge of the subject, and the caring and the commitment necessary to elevate their students to another level.

It takes a team a long time to build up such a program, yet one administrator can demolish it in no time. With the proper administrative support, this kind of program could function well in any of the barrio or ghetto schools in this country.

James Barham
Any final thoughts you would like to share with our readers? What is your biggest hope for American education?

Angelo Villavicencio
Our students are the future of our country.

There are students who know they have the talent, and could eventually develop it if they wanted to. Yet, they need to be motivated, to be given the best educational tools, and to be exposed to role models—that is, to successful individuals —so they can appreciate the beauty of their own minds and their potential. Teachers need to persuade students to believe in themselves.

Students need to be made aware of the unimaginable essence that the mind has.

I do hope that through education our professionals, technicians, and all the people in our country will learn to appreciate our planet and our human condition a bit more. We all need to think as human beings living together on one planet.

The blue planet is all we have.

Appendix 4: Ben Carson Interview

Ben Carson, M.D., is a world-famous pediatric neuro-surgeon and professor of medicine (now retired from Johns Hopkins Hospital and the Johns Hopkins School of Medicine), the author or co-author of multiple books, a recipient of the Presidential Medal of Freedom, and a former Secretary of Housing and Urban Development. He is the co-founder, with his wife Candy, of the Carson Scholars Fund, an initiative that reflects his educational philosophy.

This is the transcript of an interview with Ben Carson that took place at an annual awards banquet of the Carson Scholars Fund (May 24, 2015 in Pittsburgh). James Barham conducted the interview. The interview was posted for a time on an educational website but eventually removed for business reasons because it did not fit with the website's marketing model. In this interview, Barham and Carson have a poignant and insightful conversation about education that is as relevant today as it was when it took place ten years ago. Some light copyedits have been made for readability and timeliness.

1. Education & Success

James Barham:

Dr. Carson, thank you very much for agreeing to this interview. It is an honor for us to be able to share your thoughts on education with our readers.

Ben Carson:

I'm delighted. Thank you.

James Barham:

Despite growing up poor in Detroit, you became a gifted pediatric neurosurgeon and professor of medicine at a world-renowned institution, Johns Hopkins University. What were the key points in your education that led to this remarkable success?

Ben Carson:

Well, the big thing was, I was not a very good student. My mother, who only had a third-grade education, always had a feeling that education was important. She worked as a domestic, cleaning people's houses. She noticed that those people who were very successful did a lot of reading. They didn't sit around watching TV a lot. And, after praying for wisdom, she came up with this idea: that *we* needed to be readers, and we needed to watch much less television. Now, my brother and I weren't all that enthusiastic about that idea, needless to say. But in those days you had to do what your parents told you! So, we had to read the books.

And, I've got to say, after a while, I actually began to enjoy it. We were very poor, but between the covers of those books I could go anywhere. I could do anything. I could be anybody. I began to know *amazing* things. I used be so enamored of the smart kids because they knew so much. But all of a sudden, I knew stuff that they didn't know! And I said: "The reason for that is because you're reading. It got to the point where my mother didn't have to make me read—she was saying, "Benjamin, put the book down and eat your food!" I was always reading.

And it really changed the trajectory of my life. Even later on, when I got to high school, and a lot of times the teachers were not able to teach because they spent the whole hour disciplining people. By that time, I was firmly into getting a good education, so I would go back after school, talk to my teachers, and say, "What were you *planning* on teaching?" They would always look forward to seeing me and knowing that they could share their lesson plan with somebody. I got a lot of extra tutoring. So, even though I was in an inner-city high school that wasn't known for academics, I was able to get the kind of preparation that allowed me to get through Yale University.

2. Is Homework Too Demanding?

James Barham:

You have noted that in the 1800s, even people with only a grade-school education were well educated by today's standards. As watered down as the curriculum is by comparison with former times, some professional educators argue it is still too demanding, and thus "unfair" to minority and poor students. For example, one vice principal of our acquaintance thinks that homework should be abolished for the sake of inner-city, mostly African-American grade schoolers. What would you say to her?

Ben Carson:

I would say that probably is a very archaic attitude: to believe that African-American students cannot achieve at a high level. There was a school that I visited in Dallas. The principal, Roscoe Smith, had been assigned there. It was the worst school in the Dallas area in terms of standardized testing. Terrible area, a lot of crime, teen pregnancy, etc. He went in there and he started cleaning up the graffiti and telling the students, "This is your school." He got them involved. They had a little bit of pride in what was going on. He taught them slogans, such as "Obey your parents." Always he ended with "Obey your parents."

That perked up the ears of the parents, many of whom were not high-school graduates. But he wanted them to come to the school because he had programs designed to help *them* to learn, so that they could then in turn get more interested in what their children were doing. But the most important thing he did is this: he went out to the Dallas community, and he found people who came out of *that* neighborhood who were successful. He said, "I want you to come to my school. Just give me an hour's notice—I'll have all the kids in the auditorium. Tell them what you did. Tell them how you did it." And he had a lot of people coming in there. Long story short: within a space of three years, they went from the bottom in the state in standardized testing to third from the top.

So, can they learn? Of course they can learn!

James Barham:
Of course they can.

Ben Carson:
But you have to provide the correct environment.

James Barham:
You think that homework is a part of that environment?

Ben Carson:
Of course it is. You know, you need to set the bar a lot higher. The expectations need to be much, much higher. People will rise to expectations or they will lower themselves to expectations.

3. The Role of Discipline in Education

James Barham:

In the same inner-city school district, it was recently forbidden to discipline students for such "minor" infractions as talking loudly during class, walking around the room, swearing at the teacher, even throwing objects across the room. What are your views on the place of discipline in establishing a classroom atmosphere conducive to learning?

Ben Carson:

Well, obviously, discipline is necessary for children. Training is necessary for children. Just like if you want to train a vine, you have to apply physical manipulation to get it to go where you want it to go, but as it learns, then you don't have to do that. And I think it's one of the reasons that a lot of people are opting for alternatives to the public school system, because you have so many progressives with this mindset that somehow all you've got to do is let the kids express themselves, and everything will be great.

But that just doesn't work. And so, that's one of the reasons that I push the whole idea of school choice and vouchers—to give people an opportunity to get out of those situations where their child is not likely to learn. You've probably noticed (you see it on television all the time): a new charter school is opening in one of the inner cities, and you've got lines and lines of people trying to get their kid in there.

4. Reading, Books, and Learning

James Barham:

You frequently recount how your mother made you and your brother turn off the television and read two books a week. You then had to submit book reports to her, which she pretended to read and grade. In a similar way, you challenge young people today to turn off not only the TV, but also their computers, iPhones, and other electronic gadgets, and pick up a good book. What do you regard as the benefits of reading books? And how would you distinguish the sustained reading required by books from the fidgety reading characteristic of electronic technologies?

Ben Carson:

Well, you know, our society has changed quite a bit. Before I retired, I noticed a lot of parents were coming to me, saying, "Should we put our kids on this [drug], because they've been diagnosed with Attention Deficit Disorder?" You know, that used to be a *rare* thing, and now it's like every fourth kid. And I'd ask them a couple of questions: I said, "Can they watch a movie?" "Oh yeah, they can watch movies all day." "OK. Can they play video games?" "All day and all night." I said, "They don't have ADD." I said, "Here's what I want you to do: wean them off that stuff and substitute time with you, reading a book and discussing it. And then let's talk about it in three months."

Almost to a person, they would come back and say "it's a different kid." Why? Because nowadays as soon as a kid can sit up, we prop them in front of the TV. And what do you see? Zip, zip, zip; zoom, zoom, zoom. As soon as they get a little older, and they have some dexterity, we give them the controls for the video games. Zip, zip, zip; zoom, zoom, zoom. Now they're in school, there's a teacher up front, not turning to something every few seconds. You think they're going to pay attention?

Their brain is on "super zoom," so they're not going to pay attention. You've got to slow it back down, and get it to a point where it can now grasp and digest the material. And you'll find that reading is actually much more entertaining than the electronic media because you have to use your imagination to *create* the scenery, and you can create it the way you want, and it's really a lot more fun. You've just got to slow them down long enough to get them involved in doing that.

5. What Happened to Respect for Education?

James Barham:

In your book, *One Nation,* you write movingly of the respect that your mother and other members of the African-American community in Detroit while you were growing up had for education. We can confirm that this was a common attitude among poor white folks as well, at least up until the 1960s.

What happened? Why, generally speaking, is that respect for education no longer there among poor people, black or white? And what can we do to restore it?

Ben Carson:

One of the things that really began to happen in a big way in the '60s, which hadn't been going on before, is that we began to really *idolize* sports stars and entertainers—lifestyles of the rich and famous. And those things became much more important to us than the scientist and the doctor and the professor and people who utilize intellect in order to achieve things. And this is not to say that no one in sports or entertainment is intellectual, but that's not the aspect of their lives that's emphasized.

And consequently, you've got so many of these young boys running around—for instance, in the inner city—thinking that they're going to be the next Michael Jordan, or the next Michael Jackson, or somebody. I mean, if you can do that, and people are paying you millions and millions of dollars, you'll think to yourself, "Why do I need to bother with algebra, grammar, and all this stuff? I don't need to do that. I can buy and sell any school that I want."

But what they don't realize is only seven in one million will make it as a starter in the NBA. One in ten thousand will have a successful career in entertainment. So, your odds are not very good. Less than one percent of people who go to college on an athletic scholarship end up playing professional sports—and if you do end up playing, your average career span is three and a half years. So, we need to reorient people in terms of what real success is all about.

6. What is the Carson Scholars Fund?

James Barham:

The Carson Scholars fund gives awards to exceptional students and sets up reading rooms across the country. Could you give us an overview of this organization, especially how you came to start it and your aspirations for it? What are some of the success stories of the Carson Scholars Fund?

Ben Carson:

I would go into schools, and I would all see all these trophies: All-State Basketball, All-State Wrestling, State Baseball Champions. But there was never any hoopla about the *academic* superstars. At the same time, I was aware of many international studies that showed us languishing near the bottom of the list in terms of achievement—particularly in STEM areas.

My wife and I became concerned, and we said, "We have to do something about this." So, we started 19 years ago giving out Scholar awards to children starting in the fourth grade for superior academic performance *and* demonstration of humanitarian qualities. They had to show that they cared about other people because we didn't want people who were just smart but also selfish. We're trying to establish the leadership for this country going down the road.

Now, we have over 6,700 Scholar awards given out in all 50 states and the District of Columbia. The program has won several national awards like the Ronald McDonald House of Charity Award (only one organization a year) and the Simon Award (one organization per year). Both of these come with six-figure checks. But obviously we don't do it for the rewards —we do it for what *happens*.

You know, the teachers tell us that in many cases the GPA of the whole class goes up over the next year because now it's not *just* the quarterback, or the baseball player, that everybody wants to be like. It's the scholar who has brought to their school this big, fancy-looking trophy that sits right out there with all the sports trophies. And the kids get to wear a medal. They go to a special banquet like the one that we're out here for today. We try to put them on the same kind of pedestal as we do the athletes.

As far as the reading rooms are concerned, we put them in all over the country, in lots of different kinds of places. But especially we target Title I schools, where a lot of the kids come from. Homes with no books. They go to a school with no library (or a poorly furnished library). They're not going to develop a love for reading. The problem is, 70 to 80 percent of high school dropouts are functionally illiterate.

So, we're trying to truncate that downstream, so that we don't get into that problem. We change the trajectory of their lives. And in most of the schools where we have our reading rooms, the teachers will tell you that the kids absolutely love going to the reading rooms. They're decorated in ways that no kid could possibly pass up. Frequently, it reflects the character of the part of the country that they're in. So, in Denver, some of the reading rooms have teepees in them and little ponies that they can get on. It is really, really cool.

James Barham:
Wonderful.

Ben Carson:
And they get points for the number of books that they read and the amount of time they spend in there. They can trade them in for prizes (like S&H Green Stamps). In the beginning, they do it for the prizes. But it doesn't take long before it begins to change their trajectory—their grades, their self-esteem, the trajectory of their lives.

James Barham:
Just like it did for you?

Ben Carson:
Absolutely.

7. Public School & Music

James Barham:
You met your wife, Candy, who is an accomplished violinist, through your mutual love for classical music. Could you tell us how you first developed your interest in classical music? Would you like to see music training reinstated as an essential part of the elementary school curriculum as it was 50 years ago?

Ben Carson:
I would *love* to see music reinstated as an essential part of schooling. The culture that it brings; the knowledge that it brings. Just learning how to read music requires metrics, and I think that helps you with mathematics. A lot of scientists and doctors have a musical background—it's very interesting.

I got interested in classical music because I wanted to be a contestant on my favorite TV program, *GE College Bowl*. They asked questions on science, math, history, geography, and I was really good at that stuff. But they also asked about classical music and classical art, and you weren't going to learn that at Southwestern High School in inner-city Detroit. So, I took it upon myself. I would travel to the Institute of Arts day after day, week after week, month after month, until I knew every picture in there—who painted it, when they died. I always listened to my portable radio: Bach, Telemann, Mozart. And the kids in Detroit thought I was nuts: "A black kid in Motown listening to Mozart?" But I was boning up; I was getting myself ready.

It turned out to be tremendous. It opened up so many doors for me. One of the key doors it opened was when I was applying to Johns Hopkins. They only took two people a year in their neurosurgery program out of the top 125 applicants. How was I going to be one of them? Well, the fellow who was in charge of the residency program was also in charge of cultural affairs at the hospital. So, we started talking in the interview about medicine, neurosurgery—somehow the conversation turned to classical music. We talked for over an hour about different composers and their styles, conductors, orchestras, orchestral halls. He was on Cloud Nine. There was no way he wasn't taking me after that!

I always like to tell young people: "There's no such thing as useless knowledge. You never know what doors it's going to open up for you."

8. Education Reform

James Barham:

You have emphasized the importance of the role of public education in creating an informed citizenry upon which the health of our nation depends. And yet many of our public schools are failing in this task. How should American education be reformed to create an informed citizenry?

Ben Carson:

One of the things that I think we're going to have to do is to *reward* teaching, good teaching. Right now, if you're an excellent teacher, what do you get? More work to do. Pretty soon, you just start submitting to the unions and all these people who are trying to protect you (or think they're trying to protect you). And that doesn't work. We need to start thinking about new paradigms.

For instance, through virtual classrooms we now have the ability to put the very best teachers in front of a *million* students at a time instead of 30 students at a time. There are computer programs that can look at the way a kid solves five algebra problems. Based on how they solve them (or tried to solve them), it knows what they don't know. It goes back and tutors them on that, brings them up to speed, so they can solve them.

It's the same thing a good teacher can do, obviously, but a teacher can only do it for one student at a time. A computer can do it for a whole classroom or a whole school simultaneously —and at the speed of the patient ... of the student. (You see, I'm still in doctor mode here!) But utilizing technology in that way can really help close the gap pretty quickly.

9. Wisdom & Common Sense

James Barham:

For all your obvious respect for learning, you have stressed the difference between knowledge and wisdom, and have written in your book, *One Nation*, "I would choose common sense over knowledge in almost every circumstance." Yet much of American higher education puts a premium on knowledge and ideology over wisdom and common sense. What, then, would you say to our young people to help them attain wisdom and common sense, especially against the cultural forces that oppose these virtues?

Ben Carson:

I would say, "You need both. You need both knowledge and wisdom." But I know a lot of very knowledgeable people who are not very wise, because wisdom tells you how to *apply* that knowledge—how to acquire and how to apply it. I seek wisdom from the *source* of wisdom, which is God. It's a matter of looking at people around you who are successful, looking at people around you who are *not* successful, and figuring out: What are the traits that tend to characterize the unsuccessful people? What are the traits that tend to characterize the successful people? If you can then learn from that—inculcate that into your pattern of life—you're a wise person.

A foolish person has to make every single mistake themselves, and it takes them a lot longer to make progress than someone who can watch you, you, and you, and say, "That didn't work out. I'm not doing that." It makes a big difference.

10. Freedom of Thought in America's Universities

James Barham:

It's vital that higher education give unconditional support to freedom of thought and expression. Unfortunately, an increasing conformity has crept into higher education, in which ideologies rule the day and dissident voices are shouted down or driven out. You yourself were disinvited from delivering commencement addresses more than once because views you hold were unwelcome. What has happened to freedom on America's college campuses? And how can it be restored?

Ben Carson:

What has happened to it, simply, is that there are a group of people, and their philosophy is, "My way or the highway. We are all-wise, and anybody who disagrees with us doesn't deserve to be heard—needs to be shut down. If possible, hurt them." That's completely antithetical to what the founders of this country fought for!

What can be done about it? I would say we need the kind of leadership in this country at a national level that will speak out against that kind of thing—not just turn your head and look the other way. Maybe even go so far as to change the function of the Department of Education. Make one of their functions monitoring our institutions of higher education for extreme political bias. And if it exists, they're not eligible for federal funding. I think you'd find it would go away pretty quickly under those circumstances.

11. Leaders, Virtue, and Common Sense

James Barham:

On page 164 of *One Nation*, you present a wonderful summation of your moral philosophy, which centers on what you call "true compassion." You say that true compassion is a rare thing, consisting in the willingness to extend a helping hand to one's neighbor while also standing on one's own two feet as a self-reliant and productive citizen. But to instill true compassion in the next generation, we need to be able to teach the traditional virtues of courage, temperance, fairness, and wisdom. Our question is this: What will it take to win back the hearts and minds of the intellectual leaders of our society to traditional moral virtues and plain common sense?

Ben Carson:

When the people with common sense get in power, they have to take the right attitude. Not an attitude of vengeance—"You did it to us, we're going to do it to you." That's the wrong attitude. The right attitude is to show everybody (including those individuals you just talked about) the benefits of doing things the right way, of having morals and values, of saying there *is* something that's right and there *is* something that's wrong—of recognizing the Judeo-Christian values upon which this country was established, and which allowed us to rise to the pinnacle of the world (and to a higher pinnacle than anyone had ever risen) much faster than anyone had ever gotten there. To throw these things out is stupid. But what we have to do is, while we embrace these things, let anybody else do whatever they want to do. And then it becomes very clear what the advantages are.

12. The Shackles of Ignorance

James Barham:

You mentioned that in the 1800s, back when slavery was a reality, most people were far more educated than they are today, and that even the exams for passing the sixth grade were fairly rigorous, so much so that a college graduate today might not be able to pass them. You added that education liberates a child. So, what today would ignorance enslave a person to? What does a lack of education metaphorically enslave a child to? In the absence of actual, literal slavery, what is the metaphorical slavery that a lack of education shackles one to?

Ben Carson:

Education *is* the great divide in our society. It doesn't matter what your ethnic background, your economic background: you get a good education, you write your own ticket—end of story.

Unfortunately, there are a lot of people who lack information. They're very ill-informed. They're not well-educated. And that's the reason our founders put so much emphasis (particularly Franklin and Jefferson) on education—because they recognized that a well-informed populace is essential to the freedoms that we enjoy in our form of government. Why? Because *uninformed* people can be easily manipulated. For instance, in today's world, given an uneducated, uninformed, unsophisticated population, slick politicians and dishonest media will come and say: "The unemployment rate is down to 5.4 percent. Oh, how wonderful everything is!"

But, of course, *informed* people know that that's just not true. They recognize that it's the labor force participation rate —the percentage of people eligible to work who are working —that has gone down steadily since 2009, and is now as low as it's ever been in 37 years. But you have to be informed to know that kind of thing. If you're not informed, someone easily comes along and tells you falsehoods, and you just lap it right up like a dog.

13. Success & Mediocrity

James Barham:

Recently, George W. Bush gave a commencement speech. When he congratulated the *summa cum laude* and the *cum laude* students for their excellent work, he jokingly added: "And to the C students, I would say: 'You, too, can be president.'" What would you say to this valuation of mediocrity, where people are *aspiring* to mediocrity, as though just luck and pluck and circumstance can bring you all the rewards you need, and you don't have to actually have intellectual horsepower?

Ben Carson:

I would say there are probably some people who did not achieve at the highest level but who are very smart. And, you know, I've had many opportunities to sit down with President Bush, have dinner at the White House, and various things. He's always saying: "You know, all my opponents think that I'm stupid, but here's the funny thing: They're out there, and I'm in the White House." And he actually reads 90 minutes every night before he goes to sleep.

James Barham:

Does he?

Ben Carson:

And, if you probe, you'll find he's really quite knowledgeable.

14. Closing Thoughts

James Barham:

Thank you very much for taking the time to share your insights with our readers. If there is one closing thought you would like to leave with our readers, what would that be?

Ben Carson:

That would be that the person who has the most to do with what happens to you in life is *you*. You get to make the decisions. You get to decide how much energy to put into it. You don't ever need to look for anybody else to blame.

Notes

1. Renegade

1. This information about Maria Elena Tostado and her relationship with Jaime Escalante is from author interviews with Henry Gradillas November 9, 2014, Lucy Romero November 10, 2014, and Angelo Villavicencio November 11, 2014.
2. Gradillas's comment on reasons for finishing his doctorate is from author interview.
3. Quotations from "Something More Than Calculus" are by Ron La Brecque, *The New York Times*, November 6, 1988.
4. Quotations about Gradillas's reassignment are from "Praised Principal Put in Academic Siberia" by Jay Mathews, *Washington Post*, November 27, 1988.
5. Gradillas's comment about shop class is from author interview.
6. Escalante's comments about "ingratitude" and his decision to leave Garfield are from "Celebrated Math Teacher Escalante Says He'll Quit" by Elaine Woo and Larry Gordon, *Los Angeles Times*, February 22, 1990.
7. Escalante's and Tostado's comments about Escalante's final decision to leave Garfield are from "A Calculated Move: Jaime Escalante Prepares to Leave to Teach in Sacramento" by Elaine Woo, *Los Angeles Times*, June 19, 1991.
8. Lucy Romero comments about Tostado are from author interview.
9. Angelo Villavicencio comments about his departure are from author interview.

10. Don Mroscak's comment about falling standards at Garfield is from author interview, November 9, 2014.

11. Jesness's comment on Escalante's legacy at Garfield is taken from "Stand and Deliver Revisited" by Jerry Jesness, posted at https://reason.com, July 1, 2002.

12. *New York Times* obituary of Escalante was by William Grimes, March 31, 2010.

13. Villavicencio's offer to relaunch calculus at Garfield was recounted in author interview.

14. Information contained in this chapter about the life of Jaime Escalante and the history of his calculus classes at Garfield High is from *Escalante: The Best Teacher in America* by Jay Mathews (New York: Henry Holt and Company, 1988).

2. I Will Succeed

1. Burroughs Corporation history from https://computerhistory.org and from https://burroughsinfo.com.

2. Jaime Escalante's biographical information in this chapter from *Escalante: The Best Teacher in America* by Jay Mathews (New York: Henry Holt and Company, 1988).

3. Kemo

1. For more about the history of real estate covenants in Los Angeles see "A Southern California Dream Deferred: Racial Covenants in Los Angeles" by Kelly Simpson, February 22, 2012, at https://kcet.org and "Living with a Reminder of Segregation" by Jessica Garrison, *Los Angeles Times* July 27, 2008.

2. The quotation from the Continental Congress is from their papers at the Library of Congress.

3. *The Negro Family* PDF can be found at https://web.stanford.edu/~mrosenfe/Moynihan%27s%20The%20Negro%20Family.pdf; see also "The Moynihan Report: An Annotated Edition" by Daniel Geary, *The Atlantic*, September 2015.

4. This characterization of the Avilez administration is from *Escalante: The Best Teacher in America* by Jay Mathews (New York: Henry Holt and Company, 1988), 86.

5. Mathews, *Escalante*.

4. Star Rising

1. Information about the AP retest and its aftermath at Garfield is from *Escalante: The Best Teacher in America* by Jay Mathews (New York: Henry Holt and Company 1988).

2. Information about the aftermath of AP retest and Escalante's techniques and attitudes during this time are from author interviews with Henry Gradillas on November 9, 2014, Angelo Villavicencio on October 24, 2014 and November 11, 2014, Chris Martinez on February 13, 2015, and Erika Camacho on April 17, 2015.

3. Background on the film *Stand and Deliver* is from "Math Stars in a Movie" by Aljean Harmetz, *The New York Times*, March 20, 1988.

4. Jay Mathews's review of test booklets is from *Escalante* and from his reflections on the incident after a later unrelated cheating accusation in "Retest D.C. Classes That Had Dubious Exam Results in '08," *Washington Post*, September 14, 2009.

5. Angelo Villavicencio's comments on cheating are from author interview on November 11, 2014.

5. Don't Give Up

1. Review quotations from "'Deliver' Receives High Marks" are from Sheila Benson, *Los Angeles Times*, March 10, 1988.

2. Film background and commentary are from "Math Stars in a Movie" by Aljean Harmetz, *The New York Times*, March 20, 1988.

3. The Aili Gardcna quotation is from author interview, October 30, 2014.

4. Box office figures from Internet Movie Database.

5. ARCO representative comments are from "Celebrated Math Teacher Escalante Says He'll Quit" by Elaine Woo and Larry Gordon, *Los Angeles Times*, February 22, 1990.

6. The comment that Sacramento would be "elated" is from "Math Teacher Escalante Quitting Garfield High" by Elaine Woo, *Los Angeles Times*, June 14, 1991.

7. Professional friction challenges and information about Escalante's career in Sacramento are from "Success Keeps Multiplying for Jaime Escalante" by Gary Libman, *Los Angeles Times*, May 23, 1995, and "Escalante's Formula Not Always the Answer" by Amy Pyle, *Los Angeles Times*, May 18, 1998.

8. Information about Escalante's final illness and death is from "Jaime Escalante, Inspiration for a Movie, Dies at 79" by William Grimes, *The New York Times*, March 31, 2010 (cause of death given is incorrect); "Jaime Escalante Dies at 79" by Elaine Woo, *Los Angeles Times* March 31, 2010; and "Jaime Escalante dies, inspired 1988 film *Stand and Deliver*" by Jay Mathews, *The Washington Post*, March 31, 2010.

6. Teaching from the Top Down

1. Text of legislation authorizing the Department of Education is found at https://govtrack.us/congress/bills/96/s210 .

2. Historical background on the Department of Education is at https://www.archives.gov/research/guide-fed-records/groups/441.html/1000.

3. *A Nation at Risk* can be found at https://files.eric.ed.gov/fulltext/ED226006.pdf.

4. The Gerald Holton quotations are from "An Insider's View of *A Nation at Risk* and Why It Still Matters" by Gerald Holton, *Chronicle of High Education*, v49 n33, April 25, 2000.

5. "The Sandina Report and US Achievement: An Assessment" by Lawrence C. Stedman, *The Journal of Educational Research*, v87 n3, 1994.

6. The Edutopia report is at https://www.edutopia.org/landmark-education-report-nation-risk.

7. "Unprecedented sweeping oversight" quotation is from "Why America Overhauled Its Main Education Law," *The Economist*, December 10, 2015.

8. The *Education Week* quotation and background on NCLB are from "No Child Left Behind: An Overview" by Alyson Klein, *Education Week*, v24 n27, April 2015.

9. This quotation about Race to the Top is found at https://eric.ed.gov/?id=ED557422.

10. The Governor Rick Perry quotation is from "Texas Shuts Door on Millions in Education Grants," *The New York Times*, January 13, 2010.

11. The Senator Lamar Alexander quote is from the US Senate Committee on Health, Education, Labor & Pensions press release "Alexander Offers Plan that Rejects 'National School Board'," released on June 11, 2013.

12. The Lily Eskelsen García quotation is from "US Senate Passes Every Child Achieves Act, End of NCLB Era Draws Closer" by Tim Walker, *NEA Today*, July 16, 2015.

13. The House Speaker John Boehner quotation is from "Every Child Should Have a Chance at a Great Education," Speaker's Press Office, July 8, 2015.

14. The Terry Beasley quotations are from *NEA Today*, July 16, 2015 cited earlier in this chapter.

15. Author interview with Ray Mayoral, February 16, 2015.

16. Author interview with Mark Peabody, February 19, 2015.

7. The Testing Juggernaut

1. College admissions officers' remarks on the SAT by William C. Hiss and Valerie W. Franks are quoted in "Ivy League's Meritocracy Lie" by Lani Guinier at https://www.salon.com/2015/01/11/ivy_leagues_meritocracy_lie_how_harvard_and_yale_cook the books_for_the_1_percent.

2. The Iris C. Rotberg quotations in this chapter are from "A Self-Fulfilling Prophecy" by Iris C. Rotberg, *Phi Delta Kappan*, v82 n2, October 2001.

3. The Mike Rose quotation is from "How School Reform Has Failed the Test" by Valerie Strauss, *The Washington Post*, January 28, 2015.

4. The quotation to get rid of Common Core testing is from an author interview with a teacher who did not want to be identified in connection with this observation.

5. The Mary Poplin quotation is from author interview, March 16, 2015.

6. The Houston Sarratt quotations in this chapter are from author interview, January 8, 2015.

7. These Henry Gradillas quotations are from *Standing and Delivering: What the Movie Didn't Tell* by Henry Gradillas and Jerry Jesness (Lanham: Rowman & Littlefield, 2010), ch. 15.

8. The Mark Peabody quotations in this chapter are from author interview, February 19, 2015.

9. The Lucy Romero quotation is from author interview, November 10, 2014.

10. The Angelo Villavicencio quotation from author interview, November 11, 2014.

11. The Molly Slack quotation is from author interview, October 28, 2014.

12. The Karen Vogelsang quotation is from author interview, January 14, 2015.

13. The *New York Times* quotation from "Nation's Schools Struggling to Find Enough Principals" by Jacques Steinberg, *The New York Times*, September 3, 2000.

14. The PDK/Gallup Poll was published in *The Phi Delta Kappan*, vol96 n1, September 2014.

15. The story of the ten-year-old daughter is from "Everybody Hates Pearson" by Jennifer Reingold, *Fortune*, v171 n2, May 1, 2015.

16. "Four Effects of the High-Stakes Test Movement on African American K-12 Students" by Gail L. Thompson and

Tawannah G. Allen, *Journal of Negro Education,* Summer 2012.

17. The *Policy Review* quotation is from "No Excuses" by Tyce Palmaffy, *Policy Review*, January/February 1998.

18. The Kentucky assessment coordinator quotation is from Rotberg, "A Self-Fulfilling Prophecy."

19. The *New York Times* quotation about raising academic standards is from Steinberg, "Nation's Schools Struggling to Find Enough Principals."

20. Information about the Atlanta cheating scandal is from "Atlanta Educators Convicted in School Cheating Scandal" by Alan Blinder, *The New York Times*, April 1, 2015; and "How and Why Convicted Atlanta Teachers Cheated on Standardized Tests" by Valerie Strauss, *Washington Post*, April 1, 2015.

21. Information about Pearson is from Reingold, "Everybody Hates Pearson."

22. The Linda Darling-Hammond quotation is from Reingold, "Everybody Hates Pearson."

23. The Leon Botstein quotation is from Guinier, "Ivy League's Meritocracy Lie."

24. The Mike Rose quotations are from "School Reform Fails the Test" by Mike Rose, *The American Scholar*, Winter 2015.

8. Turn Back the Wheel

1. The Mary Poplin quotations are from author interview, March 16, 2015.

2. "The Lost Tools of Learning" by Dorothy Leigh Sayers can be found at https://www.pccs.org/wp-content/uploads/2016/06/LostToolsOfLearning-DorothySayers.pdf.

3. The quotation criticizing whole-language instruction is from "Whole Language, Half an Education?" by Gayle M.B. Hanson, *Insight*, February 8, 1999.

4. The Kenneth Goodman quotation is from "ABCeething: How Whole Language Became a Hot Potato In and Out

of Academia" by Christina Duff, *The Wall Street Journal*, October 30, 1996.

5. The Stephen Krashen reference and Ann Edwards quotations are from Hanson, "Whole Language, Half an Education?"

6. The PERT founder reference is from Duff, "ABCeething."

7. The Ann Edwards quotations are from Hanson, "Whole Language, Half an Education?"

8. The Project Follow Through reference is from "No Excuses" by Tyce Palmaffy, *Policy Review*, Jan/Feb, 1998.

9. The Marion Joseph quotation and cost figures for California textbooks and consultants are from "The California Story: A Very Costly Lesson" by Howard Libit and Mike Bowler, *Baltimore Sun*, November 3, 1997.

10. The information about Marva Collins is from "Marva Collins, Educator Who Aimed High for Poor, Black Students, Dies at 78" by Sam Roberts, *The New York Times*, June 28, 2015.

11. The information about and quotations by Thaddeus Lott are from Palmaffy, "No Excuses"; see also "Sounds Bad, But It Works" by William Raspberry, *The Washington Post*, March 30, 1998.

12. The study of highly effective teachers by Mary Poplin is described in "She's Strict for a Reason..." by Mary Poplin et.al., *Phi Delta Kappan*, v92 n5, February 2011.

13. For information about KIPP, see https://kipp.org.

14. The information on Success Academies and Eva Moskowitz is from "At Success Academy Charter Schools, Polarizing Methods and Superior Results" by Kate Taylor, *The New York Times*, April 6, 2015. See also Moskowitz's memoir titled *The Education of Eva Moskowitz* (New York: Harper, 2018).

15. The information about Nettlehorst Elementary is from "Nettlehorst Elementary School's Remarkable Turnaround" by Beth Wilson, *Chicago Magazine*, January 10, 2011.

16. The quotations from Senator Lamar Alexander were available at https://alexander.senate.gov/public/index.cfm / while he was still a US Senator.

17. The information on Finland is from "Finland Has an Education System the US Should Envy—and Learn From" by Linda Moore, *The Guardian*, February 15, 2013; see also "What We Can Learn from Finland's Successful School Reform" by Linda Darling-Hammond, *NEA Today*, October/November 2010.

18. The quotations about teacher mediocrity are from "Why Other Countries Teach Better," *The New York Times*, December 17, 2013.

19. Reported by Syna Sharma, "How the World's Happiest Country Supports Its Teachers," January 13, 2025, https://www.ednc.org/perspective-how-the-worlds-happiest-country-supports-its-teachers.

20. See https://worldpopulationreview.com/country-rankings/pisa-scores-by-country.

21. The Ann Davis quotation is from Palmaffy, "No Excuses."

9. The Point of Education

1. The Michael Barber quotations are from "Everybody Hates Pearson" by Jennifer Reingold, *Fortune*, January 21, 2015.

2. The Mary Poplin quotations are from author interview, March 16, 2015.

3. The information about Garfield alumni comes from author interviews with alumni as well as with Henry Gradillas, Angelo Villavicencio, and Don Mroscak.

4. The Wayne Bishop quotation is from an email exchange with Jerry Jesness, September 14, 1997.

5. The David Rose quotation is from "School Reform Fails the Test" by Mike Rose, *The American Scholar*, Winter 2015.

6. *The Tyranny of the Meritocracy* by Lani Guinier (Boston: Beacon Press, 2015), ch. 2.

7. The Madison Sarratt quotation may be found at https://s
    tudentorg.vanderbilt.edu/honorcouncil/honor-quotes. It is
    the first of many "Honor Quotes" listed there.

8. Available at https://www.pccs.org/wp-content/uploads/
    2016/06/LostToolsOfLearning-DorothySayers.pdf.

9. The James Barham quotation is from correspondence with
    author, February 1, 2015.

10. From *Lasker's Manual of Chess* by Emanuel Lasker, origi-
    nally published in German in 1925 and then translated
    into English (presumably by Lasker himself—no translator
    is listed), with a 1927 English edition published by E.P.
    Dutton. The quotations by Lasker here are from the edition
    that has a foreword by chess trainer Mark Dvoretsky
    (Milford, CT: Russell Enterprises, 2010), 248.

10. If We Know What Works

1. The Henry Gradillas quotations are from author interview,
    November 9, 2014.

2. See *The Universal History of Numbers: From Prehistory to
    the Invention of the Computer* by George Ifrah, translated
    by David Bellos, E. F. Harding, Sophie Wood, and Ian
    Monk (New York: John Wiley & Sons, 2000), ch. 22.

3. The Angelo Villavicencio quotation is from author inter-
    view, October 30, 2014.

4. The Henry Gradillas quotation is from author interview,
    November 9, 2014.

5. The Escalante quotations and descriptions are from *Es-
    calante: The Best Teacher in America* by Jay Mathews
    (New York: Henry Holt & Company, 1988).

6. The Gradillas quotation about the *barrio* is from author
    interview, November 9, 2014.

7. The Gradillas quotation about mandates is from *Standing
    and Delivering: What the Movie Didn't Tell* by Henry
    Gradillas and Jerry Jesness (Lanham: Rowman & Little-
    field, 2010), ch. 15.

8. The Aili Gardena quotation is from author interview,
    October 30, 2014.

9. See https://www.elac.edu/academics/cewd/continuing-ed/escalante and https://www.theescalanteprogram.org. The numbers here were confirmed in a telephone conversation with leadership at the Jaime Escalante Math Program on November 19, 2025.
10. The Gradillas quotation about book covers is from author interview, November 9, 2014.
11. The Gradillas quotation about being in command from author interview, November 9, 2014.
12. The Angelo Villavicencio quotation is from author interview, October 26, 2014.

11. You Can Do Anything

1. The Angelo Villavicencio quotation is from author interview, November 11, 2014.
2. Ben Carson's words here are from his interview with James Barham as found in Appendix 4 of this book.
3. The Henry Gradillas quotation is from author interview, November 9, 2014.
4. Or as great Carthaginian general Hannibal put it: "Aut viam inveniam aut faciam" ("I will either find a way or make one").

Afterword by Mary Poplin

1. For an overview of this work, see Mary Poplin and Claudia Bermúdez, eds., *Highly Effective Teachers of Vulnerable Students: Practice Transcending Theory* (New York: Peter Lang, 2019).

Acknowledgments

James Barham has been crucial to this book, bringing together and interviewing the key people needed to understand Jaime Escalante's legacy.

Henry Gradillas gave an inordinate amount of time to helping us understand the real Escalante, making us feel like eyewitnesses to Escalante's world even though by the time we approached this project, Escalante's work at Garfield High was decades in the past.

Angelo Villavicencio was likewise generous with his time and insights about Escalante. With a larger-than-life figure like Escalante, myth and hagiography come easily, yet they can also be misleading. Gradillas and Villavicencio helped us avoid this pitfall.

The interview of Ben Carson in this book was initially approached with no thought of Escalante. Yet, Carson's educational experience, as described in the interview, dovetailed so beautifully with Escalante's story that we had to include it.

Mary Poplin has done amazing work over the years tracking teacher effectiveness, especially in troubled inner-city school systems. Her afterword gives scholarly teeth to many of the lessons we draw from Escalante's example.

Jenn Finley and Rich Tatum helped bring an earlier version of this book to life. Now working for Inkwell Press, Jenn also helped bring this new version to life, as did Chloe Dembski.

Ryan Axe took terrific photos of the famous Escalante-Olmos mural in Los Angeles. We've adapted his photography for the cover of this book.

Our thanks go to each of these individuals. In addition, we are grateful to Escalante's students, who to this day testify to his immense contribution to education.

The Authors

William A. Dembski worked as a research mathematician at the height of Jaime Escalante's fame in the late 1980s. Never losing sight of Escalante's monumental success in teaching calculus at Garfield High in East LA, Dembski finally had the opportunity to pay homage to Escalante with this book. Best known for his work on intelligent design, Dembski is also an entrepreneur, focusing on the connections between education, technology, and freedom.

Alex Thomas began his career as an advertising copywriter and radio producer in Dallas and Houston. Since then, he has worn a variety of hats including music producer, radio syndication executive, publisher, editor, and communications consultant. He has a special interest in the history of education and the role of education in American culture. Alex was educated at Houston Baptist University, Vanderbilt University, and University College, Oxford.

Index

www.ingramcontent.com/pod-product-compliance
Lightning Source LLC
Chambersburg PA
CBHW060403130626
46555CB00005B/1980